MW01620181

MOSAICA PRESS

THE HUMAN CHALLENGE

BEING JEWISH IN THE 21ST CENTURY

RABBI AVRAHAM EDELSTEIN

ISBN: 978-1-952370-30-4

Published by Mosaica Press, Inc.
www.mosaicapress.com
info@mosaicapress.com

מוקדש לע"נ

משה בן מנחם מענדל ז"ל

נלב"ע בש"ק כ"ו תמוז תשס"ט

יונא בת בענדעט ע"ה

נלב"ע במוצש"ק ד' כסלו תשע"ז

זוסמאן בן צבי ז"ל

ו' ניסן תשע"ט

LEONARD FINE: While every generation has its challenges, our post-COVID era faces a paradigm shift. The way we are going to live is going to be very different to the past. I have rarely come across an intellect like Rabbi Edelstein's that has the ability to communicate the wisdom of Judaism. Now he has written a must-read for every Jew seeking answers to the relevance of Judaism to today's modern world.

Leonard Fine has consulted in strategy for over fifty years and has written and spoken extensively on the subject internationally. He is the co-founder of an Orthodox shul in Johannesburg, South Africa.

AKIVA MOSHE PRELL: Every generation needs a book that connects the wisdom and relevance of Judaism to our lives. *The Human Challenge* is that book for our time.

Akiva Moshe Prell is an author and an advisor to prime ministers of Israel, Canada, and Australia. He is a convert to Judaism.

MIRIAM KOSMAN: How does one create a readable overview to 3,000 years of Jewish wisdom? How does one introduce Judaism without dumbing it down and over-simplifying it? *The Human Challenge* manages to do just that! It is profound and revelatory—each concept meticulously sourced—yet made clear and accessible to the complete beginner.

Miriam Kosman is a popular lecturer and the author of Circle, Arrow, Spiral.

DANIELLE IMMERMAN: If Torah is a roadmap to navigating life, then that roadmap must tell us how to begin that journey. This deep yet practical book is the story of that navigation.

Danielle Immerman is a communications and media specialist.

NECHAMA BERG: I study Jewish topics every day, and yet I learned so much from this book. I was amazed at the deep insights and wonderful motivational ideas. Every Jewish educator needs this book.

Nechama Berg is a marketing consultant.

PARIS NASTER: Introducing 3,000 years of Jewish wisdom to the seeking novice and reigniting the flame for life-long learners, *The Human Challenge* is a beautifully arranged piece from which you could read every day and gain newfound knowledge of both Torah and yourself.

Paris Naster is an actor.

CHLOE BIREN: Every generation requires a book that explains the profundity and relevance of Judaism to the generation. I think *The Human Challenge* does that in our time.

Chloe Biren is a chemist.

TABLE OF CONTENTS

SECTION 1

A PURPOSEFUL LIFE

SECTION 2

HOLINESS

SECTION 3

WISDOM

SECTION 4

PATTERNS OF GROWTH

ACKNOWLEDGMENTS

This book is not the product of one person. For one, it represents the cumulative wisdom of all that my rabbis and mentors have taught me. It also represents my cumulative experience of teaching Torah, and, in particular, at Neve Yerushalayim where I serve as the Educational Director. The curiosity, thirst for Torah and desire to grow on the part of the Neve students fueled my inspiration to write this book. I am truly grateful to Rabbi David Refson, the Dean of Neve Yerushalayim, for the unique opportunity with which he has provided me. Rivka Kantor rewrote the entire first section. Rochel Abrahams made hundreds of proofreading and other suggestions. Nechama Berg went through the entire manuscript and made incisive comments. Rebbetzin Tziporah Gottlieb (Heller) did a comprehensive review of the book. So did Zelda and Leonard Fine, Daniella Immerman, Rachel Schwartz, Deborah Guida, Netanya Sacks, Chloe Biren, Paris Naster, Zoe Sabel, and Jamie Wisener. Ali Kor critiqued and helped to improve several of the chapters. My wife, Yael Edelstein, provided important insights, was a sounding board for many points, and gave me loads of encouragement.

I am indebted to the Yad Mordechai team—Anthony Moshal, Michael Setzer, and Damon Hoff—for sponsoring this work.

The staff at Mosaica Press is a team of professionals dedicated to publishing high-quality books of Jewish interest. I would like to thank Rabbi Doron Kornbluth and Sherie Gross for their guidance, critiques, and editorial comments; these have made *The Human Challenge* a much better book than it would otherwise have been.

I also want to thank Rabbi Yaacov Haber for his early encouragement of this work, and the other members of the Mosaica team who helped make this happen: the copyeditor Binyamin Lieb and the proofreader Binyomin Prenzlau, both of whom made dozens of suggested improvements and corrections; Rayzel Broyde, the art director; and Brocha Mirel Strizower, the typesetter.

It takes a village to produce a book, and a sizable village at that.

I hope this work will be a source of *nachas* for the *Ribbono shel Olam*, for it was to enable us to get closer to Him that this work was intended.

INTRODUCTION

The Treasure in Your Own Backyard

Yitzchak ben Moshe, known as Reb Ayzik (Isaac) Yekeles, lived in Krakow in the early 17th century. Night after night, Reb Ayzik had a recurring dream in which he traveled to Prague where he would find a treasure buried underneath a certain bridge. Finally, he went to the bridge in Prague he had seen in his dreams but found it guarded by soldiers. Afraid to search for the treasure, Reb Ayzik left and came back the next day, and the next, and the next, hoping in vain for an opportunity to dig unobserved. The captain of the guard stationed at the bridge noticed the stranger who came back day after day, and asked him what he was doing there. When Reb Ayzik told him the story, the officer laughed and said, "Who believes in dreams? I dreamed that I should journey to Krakow and find someone there named Ayzik Yekeles, and that if I dig in the home of that Jew, I will find a treasure under the stove."

The point of the story, of course, is that we don't need to go elsewhere to find a treasure. It is waiting for us, right "at home." This is a book for Jews who want to find that treasure.

Erich Fromm commented in *The Sane Society*, "Whereas in the nineteenth century God was dead, in the twentieth century man is dead." That was before the internet created a whole new wave of dehumanization. This is a book that shows that Judaism believes that man can be not only alive, but fully human.

To do so is to engage every aspect of oneself, as I will show, but also to engage the sparks of holiness that lie in the world around us. The Hebrew word for world is *olam* (עולם), which comes from the word *he'elem* (העלם)—hidden. And that is because real spirituality is not openly seen.[1] And yet, when we scratch under the surface of ourselves and our surroundings, it is everywhere, all over. By peering below the surface, we connect to our inner selves. This is what Micah was telling us when he said, "to walk modestly with your God."[2] The Hebrew word for "modesty" actually means hidden. So, Micah was telling us that if we want to walk with God, we have to walk below the surface of superficial reality, where spirituality resides.

Together, in these pages, we will learn where and how to look.

WHAT THIS BOOK IS ABOUT AND WHO IT IS FOR

Judaism has been something utterly profound for me. Every time that I think I have plumbed the depths of a particular issue, I turn the corner to find a whole new world of depth and meaning. As the prophet Job put it, "Its measure is longer than the earth and wider than any sea."[3] This book is an attempt to share some of that depth—to show an overview of Judaism as a way of looking at and understanding life in a way that leaps far beyond the boundaries of our initial expectations.

The question, "What are the most important things that someone approaching Judaism needs to know?" has many answers. It depends on the age, intellect, background, predilections, and commitment of the inquirer. But perhaps it is the wrong question. Real questions arise from the personal:

- What are the most pressing issues in my life and how does Judaism address them?
- How do I grow?
- How do I feel spiritual?

---

1 Rabbeinu Bachya, beginning of Genesis.

2 "And what does God demand of you except to do kindness and justice and to walk modestly with your God" (Micah 6:8).

3 Job 11:9.

- How do I become wise?
- How do I sanctify the world around me and make it a better place?
- How do I work on my character?
- How do I integrate work and food and intimacy into my life's goals?

What follows in this book is an attempt to answer these questions for an intelligent and sensitive adult reader. It draws significantly on deeper Jewish thought—made comprehensible to the novice while still giving a sense of the astonishing depth of Torah.

My hope is that it will be a rich and exciting entry to Judaism for those who are at the early stages of their relationship with Judaism. Having said that, because these chapters reflect a summary of the wisdom of the generations, this book will also be of significant benefit to those who have an extensive background in Judaism by providing a methodical and sourced overview of many topics that may otherwise have remained fragmented insights.

The content of this book is most decidedly for both genders. I often used the male pronouns "he" because the alternatives—"he/she" for example—were often awkward in their context. The English language will require a more radical makeover to accommodate all the sensitivities involved here.

The Torah that is presented here is not my own. It is all taken from many of the great books written during the last 2,500 years and going back to that greatest book of all, the Torah itself. I have therefore been careful to source everything that I have written. The wording in the contemporary idiom is mine, but I see myself as merely the faithful transmitter of timeless wisdom that ultimately comes from God Himself.

I have also tried as much as possible to go back to the source of sources—the Torah itself—and to show how the issues I bring forth emerge out of the Torah itself.

Each chapter of this book can be read independently, though the full richness of the topics will only be gained if the book is read in order.

I pray that this book transmits a message that is faithful to our profound tradition. I hope that it shows that Torah has a message that is contemporary and relevant, exciting and engaging. I have found Judaism to be so for me. I hope the reader will too.

THE CONCEPTUAL FRAMEWORK OF THIS BOOK

The innovation of this book begins with its conceptual framework. I have taken four major categories of life—a Purposeful life, holiness, wisdom, and patterns of growth—and explored the Jewish approach to them, devoting twelve or so chapters to each.

1. **Section 1: A Purposeful Life.** This deals with the big questions: Who are we? What is our purpose? Freedom, body and soul; passion and choice; relationships with God and with man.
2. **Section 2: Holiness.** This section starts with an overview of what is holiness, how we sanctify the material world, and what God's role is in this. I then move onto specific applications of sanctity—the Commandments, the Shabbat, eating kosher, physical relations between husband and wife, and the Hebrew language.
3. **Section 3: Wisdom.** Jews are about holiness, and they are about wisdom. There is the wisdom of the Written and Oral Laws; the wisdom of the heart, mind, imagination, and action; the wisdom of silence, speech, and protest. There is also the wisdom of the Kabbalah, of prayer, and the halachah.
4. **Section 4: Patterns of Growth.** How does Judaism serve as a system of growth? Where does our intense desire to express our individuality as well as our negativity come in? What are some of the big growth principles in Judaism? How should we relate to tests and challenges in our life? What is the Jewish idea of love, kindness, and charity? How do we develop our traits of modesty, humility, happiness, repentance, and forgiveness? Where does sensuality fit in?

Judaism provides a vast canopy of ideas. No one book can begin to contain them all. There is no end to the judgment calls that could be made. Why should one include this and exclude that? In the end, I made my choices based on a lifetime of involvement with Jews getting closer to their Judaism. I hope the reader looks kindly on those choices.

SECTION 1

A PURPOSEFUL LIFE

1

BELIEF AS A RELATIONSHIP

The source of my well-being, according to Judaism, is the knowledge that, since God created me, my existence is purposeful; since He is unique, He created me unique; since He created me to love me, I am intrinsically lovable; since He is all over, He will protect me everywhere.

Mrs. Shlomtzy Weisz[1]

THE MULTIFACETED RELATIONSHIP WITH GOD

It takes a lot more than simply believing that God exists in order to have a relationship with Him. Just as our relationships with our fellow humans have multiple aspects, so too, we need to explore multiple relationships with God. We need to approach Him through prayer and through the study of Torah, through the celebration of the Shabbat and through the awareness of His continuous Divine Providence. God will be the first Being we naturally turn to when we are in trouble. We may be angry with God or happy with Him—grateful, hurt, or perplexed—but, like in all true relationships, we maintain a connection.

1 "The Inevitable Emuna Workshop."

That connection triggers God's response in turn. King David stated, "God is your shadow."[2] He set up the world so that He responds to the contours of a relationship that we must initiate.[3] He waits for us to do His will so that He, in turn, can exercise His will, which is to do good for us.

The prophet Habakkuk gave us a key to unlocking all of Judaism: "A *tzaddik* (righteous person) lives by his faith."[4] One reading of this verse tells us, "Even if you are not righteous in everything, in faith you should be righteous. Be a *tzaddik* in faith."[5] Perhaps we can be mediocre in acts of kindness, in self-restraint, or in not being materialistic. But in faith we must excel. In faith, we must all be *tzaddikim*.

Let's not get this wrong. Habakkuk is not telling us to take a blind leap of faith. Faith is not a zero-sum game. It is not a case of either believing or not. There are many levels and facets to faith and many starting points:

- There is the God of comfort—the Being I turn to and talk to.
- There is the belief that God is involved in our lives, that He creates challenges for us that are just what we need—the God of Divine Providence.
- There is belief in the fact that He gave us the Torah at Sinai, and that He will unfold the Messianic Era when His unity will be revealed. This is the God of history.
- There is belief in the God of the covenant, resulting in the unique obligations of the Jewish People. The very nature of a covenant is a mutual commitment—in this case, God with the Jews.

These are just a few approaches. Faith, in fact, spreads a vast canopy that impregnates everything we do.

---

2 Psalms 121:5.

3 Rabbi Chaim of Volozhin, *Nefesh Hachaim* 1:1.

4 Habakkuk 2:4, as brought by the Talmud, end of Tractate *Makkot*.

5 Rabbi Tzadok HaKohen. According to this reading, the comma comes after the second word, "*Tzaddik Be'Emunato, Yichyeh*—A *tzaddik* (righteous man) in faith, will live." It is in faith that he is a *tzaddik*.

FAITH AND FAITHFULNESS

Of all the expressions of faith, the most important is faithfulness. When we are faithful to someone, we don't try to do things behind their back. We are loyal. We do things that we think will benefit them and don't try to harm them. We try to make them happy and to relate to their concerns. We try to nurture our connection and to take it forward. Being faithful to God is not much different. It too is a relationship. And while we can neither harm nor benefit God, we can be loyal and respond to what He wants without dreaming of cheating behind His back (so to speak).

If faith does not translate into faithfulness, it is meaningless. "Belief *that*" must translate into "belief *in*." "Belief *that*" is an abstract belief. It is the awe of God's grand cosmos. It may lead to respect but not to trust. "Belief *in*" turns my faith into a personal relationship. When I believe in someone, I must be faithful to my belief. I must show that I trust the person. And through that, I become deserving of *their* trust. In Hebrew (as in English), the two words are similar: *emunah* for faith, *ne'emanut* for faithfulness.

Believing in God is the background context in which we live; the meta-principle on which everything is based.[6] That is why the first of the Ten Commandments is in the form of a statement of fact, not a commandment: "I am the Lord your God who brought you out of the land of Egypt, out of the house of bondage."[7] God is not commanding us to believe. Rather, He is telling us that if we don't accept Him, then nothing else in the Torah is going to make sense. The first of the Ten Commandments is really an introduction to all the commandments. "I am the Lord your God."

Stated this way, the opposite of faith is not atheism. It is rather a state when one has no relationship with God and no attachment to Him.

I cannot love someone I don't trust, and I cannot trust someone I don't respect.

6 *Ramban*, glosses (*hasagot*) to Maimonides' *Sefer Hamitzvot*, positive mitzvah 1.

7 Because the wording is not in the form of a command. In fact, one of the commentators, the *Behag*, does not count belief in God as one of the 613 commandments.

WHEN TRUST BREAKS DOWN

Many of us believe in God, but we don't know how to have a relationship with Him. We believe *that* God exists, but we don't believe *in* Him. We don't know how to trust God, how to really feel that He loves us, believes in us, and is looking for us to love Him in turn. Some of us believe in God but think of Him only as this scary being, as *Malkeinu*, "our King," who sits in judgment and punishes us if we sin. But, in Judaism, we always say *Avinu Malkeinu*—"Our Father our King." We always put *Father* before *King*.[8] The relationship of a father to a child is God's starting point in reaching out to us.[9] "Every human soul that has lapsed...is His loss!"[10]

We have all kinds of relationships—with parents, spouses, children, friends, and colleagues. We can sometimes feel close to them and sometimes quite distant. If our connection with the other person goes deep enough, it will carry us through disagreements and disappointments. Even when we are hurt, we will remain committed to the relationship. But when trust breaks down, it is a different story. Trust is a precious commodity. It is hard-earned and easily lost.

What causes trust between people to break down? Often, there is an incident or series thereof—of infidelity or deep disappointment. We feel that our trust in that person was not reciprocated by his or her trustworthiness. Our trust threshold, however, will also be a function of other factors. We may have had other relationships that went sour that have made it more difficult for us to trust anyone but ourselves. Or we may live in a culture that tells us continuously to watch out for ourselves and to presume that everyone else's motives are selfish. Or we may suffer from an era when relationships are mainly superficial and hence not fully authentic.

---

8 *Avinu Malkeinu* is a famous set of appeals we repeatedly make to God on Rosh Hashanah and Yom Kippur.

9 So too, in the silent prayer, the *Shemoneh Esreh*, in the middle section of requests, we turn repeatedly to God as our father: "Return us, our Father..." "Forgive us, our Father..."

10 Rabbi Shimshon Raphael Hirsch, Passover Haggadah.

Our ability to sustain a relationship with God will be impacted by the types of relationships we have with others. If we had a poor relationship with our parents, we will have to struggle harder to have a healthy relationship with God. We won't have matured our relationship skills.

We don't need Torah to teach us the God of Einstein, the impersonal God who is behind the wondrous universe. We need it to teach us how to have a relationship with Him.

Moreover, our trust in God is a lifelong process. We may experience things along our sinuous path through life that don't make sense to us. We will then need to draw on a lifetime of faith that translates as faithfulness to our God, even in these trying times.

THE TASTE OF FAITH

King David told us *taamu u'reu*—"taste and you will understand (lit., see)."[11] Judaism requires engagement. It requires tasting. It can never be fully understood by the detached mind. I cannot explain to someone what ice cream tastes like by describing its ingredients. So too, I cannot explain the experience of the Shabbat by a verbal description.

It is one thing to show that Judaism is a rational faith. It is quite another to show the grandeur of Judaism, its profundity and acute relevance to our lives, its sophistication and depth. Only "tasting" Judaism will fully open that doorway to us. I believe in my Judaism—and in my God—in part because I have experienced both. And I have seen the effects of that experience on countless others. My Judaism works for me. And hence my faith, though it has strong intellectual components, is like an old friend.

---

11 Psalms 34:9.

2

FREEDOM

When we know our purpose, commitment
is an engagement, not a constraint.

PROGRESS AS A MEANS AND AS AN ENDS

"Death," said the American political activist Norman Cousins, "is not the greatest loss in life. The greatest loss is what dies inside us while we live."

We see our world progressing—more modern this, more cutting-edge that. Looking back in time, it is clear that humanity has come a long, long way. But where is this all going? What is it exactly that progress is bringing to the quality of mankind? Is it to live longer and healthier, with more heating and air-conditioning and connectivity?

Those cannot be the answers to this question, because they are simply means, and when we confuse means with ends, we start dying on the inside. We want to live longer and more comfortably—to do *what*? We want to have more air-conditioning—to achieve *what*? What legacy do we want to leave? What is worthy of our attention, time, and effort? Presumably, if we are serious about life, we are not simply looking to be more comfortable. Yet that is exactly what most of the things we buy are claiming to do.

THE JEWISH IDEA OF FREEDOM

The contemporary concept of freedom is based on the possibility for each to express his or her desires, creativity, and productivity. It stresses the maximum removal of external restraints. It is a combination of autonomy and means. In essence, it is a freedom from constraints—do what you want—as opposed to freedom *to* become something.[1] Yet, this contemporary framework of freedom is half-baked. It ignores the question of where this all takes us. It is "freedom from" without the idea of "freedom to."

The Jewish concept of freedom proposes a radical theology. It begins with the understanding that the freest being in existence is God. Therefore, the metric for freedom is likeness to God. It is not a freedom from, but rather a freedom to—to become as Godlike as we possibly can. It is not an emphasis on what constrains me, but rather what commitments and obligations I can make in the process of transcending myself. There is a common misconception that aligns freedom with the maximization of choices—that the more one has from which to choose, the greater his freedom. Yet, we are not free when we keep our choices open. Having an abundance of choice and failing to use that choice to commit to something produces paralysis, not freedom.

For sure, we need freedom *from*—freedom from hunger and illness, oppression, and war. But this is not the end goal. If everyone is truly free, why are we here? What do we do with our lives? Freedom makes the journey possible; it is to allow us to choose the path that will be most meaningful to our lives.[2] Perforce, that path will require commitment, limitations of options, and the undertaking of responsibilities. But this is the only

The freest being in existence is God, and therefore, the more Godlike we are, the more free we will be.

1 The Jewish-English philosopher, Isaiah Berlin, made this distinction in his book, *Two Concepts of Liberty*.

2 Freedoms *from* include from being censored, from unjust incrimination, from forced religion, respectively. It is arguable that some of the higher freedoms, like freedom of speech, the right to remain silent, and religious freedom are also essentially freedom *froms*. They are there to allow us to actualize ourselves as we see fit.

way we can release the opportunities to fulfill our potential, and that, after all, is what everyone wants from freedom.

INTERNAL VS. EXTERNAL FREEDOM

One who allows his weaknesses and whims to control him is essentially enslaved to his cravings and desires. He may be free of external constraints but feel shackled by internal ones. The same is true of someone who is given everything on a silver platter and owes nothing to his own efforts. Such a person has no control and no freedom, as his life is not driven by his personal will. He has everything but his own real self. As long as the will driving his actions is dictated by something external to himself—e.g., fashions, advertisements, and consumerism—he has not yet achieved the dignity of true freedom.

Human grandeur cannot be expressed by "Level One" freedom. Rather, we are on this earth to achieve "Level Two" freedom—of allowing our freely chosen values to define our lives and channel our actions.[3]

The way the Torah enables this is by first establishing each individual's profound worth and potential. It then provides us with a system for self-mastery. It teaches us how to control, direct, and channel our passions, drives, and compulsions.[4] It teaches us to harness our physical desires in the service of sanctity.[5] Through the Torah, we learn how to get in touch with our higher selves and connect with God, the One being that is truly free.

The Torah tells us that the Tablets were engraved with the letters of the Ten Commandments, inscribed by God Himself.[6] The Hebrew word for "engraved" is *charut* (חרות), which are the same letters that comprise the Hebrew word for "freedom"—*cheirut* (חירות).[7] (On the Tablets, as in the Torah, the vowels are not written.) The point is that to obey these commandments is to get close to the Source of freedom and to rid ourselves of the shackles of petty desires and whims. God's own engraving

---

3 *Collected Writings of Rabbi Shimshon Raphael Hirsch*, Passover.

4 See Section 4.

5 See Section 2.

6 Exodus 32:15–16.

7 *Tanna d'Bei Eliyahu Zuta* 16.

(*charut*) of the letters on the Tablets is our true liberation (*cheirut*) and empowerment.[8]

FREE TO SERVE

When God redeemed the Jews from Egyptian slavery, the pivotal moment of freedom in Jewish history was achieved. In Egypt, the Jews were a slave nation that was physically, socially, and emotionally oppressed by their Egyptian overseers. Yet, when God sent Moses to Pharaoh to demand the Jews be set free, He instructed Moses to add a vital phrase. Not just, "Let my people go," but also "*that they may serve Me* (i.e., God)."[9] But this was also a message to the Jewish People. It was as if God was saying: "If you are simply going *from* the slavery of Egypt, you will remain slaves in your heart. Your thinking will be Egyptian. Your values will be Egyptian. Your bodies will be freed, but your minds will not. The inner call of your humanity will go unanswered." Therefore, free yourself to become obligated—not as a burden but as a privilege. The privilege of responsibility.

The Jewish demand of the Pharaohs of the world is never just a release from servitude. It is the yearning for the freedom to stand at Sinai and commit to the vision and mission of God!

To our modern minds, this may seem paradoxical. How can freedom be equated with being a servant of God? But God clearly had in mind a liberation theology. Serving Him did not mean replacing one slavery with another—Pharaoh's with God's. Rather, God's message to the Jewish People is, "Serve Me and you will be free, because by following My commandments, you will unleash enormous power. You will become My partner in completing the creation of the world."[10]

THE DISCIPLINE OF FREEDOM

Have you ever witnessed a world-class pianist glide across the keyboard with absolute mastery, producing the most perfect sound? So

---

8 Talmud, Tractate *Kallah*, chap. 8.

9 This message is delivered repeatedly by Moses to Pharaoh: Exodus 7:16; 8:16, and more.

10 See Chapter 10 for a discussion of this at length.

many of us would love to be able to do that—to have that freedom to produce whatever sound we wish. But the pianist spends three to four hours a day (and a minimum lifetime of ten thousand hours) to achieve that "freedom." If I were to sit at that keyboard, I would just produce noise. I am not free to glide across the keyboard because I have not subjected myself to the *discipline* of freedom.

Take, for instance, language. "The capacity to use language" says psychologist Barry Schwartz, "is perhaps the single most liberating characteristic of human beings."[11] What is more freeing than the ability to express one's thoughts and feelings tangibly? Yet, Dr. Schwartz pins the possibility of linguistic freedom on the very fact that there are structured constraints and limitations to any given language. "The reason people can say anything and be understood is that they can't say everything."

Self-determination, he continues, also requires significant constraints, without which it can be shown that people don't function optimally.[12] We have to see this discipline as our friend, as the enabler not only to the musician and our language but also to our greatest spiritual aspirations.

The key to true freedom, the means through which we can actualize our potential to become something, is commitment. Just like the pianist commits hours upon hours to master his craft, a person who seeks to become something must dedicate himself to his values and exclude all extraneous pursuits. As mentioned previously, the Torah is the spiritual guide for achieving moral and spiritual freedom. But the Torah will not yield this freedom without commitment. This is what the Sages meant when they stated: "No one is free except he who busies himself with Torah."

For this reason, there were two stages to the Sinaitic experience. The Jews of course accepted the Torah at Sinai—or, more accurately, the

11 Barry Schwartz, "Self Determination: The Tyranny of Freedom," *American Psychologist*, 55 no. 1(2000), p. 80.

12 Ibid.

Ten Commandments engraved on the Tablets.[13] But for the whole chapter prior to this event, the Torah deals with the Jewish covenant with God.[14] "You shall be a kingdom of priests and a holy nation,"[15] i.e., you shall become not the chosen nation with a right to privileges, but the obligated nation—a nation I have chosen because of your commitment to Me and My laws.

With their redemption from Egypt, the Jewish People achieved Level One freedom. However, they can only embark on the journey to embrace Level Two freedom—the moral and spiritual vision that is the Torah—by entering a covenantal relationship with God. Though paradoxical, the commitment that paves the way for higher freedom simultaneously presents significant obligation and duty.

JUDAISM BEGINS WITH DUTIES, NOT RIGHTS

When the French Revolution announced a Bill of Rights, it also announced a Bill of Duties. The former became famous. The latter was forgotten.[16]

All societies have rights and duties. However, Western societies begin with rights and end with duties. In these societies, the first question one asks is, "What are my rights?" To preserve my rights, you—the other—have a duty not to trample on them:

- I have property. You have a duty not to trespass on my property.
- I have a right to freedom of speech. You are not allowed to shout me down.

Your duty is a consequence of my right.

In Judaism, we begin with duties, not rights. If my starting point is rights, then I need not have a vision for myself, and I don't have to have my values clear. I can choose moment by moment or year by year. My

---

13 Exodus, chap. 20.

14 Ibid. 19:5–6.

15 Ibid. 19:6.

16 In 1795, the National Convention produced a new constitution called the "Declaration of Rights and Duties of Man and Citizen." It was put to referendum and implemented.

rights grant me that and more. But if my starting point is obligation, I have to know what I am committing myself to…and why.

As a nation, we might be said to be the obligated people. As individuals, we view our personal destinies in terms of our responsibility toward ourselves as well as to the broader world. We have to develop our own potential, and by so doing we make the world a better place.

THE PRIVILEGE OF OBLIGATION

There is a fascinating blessing that mitzvah-observant Jews wish others when they see them doing a kindness or some other virtuous act. They say, "*tizku le'Mitzvot*." This translates as, "May you merit to fulfill many commandments." A mitzvah is a commandment. It is an obligation. The nicest thing you can bless a fellow Jew with is to wish him to have further opportunities to be obligated! This is the Jewish paradigm: Obligation is far from a burden. Rather, it is a privilege. How is this so?

The nicest thing you can bless a fellow Jew with is to wish him to have further opportunities to be obligated! This is the Jewish head. Obligation is a privilege.

According to Bruno Bettelheim, a Jew who survived the Holocaust, "Our greatest need and most difficult achievement is to find meaning in our lives."[17] Without meaning, there is no thread that connects all the points of my life, and I remain a fragmented being. If I do not find my past meaningful, I will not know how to achieve my future. And if I have no past and future, my present is meaningless. Meaning is what strings the fragments of our lives into a unified existence, "in true consciousness of our existence."

When someone asked Einstein what question he would ask God if he could ask one, he replied, "How did the universe start? Because everything after that is just math." After thinking for a while, he changed his mind. He said, "Instead I would ask, 'Why was the universe created?' Because then I would know the meaning of my own life."

---

17 Bruno Bettelheim, *The Uses of Enchantment: The Meaning and Importance of Fairy Tales* (Thames and Hudson, 1976), Introduction.

Uncovering the meaning of one's life is the most important pursuit for man. Rabbi Moshe Chaim Luzatto, also known by the Hebrew acronym *Ramchal*, was a prominent 18th century Italian Jewish Kabbalist and philosopher whose books are considered indispensable classics of Jewish thought.[18] In the opening statement to his work, *Path of the Righteous*, he states:

> *The foundation of righteousness and the root of pure service require that man clarifies and integrates*[19] *what his obligation in his world is and toward what he should focus his vision in all that he exerts himself all the days of his life.*[20]

The *Ramchal*'s words may appear to be the same as those of Bettelheim and Einstein, but there is a crucial difference. The *Ramchal*'s statement is couched in the language of obligation. According to the Jewish perspective, the very same goal that Bettelheim phrases as our greatest need and achievement is considered an obligation! However, this is only logical, as if one understands his purpose, how could he not feel obligated to fulfill it? This obligation is far from a burden. Rather, it is a privilege.

---

18 See Appendix for more.

19 Lit., understands to be true.

20 *Ramchal, Mesilat Yesharim*, chap. 1.

3

JOURNEY AND DESTINATION

Man attains his unique identity when, after having been enlightened by God that he is not only a committed but also a free person, endowed with power to implement his commitment, he grasps the incommensurability of what he is and what he is destined to be.

Rabbi J. B. Soloveitchik[1]

Can we understand God's mind? Can we know what He was thinking when He created the world?

Let's take a step back for a moment. If freedom and meaning are intertwined with connection to God, why would God create us on earth, a place so far removed from Him? The ways of God are further compounded when considering His essence. God is perfect.[2] He lacks nothing. Why should God create us at all? What benefit could God receive by creating man? The very notion of us, mere mortals, serving as beneficial to God would undermine God's perfection by implying that He needs something.

We can solve this dilemma by understanding the parameters of God's perfection.

---

1 "Confrontation," in *Tradition*, vol. 6, no. 2.

2 *Ramchal, Derech Hashem* 1:1:6.

Part of God's perfection is that He is "perfectly" good.[3] This trait of perfect goodness lends itself to the desire of sharing that goodness with others, for, "It is the law of the good to do good."[4] Hence, a perfectly good God who lacks nothing must have created man for man's benefit of receiving God's goodness.[5]

However, since God is not only good, but perfectly good, this will not suffice. God's perfect goodness dictates that He does the maximum good possible, and this implies that He should create man to share as many of His attributes as possible. This would make man as close to God as he could be.[6]

But there was a catch to this idea. For there is one attribute that appears to be non-transferable. God is a "bestower" of good—an active creator of good. Man is a passive recipient of that good. How can man possibly share this attribute of God's goodness if man's very creation and existence is the receiving of good? This creates a tension. For without the sharing of this attribute, there would be a fundamental difference between man and God, a vast chasm that would appear to be unbridgeable. This would implicate that God's giving is restricted; like a classic catch-22, His very giving transforms His creation into a limited receiver.

CLOSING THE GAP BETWEEN GOD AND MAN

To solve this dilemma, and to enable man to be a creator of goodness, God would need to provide man with the ability to choose equally between good and evil. Choice would become a defining feature of human dignity and completeness. If man chooses good, he is allowing for the creation of goodness by dismissing evil from staking its ground (or vice versa). Hence, man becomes a creator of good in his own right and is close to God in this respect.

---

3 Hence, the Torah, which is a revelation of God's will, begins with kindness, ends with kindness, and its middle is kindness; *Tanchuma, Parashat Vayeira* 64.

4 *Ramchal, Daat Tevunot* 18.

5 Ibid. See also *Derech Hashem* 1:2:1.

6 *Derech Hashem* ad loc.

Yet, the mechanism through which God provides this choice sustains yet another dilemma. For God must distance himself from man to allow for the goodness-creating attribute to be obtained so that evil is seen as an option for man's choices. But man would now be far away from God's other attributes! Man can have distance and choice, or closeness and no choice. He cannot have both. And either option limits God's gift to man.[7]

If God had created Man as close to Himself as possible, God would have been a creator of goodness and man would have been a created goodness.

THE TWO WORLDS

To solve this, God created man in a two-stage process. Stage One places man a distance away from God and allows man to become a God-like creator of goodness. Stage Two removes the distance and allows man to get close to all of God's other attributes.

Each stage requires a different environment. The environment for Stage One is called "This World" (*olam hazeh*).[8] The journey through This World is fueled by choice. In This World, God is distant and veils his face (*hester panim*), hiding His essence. Though created and sustained by Him, physical reality appears to take on an independent existence—with God hiding behind this veil. Man can therefore choose to distance himself from God. Yet, man can also choose to connect himself and draw closer to God, as God is only hidden and not absent.[9]

Once man goes through This World, he is ready for Stage Two. The environment for Stage Two is called "the World to Come" or "the Next World" (*olam haba*).[10] There is no choice in the World to Come. The reality of God will be so clear that no alternative will present itself. In the World to Come, we will continue to grow, constantly getting closer and closer to the Infinite God. However, this growth will not be determined

---

7 The way this is expressed in the *Derech Hashem* (1:3:3) is that the period of good (of being close to God) has to be longer than the period of earning that good.

8 Ibid. 1:3:3.

9 *Ramchal, Daat Tevunot* 40.

10 *Derech Hashem* 1:3:3.

by our choices. We will be attracted inexorably toward God, closer and closer, forever.[11]

Each environment—both This World and the Next—is impeccably tailored for its purpose. This World is perfectly designed to give man a balance of choice between good and evil, between the sensual and the spiritual, between the impure and the holy.[12] The World to Come is perfectly designed for getting close to God in all other respects, the joy of which cannot be imagined.[13]

BETWEEN THE WORLDS

The trajectory of mankind includes an additional stage, an intermediate stage between This World and the World to Come. This stage is called the Messianic Era.[14]

The Messianic Era has characteristics of both worlds:

- The laws of nature will still function,[15] economies will run and be developed, science will progress,[16] and there will still be different nations and peoples, each with a specific contribution to make.[17]
- However, during this time, man will have such an acute sense of clarity about our purpose that there will be no viable alternative to following that purpose.[18] Although we will still have the capacity for choice, man will not be attracted to anything other than connection with God.[19] As Jeremiah put it: "No longer will

---

11 *Daat Tevunot* 88. Actually, there will be a time when we will be so high that we will be above time. Time, for us, will then stop. This is called the tenth millennium.

12 *Derech Hashem* 1:2:4.

13 Ibid.

14 *Ramchal*, *Maamar Ha'ikkarim*; *Shem MiShmuel*, *Parashat Eikev* (Deuteronomy), p. 75, words beg. *v'nireh*.

15 *Maharal* of Prague, Rabbi Judah Loew ben Bezalel (1520–1609). *Netzach Yisrael*, chap. 50. The *Maharal* is best remembered for his many books on Jewish thought, in which he gives deep and profound insights into seemingly every issue. We will refer to him many times throughout this work as the *Maharal*; see Appendix for more.

16 Maimonides, *Mishneh Torah*, Laws of Kings 12:1, Laws of Repentance 9:2.

17 *Ramban*, *Sefer Havikuach* 39.

18 *Ramban*, Deuteronomy 30:2.

19 Maimonides, *Mishneh Torah*, Laws of Kings 12:5.

> man teach his friend, nor man his brother saying, 'know God,' for everyone will know Me from the youngest to the eldest."[20]

In the Messianic Era, the entire history of creation will be brought to a state of holistic completion, what is known as the *tikkun haklali*, the repairing of our fractured world.[21] At this time, we will understand the world as a grand symphony where each person plays his or her part to produce this big picture of pure spirituality.[22] Because everyone will have the same goal, there will be no wars, no arguments, and no tension between one person and the next. All of mankind will be dedicated to producing more and more spirituality.

In the beginning, God created the goals toward which man should aspire, as well as the means to achieve those goals.

As the Messianic Era unfolds, our understanding that everything connects back to God will become more and more profound. We will look back on all history and find that even when and where He seemed hidden, He was in fact completely behind all that happened and existed.[23]

DESTINATION BEFORE JOURNEY

The final destination of complete and unadulterated closeness to God preceded all of creation. God indicates this in the very first verse of the Torah before the world began. This verse reads: "In the beginning, God created the heavens and the earth."[24] The Hebrew word for heavens, *shamayim* (שמים), shares the same root as the word *sham* (שם), which means "there." This suggests that the heavens are the ultimate "there"—the destination and goal. The Hebrew word for earth, *eretz* (ארץ), is etymologically related to the word *ratz* (רץ), which means "run," alluding to the purpose of the earth as the place in which we run and advance toward our goals.

---

20 Jeremiah 31: 33. When Jeremiah says "Me," he is producing, through prophecy, God's words. There are many other verses in *Tanach* that refer to this idea. See for example, Isaiah 2:2–3, 11:9, 66:23; Zephaniah 3:9; Zechariah 14: 9. See also *Mishneh Torah*, Laws of Kings 12:1.

21 *Ramchal*, *Kelach Pitchei Chochmah* (*Petach* B, p. 6); *Daat Tevunot*, p. 32.

22 *Ramchal*, *Daat Tevunot*, 168.

23 Ibid.

24 Genesis 1:1.

With this insight, the initial verse of the Torah translates as "In the beginning, God created the goals toward which man should aspire, as well as the means to achieve those goals." The chronology of the verse states that the heavens, or the goals, were created before the earth, or the means. God knew at the outset why He was creating the world.

We too must know at the outset of our journey of life why we were created. For if we don't, we remain clueless as to where we need to go. Or, to paraphrase the Cheshire Cat's wisdom from *Alice in Wonderland*, if you don't know where you are going, any road will take you there.[25]

If you don't know where you are going, any road will take you there.

The great Kabbalist of Safed, Rabbi Shlomo Alkabetz, referenced this concept in his famous composition, the *Lecha Dodi* song. The Kabbalists were known to go out to the fields surrounding Safed as the sun would set on Friday and sing *Lecha Dodi* to usher in the Shabbat. One of the stanzas concludes by saying: "The end of the action was in the thought at the outset."[26] God knew at the outset of His thought what the end of His action would be. On the Shabbat, when we take a step back and get our goals right, we too have an opportunity to see the horizon—the goals that will guide our actions, the vision that will propel us forward. That vision ought to inform everything else we do. As Michel De Montaigne, the French Renaissance philosopher, put it, "The great and glorious masterpiece of man is to know how to live life in purpose."

---

25 Lewis Carroll, *Alice in Wonderland*: "Would you tell me, please, which way I ought to go from here?"
"That depends a good deal on where you want to get to."
"I don't much care where—"
"Then it doesn't matter which way you go."

26 Friday night service, *Kabbalat Shabbat*: "*Sof maaseh be'machashavah techilah.*" It is thought to be based on the *Zohar* (vol. 3, 238:1): "First in thought; last in action."

4

WHO AM I?

Today you are you. That is truer than true.
There is no one alive that is youer than you.

Dr. Seuss, Happy Birthday to You

BEING TRUE TO ONESELF

Rabbi Shlomo Wolbe, one of the great sages of the last century, made a remarkable statement: "I, with all my abilities, potentials, and talents, both physical and spiritual, am unique in the universe. Amongst all those alive today, there is no other me. In past generations, too, there was no other me, and until the end of time there will be no other me." This uniqueness is not an accident, the random outcome of genetic variation. Rabbi Wolbe continues, "And if so, the Master of the Universe must certainly have sent me here on a special mission that could be fulfilled by no one else but me—with all my uniqueness."[1]

To be true to myself, I cannot be the way I am because of what someone else does. Nor can I determine my self-worth by comparing myself to others. The great Chassidic master, Rabbi Menachem Mendel of Kotzk, stated, "If I am I because I am I and you are you because you are

1 Rabbi Shlomo Wolbe, *Alei Shur*, vol. 1, p. 68.

you, then I am I and you are you. But if I am I because you are you and you are you because I am I, then I am not I and you are not you."

The point is that I must actualize my own God-given potential and not to try and become someone else. Only then can I live authentically and with the appropriate human dignity. There will only ever be one Abraham and one Moses. This is because there is only one of each of us. Hence, I am not meant to become Abraham or Moses. I am meant to become...me![2]

I am not meant to become Abraham or Moses. I am meant to become me!

RESISTING SOCIAL MESSAGES

If all of my distinct aspects enable me to do what no one else can, I have to embrace my uniqueness. I have to own it. I have to dig deep to know what motivates me. Am I just trying to fit in because of my intense need to be accepted? Or worse, do I follow the crowd because I am worried of being laughed at for my differences? The vision of ourselves lies not in the society beyond but within the deepest recesses of our souls.

Our deep desire to be accepted by others takes on many guises and can even pose as a way of being unique. Take the infiltration of jeans into the former Soviet Union. Symbolizing the freedom of the Western world, jeans became a hot black-market item in Communist countries, as they represented the rebellious.[3] Yet, in the name of that rebellion, everyone became the same. They *all* wanted to wear jeans. Many Soviet youths made their wardrobe choices thinking that they were being individuals, going against the grain of society, but in truth they were just following the crowd.

---

2 Based on the Vilna Gaon.

3 See Niall Ferguson, *Civilization*, pp. 240–50. On p. 249, he discusses why jeans were such a threat to the Soviet system.

I AM MY REALITY PLUS MY POTENTIAL

If we are to be true to ourselves, we need to get to know ourselves.[4] And once we have met ourselves, we need to like what we see. But that is just the beginning. We need to also believe in our almost-endless capacity to become more than we can imagine. We must develop what the Kabbalists call *mochin d'gadlut*—"greatness of thinking"—an expanded consciousness.[5] "God made the human upright," said the Kotzker Rebbe, "unlike the animal who walks on all fours. While the beast sees only the earth, man can also look up toward the heavens," i.e., toward a greater vision of himself.[6]

In fact, believing in ourselves is part of believing in God. I must believe that God wants *me* with my individual makeup, and He delights in *me* when I am true to myself, thus fulfilling His will.[7] He is the "God of faith."[8] Every person's creation was preceded with God's faith. God trusts us, and we must hence believe in ourselves.

Fulfilling our mission in life is not about our skills, charisma, power, or status. It is first and foremost a function of our own moral and spiritual worth.

In the *Modeh Ani* prayer, the first words a Jew says upon waking are:

> *I thank you, O living and eternal King, for You have returned my soul within me with compassion—abundant is Your faithfulness.*

As each day dawns, God expresses his faith in us—that we will do good and are therefore worthy of getting our souls back. We are expected to similarly renew our faith in ourselves. Each one of us must believe that we are the person that God was waiting for.[9]

4 Rabbi Shlomo Wolbe, *Alei Shur*, vol. 1, Gate 3.
5 *Zohar*, Genesis 1:73.
6 Quoted by Menachem Posner, Chabad.org, based on *Kochav Hashachar*, by Simcha Raz.
7 Rabbi Tzadok HaKohen, *Tzidkat Hatzaddik*, p. 154.
8 *Sifri*, brought by Rabbi Michoel Ber Weissmandel.
9 Rabbi Michoel Ber Weissmandel, *Ish Hachamudot*, in the *Yiddishe Velt*.

OUR PROFOUND INTERDEPENDENCE

Judaism believes that everyone has a double role to play in the world. We have to fulfill our individual potential—our personal *tikkun* (reparation). In addition, each of us has a unique contribution to make to the general *tikkun* that will bring the world to completion.[10] This means that we are all interdependent in a profound way. I need you to fulfill your potential as much as you need me to fulfill mine. My responsibility to help you is an extension of my personal God-given mission.

MISSION IMPERATIVE

On Rosh Hashanah, God looks at "Man's doings and [the] charge [placed in his hands]."[11]What does this mean? We are held accountable both for our deeds in general, as well as how we carried out our "charge"—our unique mission.

Moses' encounter with God at the Burning Bush was a lesson for eternity on just this issue. God requested of Moses to approach Pharaoh and demand the Jews be freed from Egypt. Moses retort was "*Mi anochi*—Who am I?"[12]

Moses' first concern was not his skill set, charisma, or status, or whether he had enough experience negotiating slave-releases.[13] Moses was saying, "Who am I to be worthy of such a mission?"[14] Fulfilling our mission is first and foremost a function of our own moral and spiritual worth. We need to "merit" success. But success itself should not be at the forefront of our calculation. We are to do what we can and then turn to God and say, "This is as far as I can go. The rest is up to you." We are not ultimately in charge of the results, only the effort.[15]

---

10 *Ramchal*, *Daat Tevunot* 44.

11 מַעֲשֵׂה אִישׁ וּפְקֻדָּתוֹ—Rosh Hashanah prayers.

12 Exodus 3:11.

13 Although some commentators do opine that it was just this that Moses meant when he said, "Who am I?"

14 *Bechor Shor*, Exodus 3:11.

15 *Ramchal*, *Mesilat Yesharim*, beg. of chap. 26.

But Moses had another concern: The Jewish People, the very ones I am trying to help, "will not believe me and they will not heed my voice."[16] I may believe in myself, but why should anybody else believe in me?

God's response was astonishing.

As one of three signs, God instructed Moses to put his hand in his bosom and it emerged with a kind of skin disease called *tzaraat*.[17] God told Moses to repeat the action, and his hand was cured.[18] *Tzaraat* is the punishment for speaking negatively (*lashon hara*) about someone. God was showing Moses that he was being misled by his internal snake (God had turned Moses' staff into a snake)—an external message of his internal state—which caused him not to trust his people.[19] As people echo our trust, the reason the Jews might not believe him is because he did not believe in them. God later instructed Moses to write this incident in the Torah as an eternal lesson to us to believe in people.

Hidden in this message was another—that Moses' personal growth would only be achieved when he engaged the Jewish People, when he turned his "me" into a "we."

In essence, God's response amounted to, "If you will believe in them, they will believe in you."

Moses was not done. He claimed that he didn't have the right personality and talent: "I am not a man of words…for I am heavy of mouth and heavy of speech."[20] He wasn't the articulate, charismatic leader type. Note that it is only at this stage that Moses makes this claim.

God answered him, "Who makes a mouth for man, or who makes one dumb or deaf, or seeing or blind? Is it not I, God? So now go! I shall be with your mouth and teach you what you should say."[21] In fact, many great leaders were not charismatic. Believe in your cause, be courageous and humble, and people will follow.

---

16 Exodus 4:1.

17 Ibid., v. 6. *Tzaraat* is often incorrectly translated as leprosy.

18 Ibid., v. 7.

19 *Rashi*, Exodus 4:3, 6.

20 Ibid., v. 10.

21 Ibid., v. 11–12.

Moses tried one more argument. He suggested a better candidate. "Maybe I could do it. But my brother Aaron is more equipped than I am."[22] This solicits "the wrath of God."[23] One cannot play God, pretending to know the potential and the mission of every person.

The Torah, known for its conciseness, describes Moses' argument with such detail as a mirror of our own self-doubt. We don't, of course have burning bushes to make things clear. But neither did Rabbi Yochanan ben Zakkai, who was a businessman until the age of forty, then became a Torah student until he was eighty, and only then was called Rabbi.[24] Rabbi Akiva hated rabbis when he was younger and only started studying (also) at forty.[25] Both became leaders of Torah in their generation.

Just as a person is obligated to believe in God, so one must then believe in oneself.

We cannot, as Jews once did, go to a prophet to find out our mission in life. But, often enough, it is clear what we are responsible for—be it ourselves, family, or society. How often do we shy away from responsibility because we doubt our worthiness, don't think others will believe in us, feel that our resume is not up to snuff, or pinpoint someone better for the job? But the story of Moses shows us that none of us can escape our mission. If we can make a difference, we should feel the privilege of obligation.

WE NEVER HAVE TO GO IT ALONE

God assured Moses not only that He believed in him, but that "I will be with you."[26] God stated, "I will be as I will be."[27] This means, "I will be with you in future situations just as I am with you in this one."[28] You need not play God. I will be there. Audrey Hepburn once stated, "Nothing is impossible; the word itself says 'I'm possible'!" That statement only

22 Ibid., v. 13.
23 Ibid., v. 14.
24 Talmud, Tractate *Sanhedrin* 41a–b.
25 *Avot d'Rabi Natan*, chap. 11.
26 Exodus 3:12.
27 Ibid., v. 14. *Chizkuni* and others translate this as "I will be *because* I will be."
28 *Rashi*, ibid.

makes sense when you know that you have God on your team. On our own, we are all too often too vulnerable and overwhelmed, or have too much baggage, or are pursuing the wrong things to begin with. He is, as we say in the first blessing of the silent prayer, our "helper, redeemer, and shield." God will empower us when we are on the right track (our "helper"); save us when we are on the wrong one (our "redeemer"); and protect us from getting into situations that we are not capable of dealing with to begin with (our "shield").

5

BODY AND SOUL

A blind man and a lame man steal some fruit from an orchard guarded by a high fence. They do this by joining forces. The lame man climbs onto the shoulders of the blind man and guides him toward the fruit. When caught, each of them claims that he is obviously unable to commit the crime due to his disability. The orchard owner places the lame man on the back of the blind man and they are judged as one. [A parable to the soul and the body]

Talmud, Tractate Sanhedrin 91a

THE THIRD DIMENSION

Kabbalistic wisdom states that this world is comprised of three dimensions: time, space, and soul.[1]

These three dimensions are inseparably linked. Einstein demonstrated this connection with regard to time and space, declaring that one cannot accurately describe one without the other. There is not time and space. There is only space-time.[2]

---

1 *Sefer Hayetzirah* 6:1. In Hebrew, this is known as *Olam* ("world"—space), *Shanah* ("year"—time), and *Nefesh* (one of the words for soul).

2 This was a part of Einstein's General Theory of Relativity, which he announced in 1915.

Likewise, from the Jewish perspective, one can only speak of time-space-soul.[3] In fact, it goes further than simply linking these dimensions together. Kabbalah states that the energy source sustaining the world is the soul. It is the internal spiritual dimension that sustains the other two.[4]

BODY-SOUL INTEGRATION

We are created as two seemingly contradictory parts: body and soul. Our bodies, which are very physical, are created by God's "hidden face." Our souls are created by His "revealed face."[5] The body is an exact replica of how God hides His face in the world, and the soul is an exact replica of how God shines His light in this world.[6]

Neither alone can define us. We are not our body. The body is a transient creation, made from the dust of the earth.[7] When its time on earth expires, it will return to the dust of the earth.[8] However, we can't be our soul either. When saying the morning blessings, one declares: "God, the soul that you have placed in me is pure."[9] If so, there must be a "me" external to the soul that can receive it.

In this world, body and soul are in constant tension. Each of us—the being that is made of these two elements—is essentially a paradox. The miracle of man is that God integrated the soul and the body into one being. When we think of ourselves, we don't think of two beings—a body and a soul. They are both just us. One who cannot think this way will be alienated from his own being. (Alternatively, he may be an existential

---

3 *Yosher Divrei Emet* 53.

4 See below.

5 *Ramchal, Daat Tevunot* 80.

6 Ibid.

7 Genesis 2:7: "And the Lord God formed man dust from the earth and He blew into his nostrils the breath of life." The body was from the "dust of the earth," while "the breath of life" refers to the creation of the soul.
See also ibid., v. 17, where God also forms the animals from the ground. However, the term "dust of the earth" is only used with reference to man.

8 Genesis 3:19: "By the sweat of your brow you will eat bread until your return to the ground, for you were taken from it, for you are dust and you will return to dust."

9 Prayerbook, Morning Blessings.

philosopher.) If man thinks he is only his soul, then when his body acts with sensual passion or craves materialism, or wants to sin, who is that?

If we want to integrate the multiple facets of our being and still be the same person, we have to become soul-people. Only then can we connect all the dots of a self that is part angel and part animal. Only then can we stay true to ourselves across the spectrum of our lives.

THE WONDROUS CREATION

How this works—how body and soul come together to create "me"—is one of the ineffable mysteries of the creation.

There is a blessing that is said after using the bathroom, in which we praise God for allowing our bodies to work properly. We declare that should any opening of our bodies be clogged or anything ruptures, we would cease to exist, and it is God who maintains our existence. This blessing ends: "Blessed are You, O God, Who heals the flesh and acts wondrously." While there are many blessing of praise to God, the inclusion of "wonder" is unique to this blessing. What is the wonder here?

In the early morning, this blessing of the body is followed directly by the blessing of the soul. The wonder is that these two—body and soul—come together in a new synthesis. God "acts wondrously" and man remains mystified. Recognizing this, we choose to bless God appropriately.[10] The very mundane act of going to the bathroom stimulates our sensitivity to this wonder of the creation.

THE LIMITATION OF THE SOUL

While we are composed of both body and soul, the soul is the component that defines us. Because of its spiritual nature, the soul is much closer to the source of ultimate energy—i.e., God Himself—and hence is much more powerful than the body.[11]

We are first and foremost soul-people.

10 Rabbi Moshe Isserles (the *Rama*), glosses on the *Shulchan Aruch*, *Orach Chaim* 6:1.

11 *Ramchal*, *Derech Hashem* 1:3:13.

In a statement that is both profound and multifaceted, the Sages describe the relationship of the soul to the body as similar to the relationship God has with the world:

> *To whom was [King] David referring to in these five [verses beginning with] "Bless the Lord, O my soul" (Barchi Nafshi)?*[12] *He was alluding only to the Holy One, blessed be He, and to the soul.*
>
> *Just as the Holy One, blessed be He, fills the whole world, so too the soul fills the body.*
>
> *Just as the Holy One, blessed be He, sees but is not seen, so too the soul sees but is not itself seen.*
>
> *Just as the Holy One, blessed be He, nourishes the whole world, so too the soul nourishes the whole body.*
>
> *Just as the Holy One, blessed be He, is pure, so too the soul is pure.*
>
> *Just as the Holy One, blessed be He, abides in the innermost precincts, so too the soul abides in the innermost precincts.*
>
> *Let that which has these five qualities come and praise He who has these five qualities.*[13]

This means that the soul's spiritual energy is comparable to God's expression in the world. Given this, it is so much stronger than the body that, left to express itself fully, it would immediately "whoosh" the body up to the highest spiritual levels possible.[14] There would be no choice, no ethical struggle, no world as we know it here.[15] The purpose of creation—that we choose to do good and reject evil—would be defeated.

To level the playing field between soul and body, the soul is artificially restrained by God,[16] "its power is obstructed and its brilliance reduced."[17]

---

12 Psalms 103:1, 2, 22, 104:1, 35.

13 Talmud, Tractate *Berachot* 10a.

14 Ibid.

15 *Ramchal, Derech Hashem* 1:3:1–2.

16 Ibid., no. 13.

17 Ibid.

This allows for a balance of choice between the good and the bad—a perfect environment for choice that is delicately balanced between the possibilities of good and evil.[18] The result is that two voices whisper into our ears at every turn, and every choice matters, moving us higher up toward the soul-reality or further into the material-reality.[19] If we choose to do good, the soul gradually elevates and purifies the body.[20] The body then also becomes a force for good.

In the World to Come, the soul will be allowed to express itself fully and the body will move in total harmony with it, inexorably toward God.[21] The World to Come functions entirely under the "revealed face" of God. With absolute clarity of God as the Source of everything,[22] there will be no alternative to drawing close to God. There will be no choice.[23] The soul will express itself freely, rendering the body powerless.[24]

The various stages of history can then be described as stages of the soul becoming increasingly more dominant with respect to the body. The body becomes increasingly purer as a result.[25]

---

18 Ibid., no. 2–3.

19 Ibid.

20 Ibid., no. 7.

21 Ibid.

22 Ibid., no. 4.

23 The lack of choice already begins in the Messianic Era; *Ramban*, Deuteronomy 30:2.

24 Ibid. See above, "The Limitation of the Soul." The *Ramchal* (*Daat Tevunot*, 88) describes the relationship of the soul to the body in five different stages:

1. The time during the soul's sojourn in This World, a period of six thousand years: The body has significant control, and it is the job of the soul to channel the urges and passions of the body toward sanctity.
2. The Seventh Millennium, the Messianic Era: All body faculties are present but not necessarily operative. The soul is clearly the leading force.
3. The Eighth Millennium, the beginning of the World to Come (after Resurrection of the Dead): We are now in a world of pure and fine spirituality. The soul is the driving force and the body is hence also able to enjoy the spiritual rewards of this world. The body, at this stage, still has limited control with respect to some details.
4. The Ninth Millennium: a deepening of whatever happened in the Eighth Millennium.
5. The Tenth Millennium: By now, there is no control exerted by the body, which is now completely annulled to the soul.

25 See previous footnote. However, there will always be a slight difference between the body and the soul. *Ramchal, Daat Tevunot* 80 (p. 67), last paragraph.

This is only logical. The highest parts of any creature represent their essence, otherwise, why would they be endowed with that extra capacity?[26] Our bodies may be physical, but they are filled up by our souls.[27] The shape of our bodies reflects that.[28] Our body, in essence, is just a garment for the soul.[29]

THE SOUL IS HOLISTIC—THE BODY IS FRAGMENTARY

If we define ourselves in any way that deviates from our spiritual authenticity, we will simply not be satisfied. We may become rich or famous or successful, but there will always be a voice inside that proclaims that we are missing out on whom we really are. I have met numerous people at the very top of their professions—doctors, business people, artists, architects—and they all told the same story. They always believed that reaching the top was the key to happiness—until they got there. They were stuck on the classical within-the-paradigm. They had been primed for only one mission, and when they fulfilled that mission, they found it wanting. This is part of the reason why Olympic participants often get depressed after the Olympics.[30] There was all that training and expectation, that rush of adrenalin during the games...but then what? They hadn't become better, more fulfilled, spiritual people. They were not their biceps or their legs or whatever else they used to get to the Olympics. Their essence had simply been ignored.

We need the fulfillment of the soul rather than that of the body, because the body, being physical, is subject to the fragmentation and atomization of this world. The eye sees and doesn't hear. The ear hears and doesn't see. The soul, on the other hand, being spiritual and a part of the Oneness of God, is intrinsically holistic.[31] Even when it expresses

---

26 *Maharal, Tiferet Yisrael*, chap. 1.

27 Rabbi Tzadok HaKohen, *Machashavot Charutz*, no. 4.

28 *Maharal, Tiferet Yisrael*, chap. 4.

29 Rabbi Shneur Zalman of Liadi, *Tanya*, chap. 23.

30 See, for example, https://www.theatlantic.com/health/archive/2016/08/post-olympic-depression/496244/

31 *Daat Tevunot* 80 (p. 68), first paragraph. This is because the soul was created as a *chelek elokah mi'maal*—a part of God from above, and just like God is indivisible, so too is the soul.

itself in different ways, it is the whole soul operating.[32] If we want to feel whole, if we want to feel a sense of unity between the different aspects of ourselves, we need to be soul-people.[33]

Only when the body is an instrument of the soul can we be whole with our body as well. Many artists, dancers, and gymnasts have told me that they feel that they are doing something essentially spiritual, not physical; what moves them are the deepest wellsprings of their selves.[34] They are able to transcend the physical act and impregnate their actions with meaning. The artistic expression becomes the vehicle to express their soul. It is no longer just physical prowess or dexterity that is being displayed. It is no longer just to show others what their body can do, but rather to show themselves whom they are.

But this, too, will not suffice, for the body provides decreasing returns. Sooner or later, even the greatest dancers or sports-people find that their expression is more limited. They begin to live in the past, nurturing the memories of what they once were. Their life, as they defined it during those heroic years, is over. On the other hand, the person whose core is the soul keeps on growing until the end of his days.

The body is still an integral part of who we are, and it is important that we ensure its health and good shape. But this is just so the body will cooperate with the dreams of the soul.

We are first and foremost soul-people.

---

32 Ibid.

33 Rabbi Shneur Zalman of Liadi, *Tanya*, chap. 23.

34 I showed this sentence to a world-class dancer, Eliana Girard, who also studies Torah. Her response: "I completely agree with that statement. Dance brings me into a quiet space in my mind where I hear Hashem without my ego contradicting my thoughts."

6

THE THRESHOLD OF CHOICE

Between stimulus and response there is a space.
In that space is our power to choose our response.
In our response lies our growth and our freedom.

Viktor E. Frankl

CONDEMNED TO CHOOSE

Jean-Paul Sartre claimed that we are "condemned to freedom." By this, he meant that I am not free because I *must* make choices, all the time, even when I think I have no choice to make.[1]

Is this so? We don't get to choose birth, our first language, intelligence, basic personality—our whole genetic make-up. No one gets to choose who their parents are or whether their family would be nurturing and balanced, or rough and dysfunctional. These were God's choices, not my own, and since God chose them, I am not responsible.[2]

The prophet Jeremiah exhorted us: "Let not the wise person glory in his wisdom, nor the mighty man in his might, [and] let not the rich man glory in his riches,"[3] since these are all determined before a baby

1 William Egginton.

2 Maimonides, *Mishneh Torah*, Laws of Repentance 5:4.

3 Jeremiah 9:22.

is born.[4] "But let he who glories, glory in this: that he understands and knows Me, that I am the Lord that exercises on earth loving-kindness, justice and righteousness; for on these things I delight, says God." Just because God delights in these values, He gave us complete moral autonomy over them. "Everything is in the hands of Heaven except for awe of God," i.e., moral behavior, which is in the hands of man.[5]

God tells me what He wants my potential to be. Amongst other things, he chooses that potential based on my allotted contribution to the general fixing of the world. This potential determines my particular range of choices. But the choices I make within my range of choice define me. God chooses and I choose. My choices are critical in determining who I am as a moral and spiritual being.[6] And here lies the interesting thing. We all have a different *range* of choice; but the *amount* of choice we all have is the same.

GENERAL, PARTICULAR, AND IRRELEVANT CHOICES

Animals get to choose whether they are going to hunt or sleep, to play or lie in the sun. This is not what we mean by choice. Choice is only meaningful when it is a choice between good over evil, when it involves the choice between the inner spirituality of a situation and its outer superficiality, between being truly human and not allowing ourselves to become a commodity. As the Torah states: "Man," uniquely amongst all the animals, "has become like one of us knowing good and evil." Empowered with knowledge, man is able to act. He can choose.[7]

Some of our choices will be life-changing—what career we choose, whom we marry, where we decide to live, and how observant we are going to be. So too, there are times of the year—Rosh Hashanah in particular—when we don't look at the details of our lives but rather at the big picture of who we are and where we are going.[8]

---

4 Talmud, Tractate *Niddah* 16b.

5 Talmud, Tractate *Berachot* 33b.

6 Maimonides, *Mishneh Torah*, Laws of Repentance 5:1–3.

7 Genesis 22:3, as interpreted by Maimonides, ibid. 5:1.

8 Rabbi Eliyahu Dessler, *Michtav Me'Eliyahu*, vol. 2, pp. 67–68; Rabbi Abraham Yitzchak Kook, *Orot Hateshuvah*, p. 33.

If real choices are judged by their moral value, then this changes our perspective on what choosing a marriage partner should be based on. My personal experience is that those couples whose primary criteria is shared values and a vision for themselves and their family have the happiest marriages overall. Indeed, these choices express the essence of the human condition.

Mostly, our choices involve seemingly smaller decisions. Their cumulative impact, however, is just as central in defining our lives. We either rise up beyond the angels or down into the abyss we go. There is no human default position—a human in neutral, so to speak. Neutrality is a choice to deny our essential humanness. It is to be less than human.

THE THRESHOLD OF CHOICE

The choices that we have—those that are actually within our reach—are considered to be within our threshold of choice. Deuteronomy states: "I have placed before you life and death; blessing and curse; [therefore] choose life."[9] Choice is a necessity for man's moral integrity. Perforce we are then also free to choose poorly. Thus empowered, we are held accountable for our conduct, be it good or evil.[10]

Some things, however, are above my threshold of choice. I may love the idea that I would never get angry, or always pray to God with perfect love, or never over-eat. But it may be that these ideals are so elevated above my current spiritual level that I cannot seriously engage them. They may be a part of my long-term spiritual vision, but they are not a part of my immediate choice-reality. In other words, they are *above* my current threshold of choice.[11]

Some things may be a part of my long-term spiritual vision, but they are not a part of my immediate choice-reality.

There are other good and worthy aspirations that are *below* my threshold of choice. They are choices that are such an integral part of

9 Deuteronomy 30:19.

10 *Mishneh Torah*, Laws of Repentance 5:1.

11 Rabbi Eliyahu Dessler, *Michtav Me'Eliyahu*, vol. 1, *Kuntres Habechirah*, chap. 2.

me that I do not really choose to do them either. I may never be tempted to shop-lift, even if I am short of money, and I certainly may never be tempted to kill, even if I am super-angry with someone. These acts may be so integrated into my moral conscience that it is simply unthinkable for me to do something like that. Theoretically I could choose to do these things, but in practice, they are no longer within my range of choice.[12]

In the middle of these two categories—those that are above my threshold of choice and those that are below—lie my real struggles. These are the decisions that I struggle with that are within my threshold of choice. I may choose correctly or I may not, but the struggle itself has value. The struggle itself acts to purify me, even where I might fail.[13]

For example, I may decide that I don't want to gossip about others in pursuit of observing the laws of *lashon hara*.[14] I may sometimes succeed, and I may sometimes fail, but it is a part of my struggle. It is within my threshold of choice.

No two people have the same threshold of choice. What is important is not where our threshold of choice lies but how much growth we move through from our starting point. If our momentum is toward goodness, we have shown that our primary resonance is with righteousness over evil. This aspect of our lives is totally in our hands.[15]

The implications of this are tantalizing. It means that it is not the destination but rather the journey that we need to focus on. God says to Abraham, "Leave your land, your birthplace, and your home, and go to the land that I will show you."[16] Don't worry about which "land" now; to begin the process, begin the journey.

---

12 Ibid.

13 Ibid.

14 The words mean literally "bad language" or "evil speech." In Judaism, there is a prohibition not to speak negatively of your fellow man unless it is information that is of practical benefit to the person.

15 *Mishneh Torah*, Laws of Repentance 5:3, based on Deuteronomy 30:15.

16 Genesis 12:1.

MOVING THE THRESHOLD

As we grow, we begin to master certain areas of our moral commitment. Over time, they become a part of us. We then automatically act according to our commitments. We move that aspect of our life from within our threshold of choice—a struggle—to below our threshold of choice.[17] This frees us to take on new challenges. We are now able to take things that we previously thought were out of range—i.e., above our threshold of choice because they were too high—and move them into our threshold of choice. We remain with the same amount of choice. But we have now moved our threshold of choice upwards. The issues that we are dealing with are more sublime, more subtle, and more holy than before.

The measure of greatness is how much we move the needle. It is how much we take the challenges of yesterday that were within our threshold of choice and make them a part of our natural fiber, and how much of the things that were so above us yesterday we bring into our threshold of choice.

As a simple example to illustrate the point, two people may appear to have radically different lives:

- The first may come from an abusive family, be naturally anxious, not be very intelligent and have grown up without an exposure to Judaism. He seems to have everything stacked against him—so many challenges.
- A second person may seem to be blessed with all the advantages of life. He may have a loving, warm and balanced family; be naturally calm and highly intelligent; and have lots of access to Judaism.

Let us say that Person One is born at Level 2 on an artificial scale of 1 to 20, whereas Person Two is born on Level 12. Both grow during their lives. Person One achieves a level of 10 at the end of his life, while Person Two achieves a level of 16. Person One did not even achieve the starting point of Person Two, and yet, in heaven, he will be regarded

---

17 *Michtav Me'Eliyahu*, vol. 1, *Kuntres Habechirah*, chap. 5.

as the greater person because he moved through eight points on the growth scale, when Person Two only moved through four points. In this world, Person Two may have become a great rabbi and Person One a tailor, but that has nothing to do with how God judges us.

God decides our starting point. We decide our response. Every inch of growth counts, making us greater and putting us closer to fulfilling the unique potential that is within us. Our choices define us. But they aren't simply intellectual, for there is another important ingredient to growth...

7

PASSION—THE MISSING LINK

Let the good in me connect with the good in others
until all the world is transformed through
the compelling power of love.

Rebbi Nachman of Breslov

TO LIVE YOUR VALUES TAKES PASSION

Value-based living is a totally different ballgame than value-based believing. It doesn't take much to resonate with an idea and hold it sacred in your mind. But transitioning from the abstract to the concrete is another thing altogether. Value-based living demands commitment—the commitment to embody your vision through action. It involves feeling that without these values my life is worthless. They are not simply aspirational messages but rather they reflect my core, and hence I am willing to pursue them even if it involves discomfort.

The moment of initial inspiration quickly dissipates long before we can translate values into habituated behaviors. Neither can we resort to sheer will and determination. Fatigue quickly sets in. If we are going to take the leap from merely believing in values into the realm of actually living them, we need passion. Passion is the engine that gives depth, inspiration, and continuity. Habit may get me to repeat my good values, but only passion can humanize them. Intimacy can only be achieved with passion. If we want to really connect to our Judaism—and to our God—we have to find the fire within ourselves.

SARAH—THE JEWISH LEADER OF PASSION

While Sarah's husband Abraham was the scientist finding God behind the veils of nature, she provided passion and desire for the holy—the heartbeat of conviction.[1] Abraham passed onto the Jewish People the inheritance of straight and clear thinking. Sarah, the first Jewess, provided the inner soul, the warmth, and the flavor of belief.[2]

Make no mistake—Sarah had a towering intellect. Sarah was the first and greatest of the seven prophetesses.[3] We are taught that she was an even greater prophet than Abraham![4] This is not surprising. Prophecy per se comes to us with what Kabbalists call our female side.[5] Certainly, female prophets seemed to have achieved their prophecy more naturally than males. Miriam, the sister of Moses, was a prophetess while still a child, and Chana's heart-felt prayer reached the level of prophecy.[6] When prophecy will return in the Messianic Era, women will outdo men in prophecy.[7]

Yet these staggering levels of holiness were not her gift to the Jewish People. Sarah's legacy is her passion. She became the heart of the Jewish People. That is why not only her merits, but Abraham's merits as well, are attributed to her.[8]

---

1 *Shem MiShmuel*, Genesis, *Chayei Sarah* 5681, p. 259.

2 See Rabbi Joseph B. Soleveitchik's eulogy for the Tolna Rebbetzin, Rebecca Twersky, delivered on Jan. 30, 1977.

3 Talmud, Tractate *Megillah* 14a and Tractate *Sotah* 7a. The seven prophetesses were Sarah, Miriam (the sister of Moses), Deborah, Chanah, Abigail, Chuldah, and Esther.

4 Genesis 21:12 and *Rashi* ad loc.

5 *Maharal, Derech Chaim on Ethics of Our Fathers* 1:1 (end).

6 Chanah lived at the time of Samuel the Prophet (see the opening to the Book of Samuel). For the nature of prophecy, see Chapter 35.

7 *Ohr Hachaim*, Exodus 15:20–21.

8 *Shem MiShmuel*, Genesis, *Chayei Sarah* 5681, p. 259, in the name of the *Zohar*.

GOD TESTS SARAH'S PASSION

Sarah used her passion to achieve spiritual greatness. She was a genius of the soul. Just because of that, God tested her.[9]

Sarah was extraordinarily beautiful.[10] In fact, the Sages say she was one of the four most beautiful women ever![11] Pharaoh of Egypt and Avimelech, king of Gerar, noticed her beauty and took her against her will.[12] If not for the fact that Abraham claimed to be her brother and not her husband, they would have simply disposed of him.[13]

Sarah had passion. Because of this, she became the heart of the Jewish People.

On these occasions, Sarah was tested as to whether she would cleave to the wrong parties, i.e., to Pharaoh and Avimelech, instead of to her husband Abraham.[14] Of course, Sarah would not have agreed to such an arrangement at the outset, but being forced into this, perhaps she could come to terms with being the illustrious wife of a wealthy and powerful ruler. After all, here was Sarah, a person of intense passion, capable of embracing her new situation and the people who went with it.

Here was Sarah's big test. Would her intense passion be attached to the wrong people and to the wrong cause? To properly employ passion, one must avoid moral confusion and have absolute clarity and moral resolve. Passion can so easily drive purpose—leading us to explain to ourselves why what we are doing is really good after all.[15]

Sarah withstood this test. She remained faithful to Abraham. She made sure that her passion was driven by her values. It was this that allowed her to remain authentic to herself and to not allow her passion to cloud her vision.

---

9 In general, God tests the foremothers and the forefathers on what they excelled in. See Chapter 43.

10 Genesis 12:11, 14.

11 Talmud, Tractate *Megillah* 15a. The other three were Esther, Abigail, and Rachav.

12 Genesis 12:15, 20:2.

13 Ibid. 12:13; 20:2.

14 *Shem MiShmuel* ad loc.

15 Hence the Sages say, "The sons of Israel only served idolatry to permit public licentiousness." The idolatry was simply a justificatory ideology for illicit behavior; Talmud, Tractate *Sanhedrin* 63b.

Sarah was a master of moral clarity. In his eulogy for Sarah, Abraham says, "She seeks out wool and linen."[16] Jewish law prohibits the use of *shaatnez*,[17] garments that are made of wool and linen together. This retains our sensitivity to the order and balance of the creation.[18] The Sages interpret Abraham's reference to these materials as Sarah's ability to have moral clarity—to separate what was good from what was bad.[19] Sarah's passion made her great because she combined it with absolute moral clarity. She never fooled herself, and she never got sucked in.

SARAH'S DECISIVENESS DEFINES THE JEWISH PEOPLE

Moral clarity operates hand-in-hand with distinct boundary setting. Sarah's moral clarity challenged her numerous times to draw a line in the sand. When Ishmael, the child of Abraham and Hagar,[20] began to drift toward sinful behavior, Sarah drew a clear line and demanded his expulsion from her home.[21] Abraham still wanted to keep Ishmael close and make him a part of the future of the Jewish People,[22] but Sarah, with her moral clarity, made the difficult decision to oppose this, realizing that Ishmael's behavior contradicted everything that she and Abraham lived for.[23]

Sarah's disagreement with Abraham was hardly some local domestic disagreement. It was about the very borders and parameters of the Jewish People with mind-boggling ramifications. Would Ishmael and

---

16 Proverbs 31:13. This is known as the *Eishet Chayil* ("Woman of Valor") song, which we sing every Friday night around the Shabbat table. The *Yalkut Shimoni* tells us that the song is about Sarah. *Midrash Tanchuma, Chayei Sarah*, chap. 4, tells us that it was first composed by Abraham and was later included by Solomon at the end of his book of Proverbs.

17 Deuteronomy 22:11.

18 Rabbi Shimshon Raphael Hirsch, ibid.

19 *Tanchuma* ad loc.

20 Hagar was Sarah's maidservant whom she gave to Abraham to produce a child when she seemed not able to; see Genesis 16:1–4.

21 Genesis 21:10.

22 Ibid. 21:11.

23 Ibid. 21:9. See *Rashi* ad loc., who states that the words used by the Torah, *metzachek*, refers to the three cardinal sins. However, at the end of his life, Ishmael repented. We learn this from Genesis 25:17, where it uses the term *va'yigva* for the death of Ishmael. *Rashi* there tells us that this word is only used with reference to the death of the righteous.

his descendants contribute their enormous civilization-energy as a part of the Jewish People? Or would they develop a civilization of their own?[24]

God clearly came out on the side of Sarah. He tells Abraham to listen to his wife—and history was forever changed.[25] God gives Ishmael his own blessing, and hence he became the forefather of the Arab nations and, ultimately, Islam.[26]

With this action, Sarah set up a pattern of history.[27] From then onwards, Jewish lineage is determined by the mother and not the father.[28] This was part of Sarah's ability to create parameters and define the borders of expression of human behavior. Sarah's very name was given by God and came from the Hebrew word meaning "to rule over."[29] As the matriarch of all Jewish women, Sarah bequeathed these qualities to all future generations of Jewish women. This is part of the Jewish conception of female power.[30]

FEMALE POWER

Female power is not just engaged in creating life-environments; it is that which creates life to begin with. The male contribution to the fertilization of an egg cell is infinitely small. It contains no effort and no pain. Not so the female. She has the ability to absorb this minute speck within herself and build from it a completely new life. The child is formed physically within the mother over a considerable time; effort and pain are involved, and finally a child is born.

The female is the one who nurtures. During pregnancy, the womb provides a total environment for the fetus—its food, oxygen, warmth, and blood supply. This has to do with creating environments and providing

---

24 *Tanchuma*, *Chayei Sarah*, chap. 4.

25 Genesis 21:12.

26 Ibid. 21:18.

27 This is based on a principle that "the actions of the fathers are a sign to the children," and is used extensively by the commentators throughout their commentaries on Genesis. See, for example, *Ramban* 26:1; the *Netziv*, *Haamek Davar* 18:15 and 30:40; *Meshech Chochmah* 15:15; *Taz* 45:14. This is based on the Talmud, Tractate *Sotah* 34a.

28 Talmud, Tractate *Kiddushin* 68b (chap. 3, mishnah 12), based on Deuteronomy 7:3–4.

29 See *Rashi* on Genesis 17:16, where God himself changes her name from Sarai to Sarah.

30 See Chapter 30 for more on this.

boundaries. But there is an extra element: the element of mercy. Mercy is a fine-tuning of the environment, allowing general principles to be applied according to the specific needs of each individual situation. Hence the Hebrew word for womb, *rechem* (רחם), is related to mercy, *rachamim* (רחמים).[31]

PASSION FOR THE WEEK

We begin every week by making the blessing of Havdalah at the end of the Shabbat. Included is the blessing *Borei Meorei Ha'aish*—"He who created the lights of fire." What we are really saying is, "May we have the right passion for the week." When we are passionate about our beliefs, we are truly alive, seeing even ordinary moments as enchanted. Our spiritual future is dependent on female nurturance—"the Torah of your Mother"[32]—to direct our passion toward our value-based goals.

---

31 Talmud, Tractate *Chullin* 63a, discusses a non-kosher bird called *racham* (Leviticus 11:18) and relates that to the word *rachamim*.

32 Proverbs 1:8.

8

THE NEGATIVE INCLINATION

"And behold it was very good." This is the yetzer hara (the bad inclination)…[For] without the yetzer hara, a person would not build a home or marry a woman; he would neither have children nor engage in business.

Midrash Rabbah Genesis (9:7)

The deepest part of us—our souls—genuinely wants to do the right thing. However, there is another side to us, the *yetzer hara* (the negative inclination).[1] The *yetzer hara* may take many forms. The main tool of the *yetzer hara* is not frontal seductions and overwhelming desires; it is thoughtlessness. And thoughtlessness is achieved by busyness—by making sure that our every waking moment is filled with work, texts, driving, checking our various social media accounts. Through this, it ensures that we never find the time to take a step back, establish our goals, and assess whether we are on track.[2]

The *yetzer hara* also chips away at our commitment to create ambiguity. It then exploits that ambiguity. For example, we may know that it is wrong to speak negatively about someone else (*lashon hara)*. However,

1 See, for example, Talmud, Tractate *Bava Batra* 16a as per the verse in Genesis 8:21: "For the inclination of the heart of man is evil from his youth."

2 *Ramchal, Mesilat Yesharim,* chap. 2.

the *yetzer hara* alerts us to just how delicious it is to share salacious news with a friend. It then chips away at our commitment by ensuring that we remain a non-contemplative person. We act negatively once, and the second time gets easier. We begin to find ways of justifying the behavior to ourselves as not being prohibited at all.[3] The *Ramchal* tells us that the non-contemplative person is like a blind person walking on the narrow path at the top of a windy river-bed. One wrong move, one stumble, and the consequences can be disastrous.[4]

The *yetzer hara* will exploit any opening we give it. It exploits our hurt pride to get us to react with anger or withdrawal. It turns our fears or insecurities into resentment. It tells us that we are too tired, too hungry, too angry, or too overwhelmed to do something good. It activates our cynicism to insulate ourselves from corrective messages.[5] "There are not enough sacks in the world to contain the wily arguments of the bad inclination," said the Kotzker Rebbe.[6]

This is the superficial us, and we have to get past this if we are to live a life of real meaning.

The *yetzer hara* ensures that we have a balance of choice. Things got more complicated after the sin of Adam and Eve when good and bad were mixed up, making moral clarity an even greater challenge.[7] Instead of being a voice outside of ourselves, we now began to identify with the *yetzer hara*. It is no longer an external voice whispering in my ear telling me to spend the day in bed and do nothing on a cold day. Rather, I say, "*I* don't want to get out of bed." And it is seemingly no longer my real self telling me that I should nevertheless get up, but rather a moral imperative outside of myself: "But you should get up anyway."

But, the *yetzer hara* doesn't only seduce us to do the wrong thing. It also tells us what is bad about the good. It confuses us.[8] "I get prayer,

---

3 Talmud, Tractate *Kiddushin*, p. 40a.

4 *Ramchal*, ibid.

5 *Ramchal, Mesilat Yesharim*, chap. 5.

6 As brought by Menachem Posner, Chabad.org, based on *Kochav Hashachar*, by Simcha Raz.

7 *Ramchal, Maamar Hageulah*, chap. 2.

8 *Ramchal, Mesilat Yesharim*, introduction.

but why should the services be so long?" "I get the commandments, but I don't want to be told what to do."

This is one understanding of what the Sages meant when they said: "Average (neither righteous nor bad) people are governed by both their good and bad inclinations."[9] True, our *yetzer hara* can incite us to do bad. But much more insidious for the average, good person is the ambiguity and doubts that eat away at our commitment, sap our energies, and undermine our motivation to do good. It allows us to settle for inconsistency or mediocrity and—eventually—to suffer from moral fatigue.

More than the *yetzer hara* wants to make a person sin, it wants him to fall into sadness because of the sin. The sadness comes through the feeling of inferiority one feels after doing the sin.[10] It deprives us of the moral courage to get up, dust ourselves off, repent, and engage once again in our essential goodness.

THE BAD INCLINATION MADE THE CREATION "VERY GOOD"

When the Torah details the creation of the world, it states numerous times that "God looked and He saw that it was good (*tov*)." However, the creation of man didn't elicit this response. God endowed man with the awesome power to make choices, which includes bad choices. Hence, man was not yet in his final state of good.

However, the Torah then states: "God saw everything that he had created and it was 'very good' (*tov me'od*)."[11] The Sages say that the final ingredient that turned the world into "very good" was the bad inclination—man's *yetzer hara*.[12]

How can this be? How could the force pushing man toward bad be branded as very good?

The Sages explain that if not for the *yetzer hara*, no one would build a house, marry, have children, or engage in commerce.[13] Though our

---

9 Talmud, Tractate *Berachot* 61b.

10 "Know Yourself," by the author of *Bilvavi*, p. 45.

11 Genesis 1:31; see the *Ramban* ad loc.

12 *Midrash Rabbah*, Genesis 9:7.

13 Ibid.

impulses for ownership, sex, and wealth can lead us down the path of bad, these very same desires can be channeled for good.[14] In fact, if these desires did not exist, we would not engage in worldly endeavors, be they positive or negative. Instead, desiring to do good, we would withdraw from the world to the nearest ashram or cave. For that, God doesn't need humans. Angels would be better!

And so, the *yetzer hara*—that bundle of passions that takes us to all the wrong places—can also be turned around to face the other direction. The *Shema*, which is recited daily, states, "You should serve God with all of your hearts,"[15] implying that we all have at least two hearts. These, say the Sages, are our *yetzer hatov* (good inclination) and our *yetzer hara* (bad inclination).[16] The *Shema* tells us to serve God with both hearts. We have to channel the desires of our *yetzer hara* so that it too produces good.

Take food as an example. Food is one of our basic sensual desires, and there seems nothing more grossly physical than someone who chronically gorges himself on food. But, just because of that, God directed us to elevate it to holiness. We make special foods for the Shabbat and *chagim* (festivals). On Pesach (Passover), many of the mitzvot that we do are food based, e.g., eating matzah and maror (bitter herbs), and drinking the four cups of wine. We also make a blessing over wine on many special occasions, e.g., at a wedding, a *brit milah* (a circumcision[17]), for Kiddush on Shabbat and the *chagim*, and several other occasions.

What this means is that we are taking our physical drive to eat for sustenance plus our desire to want culinary experiences and harnessing that to drive holiness. When we do that, the food itself becomes holy, and so do we.

---

14 *Yefeh Toar*, ibid.

15 Deuteronomy 6:5.

16 *Rashi*, ibid.

17 Lit., "a covenant of circumcision."

IMAGINATION

The great motivator of sin is our power of imagination.[18] Imagination is that which allows us to make a leap beyond ourselves and be God-like. In fact, the Hebrew word for "imagination," *dimyon*, is related to the word *adameh*, "I will be like."

Still, imagination is a double-edged sword. We can use our imagination to have all kinds of fantasies, such as lusting after power or sensual encounters. The snake activated Eve's imagination when he told her how she and Adam could literally be gods (and not just God-like) if they ate from the forbidden fruit.[19]

It is imagination that fools us into absorbing the advertising messages so cleverly targeting us. It is that which leads us to naturally judge our actions favorably (or at least to identify every extenuating circumstance) while finding it so difficult to give our fellow man a similar benefit of the doubt.[20] If we see our friend smoke ten cigarettes, we'll label him a chain smoker in danger of dying of cancer, but the chain smoker himself convinces himself that smoking isn't so dangerous. His cognitive dissonance forces him to reinterpret the information in his favor.

Our imagination is used by our *yetzer hara* to dream of being rich and famous as secrets to happiness. It is that which provokes a man into imagining that the scantily dressed girl who just crossed the street is trying to attract just him. The *yetzer hara* activates our imagination to picture an alternative life full of sensuous or other gratifications.

It was this that was the legacy of the sin of Adam and Eve. From then on, all fruits—i.e., all physical phenomena—were tainted with the sensation of physical pleasure disconnected from their spiritual purpose. "I have eaten (from the forbidden fruits) and I will eat again," says Adam[21]—not out of defiance, but in recognition of the new reality. As

---

18 Rabbi Shlomo Wolbe, *Alei Shur*, vol. 2, p. 43.

19 Maimonides, *Guide to the Perplexed* 2:30.

20 This is known as the actor-observer bias.

21 *Midrash Rabbah*, Genesis 19:22.

if to say, "Now that I have tasted the fruit, I shall never again be able to eat without this sensation recurring."[22]

AN OLD FRIEND

When Rabbi Yitzchak Hutner was a student in Hebron Yeshiva, his mentor saw him talking as if to someone else.

"Who are you talking to?" his mentor inquired.

"I am talking to my old friend," the young Yitzchak Hutner answered.

"And who might that be?"

"My *yetzer hara*," came Yitzchak Hutner's reply.

"And why is your good inclination not your friend?" inquired the mentor.

"My good inclination is a fair-weather friend," came the insightful reply. "But my evil inclination is always with me. He never leaves me. He is forever loyal."

The *yetzer hara* is called three things: a king, an old man, and a fool (*melech*, *zaken*, *u'chesil*):[23]

- A "king" because everyone listens to him.
- "Old" because he is with the person from birth to old age.[24]
- A "fool" because we can outwit his seductive voice with counter messaging through our authentic voice of goodness.

In fact, just because he is an old friend, he is a fool. We can easily get to know exactly how he operates, turning his very instruments against him. We can use that same power of imagination to do good instead of bad.[25] We can imagine holiness and realize that it is far sweeter, more profound, and more enduring than the futilities of our *yetzer hara*.[26] The *yetzer hara* has been around since the beginning of time, but he experiences no learning curve. He is the ultimate fool.[27]

---

22 Rabbi Mordechai Miller, *Shabbat Shiurim*, vol. 1, Genesis.

23 *Kohelet Rabbah* 4:13.

24 Whereas the opposite inclination, our *yetzer tov* (our good inclination), is only fully active from bat/bar mitzvah.

25 Rabbi Shlomo Wolbe, *Alei Shur*, vol. 2, p. 43.

26 Ibid., pp. 44–45.

27 *Kohelet Rabbah* 4:13.

9

MAN—THE FOREVER INCOMPLETE BEING

A wise man, Reb Zusha, once said of himself: "When you go up to heaven, you will not be asked why you were not Moses. You will be asked why you didn't become yourself."

As humans, we are spiritually dynamic—something that cannot be said about any other creature. When it comes to spiritual growth, animals are completely static. While they can develop emotional relationships, acquire new skills, and mature both physically and intellectually, they cannot grow spiritually. The Hebrew word for "animal," *beheimah* (בהמה), reflects this reality. The word *beheimah* is made up of two words, *bah mah* (בה מה), which means, "in it, there is 'what.'" The total reality ("whatness") of the animal is already inside the animal. It has no growth potential.[1] Animals are incapable of having a moral vision or of pursuing a spiritual trajectory. You will never find a lion sitting on a rock having an existential crisis about the meaning of life. From a spiritual point of view, animals are born complete.

---

1 *Maharal, Tiferet Yisrael*, chap. 3.

The same is true about angels. Although much more spiritual than animals, angels cannot grow spiritually. The prophet Zechariah contrasts the angels with man. Angels are creatures that stand, while man walks.[2] Angels praise God standing with their feet together, in a position of no movement and no growth, because that is what they were created to do.[3]

In a way, angels and animals are actually very similar. Angels see God so clearly that they have no option but to cleave to God. Animals are so moved by their instinct that they are pre-programmed to do God's will. The former's intelligence and clarity are their instinct; the latter's instinct is their clarity and intelligence.[4]

But man is different. Man cannot find redemption by simply being. Man is called *adam* from the word *adamah*, which means "ground." Just like the ground has to produce its potential by yielding its crops and fruits, so too, man's very name reflects the idea that he starts out as all-potential.[5]

To be human is to grow. Man needs to give birth to himself, again and again.[6]

ADAM—THE POTENTIAL BEING

We humans have an almost infinite soul. This means we can be growing our entire lives, always discovering new aspects of ourselves. And if we could, we should. To be human is to sense the gulf between the "is" and the "ought"; between what we have already become and our as-yet-unfulfilled potential. We really should not be calling ourselves human beings, but rather human becomings.

---

2 Zechariah 3:7; Isaiah 6:2 also describes one category of angels, the *seraphim*, as standing.

3 *Beit Elohim of the Mabit*, chap. 5.

4 Rabbi Alexander Safran, *The Kabbalah: Law and Mysticism in the Jewish Tradition* (Feldheim).

5 *Maharal, Tiferet Yisrael*, chap. 3. Hence, the creation of the body of man is uniquely called "dust from the earth" (Genesis 2:7), even though all living beings were similarly created; *Maharal*, ibid.

6 *Maharal, Gur Aryeh*, Genesis 6:15.

At the end of creation, the Torah states, “God saw everything that He had created and it was “very good” (*tov me’od*).[7] A more accurate definition of *me’od* is “more and more.”[8] The Hebrew letters of this word *me’od* (מאד) are the same letters as *adam* (אדם), man.[9] The essence of being human is this ability to continuously fulfill our potential—to become more and more.

It is only in the spirit that we excel as uniquely human.

GREATNESS IS NOT AN INSIDERS CLUB

There is no special club to becoming spiritually great. It is a system that is open equally to all. You don’t have to have any degrees or be a rabbi or rebbetzin. Illustrious lineage does not guarantee greatness. Moses dreamt that his sons would succeed him, but Joshua was greater and therefore took the reins of leadership.[10] Over the last two thousand years, the children of the greatest rabbis who became the greatest rabbis of the next generation were the exception rather than the rule. As the Sages put it, a mamzer[11] who becomes a wise man is greater than a High Priest who remains ignorant.[12]

Anyone can learn Torah and become a wise person. There are no favorites, elites, or hierarchy of access.

The “crown of Torah” is available to all.[13] Anyone can learn Torah and become a wise person. Anyone who applies that Torah can become righteous. There are no favorites, elites, or hierarchy of access.

And there is no age. There is no one who can say that they have missed the boat, that had they been younger, they would have considered embracing Judaism. Abraham was already a mature seventy-five years old when God told him to make a completely new beginning: “Go from your

7 Genesis 1:31; see the *Ramban* ad loc.

8 Rabbi Moshe Shapiro.

9 In Hebrew, the letters for both are *mem*, *aleph*, and *dalet*.

10 *Rashi*, Numbers 27:16.

11 A *mamzer* is born of his married mother’s incestuous or adulterous relationship with another.

12 Maimonides, *Mishneh Torah*, Laws of Talmud Torah 3:2 (based on Talmud, Tractate *Horayot* 13a).

13 Ibid. 3:1.

land, from the place of your birth, from the house of your father." At an age that many of us are settling into retirement homes and touring Alaska, Abraham was just beginning the part of his life that the Torah writes about.[14] As Warwick Schiller said, "You can learn new things at any time in your life if you are willing to be a beginner."

We know from the midrashic literature that Abraham had been growing since he was three years old when he first started believing in God.[15] We know that he had already actively confronted his idolatrous surroundings, risking his life. And yet, it is as if God is telling him, "You are just beginning. Now you are ready to go." Until then, the Torah only makes passing mention of Abraham. The most dramatic moments of Abraham's life—his circumcision, his encounter with the angels, and the near-sacrifice of Isaac—were way ahead of him.[16]

God's words to Abraham are really *Lech Lecha*, "Go to yourself."[17] Go discover yourself. Raise yourself above your egocentricity and go toward your purpose. Stop thinking within the narrow confines of your birthplace.[18] Go to your potential!

GROWING INTO GREATNESS

To understand the Torah's vision for man, let's go back to Moses. Moses didn't just become the Moses we know. He had to work hard over a long period of time to get there. He started out by being called an Egyptian man,[19] and only much later was he called a man of God.[20]

Moses' growth began with him looking outward—from Pharaoh's palace where he had been brought up[21]—and seeing the suffering of his enslaved brethren. He began to feel their pain. He would leave his

14 Genesis 12:1–4.

15 *Raavad*, glosses to *Mishneh Torah*, Laws of Idolatry 1:3.

16 The first two incidents happened when Abraham was ninety-nine, the latter when he was a hundred.

17 Genesis 12:1. *Lech* means "go"; *lecha* means "to you" or "for you."

18 *Rashi*, Genesis 15:5.

19 Exodus 2:19, by Yitro's daughters.

20 Deuteronomy 33:1.

21 Exodus 2:5–10.

privileged existence of the palace and help the Jews achieve their quota of work for the day.[22] Moses was becoming an other-centered person.

One day, Moses saw an Egyptian overlord hitting a Jewish slave.[23] Moses could bear it no longer. After determining that no future righteous person would come out of this Egyptian,[24] he killed him.[25] With this, Moses began not just helping but taking responsibility—the most important ingredient for any leader.

The very next day, he saw two Jews arguing.[26] Now, to save your fellow Jew from a hated Egyptian was one thing, but why get involved if two of your country-men are arguing? The good side and the bad side are no longer obvious. Not only that, but the previous day Moses had committed a capital offence. One would have thought that Moses would lay low, at least for a while.[27] Moses, however, took the next step in his growth. Other people's problems were his problems. And so, he intervened.

Word had gotten out about his slaying of the Egyptian, and so Moses had to flee the country.[28] He fled to a strange land, Midian.[29] Despite being a destitute refugee, Moses intervened once again to prevent injustice.

The male shepherds were chasing away the weaker female shepherds from the watering well.[30] Moses had every reason to believe this was none of his business. He was a stranger to the land, and, after all, he was in this foreign land because of his intervention in Egypt! But Moses could not look at injustice, even to strangers, and just turn the other

---

22 *Yalkut Shimoni*, chap. 2.

23 Exodus 2:11.

24 *Rashi*, ibid. This included a greatness in future generations as well. Although Moses was not yet a prophet, he may have received this insight through *ruach ha'kodesh*, the "holy spirit"—a level just below the level of prophecy.

25 Exodus 2:12.

26 Ibid., v. 13.

27 *Yalkut Shimoni*, ibid., as explained by the *Maharal*, *Gevurot Hashem*, chap. 18.

28 Exodus 2:14.

29 Ibid., v. 15.

30 Ibid., v. 16–17.

way.[31] He helped the female shepherds and went even further: watering their sheep himself.[32]

Then Moses took another step. He became a shepherd.[33] Looking after sheep in a desert was a new level of care—not one-time interventions but the thankless task of 24/7 care. It was only after that that God appointed him to save His people at the burning bush.

Greatness did not fall into his lap. It was a lifetime of work. And this was just the beginning.[34]

NO ONE GETS TO DO IT ALL BY HIMSELF

Moses changed the course of history, and in so doing he seemed to transcend his own humanity. But the Torah stresses that, for all his unfathomable greatness, he was not so much different than us. He struggled and sometimes failed. He achieved mind-boggling levels of spirituality but ultimately died with still more to do. In the end, even the man who had brought God's Torah down to earth could not escape death. He desperately wanted to finish his mission by taking the Jewish People into Israel, but that was not to be.[35]

The Torah ends with Moses' death.[36] Man is God's partner, but no one person will get to do it all. If that is sobering, it is also inspiring. We all get to play a part. We all really count. Moses made his contribution; you and I will make ours.

God instructed that Moses' life be written for eternity—not so that we would idolize him, but so that we would see what it looks like when one person follows God's plan for him. We must know that the purpose of the world requires something greater than any one of us, but we must also know that each one of us is vital for that plan. God whispers in our ear, and we must strive for the sublime.

---

31 Maimonides, *Guide to the Perplexed* 2:45. Caring for others with worthy acts of kindness, says Maimonides, is one of the pre-conditions for prophecy.

32 Exodus 2:19

33 Exodus 3:1.

34 *Chatam Sofer*, commentary on Chumash.

35 Deuteronomy 34:1–6.

36 Ibid., v. 5–12.

10

A KABBALISTIC VIEW OF THE WORLD

MAN—THE SOUL THAT SUSTAINS THE WORLD

The first person ever was created as a solitary male-female being.[1] God initially avoided creating Adam and Eve as separate beings to send us an important message: each and every one of us has individual responsibility for the entire universe as if they were the only human in the world.[2]

If God gave us this responsibility, He must have given us the capacity to implement this as well, and hence the Torah tells us that when God created man: "And God blew into man the soul of life and man became a living spirit."[3] The verse does not say that the soul became a living spirit *in* man.[4] Rather, it says that man himself became the living spirit. Through the soul of life that was in him, man became a living soul sustaining the world.[5] Man became the central point that would draw all the other threads of reality together.

---

1 Genesis 2:21–22.

2 Talmud, Tractate *Sanhedrin* 37a; *Rashi*, ibid.

3 Genesis 2:7.

4 That would have read *va'yehi **ba**'adam*—ויהי באדם. Instead, it is written *va'yehi **ha**'adam*—ויהי האדם.

5 Rabbi Chaim of Volozhin, *Nefesh Hachaim* 1:4.

The universe of spirituality extends far beyond what the eye can see. All that we can sense is but a small part of this. The spiritual universe is composed of four worlds, each layered one atop the other, topped by huge expanses of spirituality.[6]

PARALLEL WORLDS

In the Kabbalistic literature, the world we inhabit is called the World of Action. In ascending order, it is followed by the World of Formation, the World of Creation, and the World of Emanation.[7] These worlds are parallels of each other.[8] Each one replicates the other at a higher spiritual level and level of completeness.[9] Each world above the other reflects an increasing amount of God's light.

When God said, "Let us make man," He was calling on all of the cosmos to join in and contribute their power and potential into this one being.

God hides Himself in all these worlds, but at different levels. God manifests His Will at a very high level, which then descends throughout all the worlds. Each level of descent brings about an increased level of hiddenness.[10] Our world, the World of Action, receives God's light in a significantly hidden form, yet it is only because of this thick mask that our world could be created and impurities are allowed to exist.[11]

These worlds are also linked; an action in one world ripples into those above and below it.[12] The filtering of God's light is an example of how

---

6 This level of spirituality is called *adam ha'kadmon. Nefesh Hachaim*, ibid., chap. 14, states that we cannot conceive of anything above the World of Emanation.

7 *Pardes Rimonim* 16:1. In Hebrew, these four worlds are called *Olam Hamaaseh* (עולם המעשה), *Olam Hayetzirah* (עולם היצירה), *Olam Habriah* (עולם הבריאה), and *Olam Haatzilut* (עולם האצילות).

8 The names of these worlds are based on the verse in Isaiah (43:7): "Everything that is called by name and for my honor, I have created, formed, and even made," where "honor" refers to the highest world, and "made" refers to the lowest world.

9 Rabbi Chaim of Volozhin, *Nefesh Hachaim* 1:6.

10 Rabbi Shneur Zalman of Liadi, *Tanya* 3:6. This phenomenon is known as "chaining down." Just like a chain is linked, with each link entering the one below it, so too, the bottom of each world enters into the top of the world below it.

11 Ibid.

12 *Ramchal, Derech Hashem* 1:5:2, 5.

this works moving downwards. But it also works in the opposite direction. When we make a choice in our World of Action, the effects of those choices soar upwards and affect all the worlds above. The smallest action on earth filters all the way up to the highest spiritual levels.

This structure allows man to take his place as the center of the creation. It explains how we—seemingly an insignificant speck in the cosmos—are the primary movers and shakers of the universe.[13]

MAN—A MINI-WORLD

The soul is a complex entity which contains five levels. These are (in ascending order) the *nefesh*, *ruach*, *neshamah*, *chayah*, and *yechidah*.[14] The top two souls are not contained within the body but are rather connected to it.[15] The higher parts of man's soul are way above the spiritual level of the angels.[16]

Each one of the four lower souls is connected with one of the four ascending worlds of spirituality, as depicted in the table below.[17] The fifth and highest level of the soul, the *yechidah*, exists on a plane that is an absolute unity, the Fifth World, known as *adam ha'kadmoni* or Primordial Man.

SOULS	WORLDS
Yechidah	Primordial Man
Chayah	Emanation
Neshamah	Creation
Ruach	Formation
Nefesh	Action

The parallels between the five souls and the five worlds prompt the Kabbalists to declare man to be the Mini-World, while the world outside

---

13 Ibid. 1:5:2.

14 *Derech Hashem* 3:1:4 (end).

15 Both these souls live in spiritual planes that are so high that each soul is not clearly differentiated from the unity of souls at this level.

16 These operate mainly on the level of the second world from the bottom, *Olam Hayetzirah*.

17 *Zohar* 2:94b.

of man is called the Big World. These two worlds—the Mini-World and the Big World—parallel each other.[18]

Man contains the full range of material and spiritual gradations within him. Man is therefore a replica of the world external to him, or the Big World.[19] The German philosopher Immanuel Kant once said: "Two things fill the mind with ever-new and increasing admiration and awe the more often and steadily we reflect upon them: the starry heavens above me and the moral law within me." According to Judaism, these are two reflections of the same reality. We have an entire world within ourselves with all five levels that we see outside of ourselves. It means that we can find within ourselves a point that can connect with any level of spirituality outside of ourselves. We will see the significance of this below.

Man is a mini-world, and all the forces that are found within him parallel the forces that are found in the big world outside of him.

Here is how this unfolded in the creation:

When God created man, He "appealed" to all the elements of the universe to contribute their power and potential into this one being.[20] All these elements are represented within him. Our spirituality extends through all of reality. Because of this, we have the power to pull all the spiritual threads of the universe together, for there is always a point within ourselves that we can connect with and hence elevate the Big World beyond ourselves.[21] Nothing is out of our reach.

This is the deeper message of Jacob's dream of the ladder. Jacob saw angels climbing up and down on a ladder stretching from the earth to heaven. This ladder is man's ladder. We are the soul of the world.[22] Our human impulse to innovate lies in our sense that this is true.

---

18 Ibid., p. 100a.

19 Rabbi Chaim of Volozhin, *Ruach Chaim on Ethics of Our Fathers* 5:1.

20 Ibid.

21 *Nefesh Hachaim* 1:6.

22 *Zohar, Parashat Naso* 123b; see *Ruach Chaim*, ibid.

MAN COMPLETES THE WORLD

As Jews, we stand for certain things. One of them is that all the threads of our messy history are being combined under the surface to reveal, at some stage in the future, God's grand vision. For now, God is hidden below the surface. This, which is referred to as His hidden Face (*hester panav*), is the source of all deficiency. Thus, the resolution to this is the revelation of God, known as the shining of His Face (*hearat panim*).[23]

Why did God do this? Because He deliberately created our world incomplete[24] so that we could complete the world and become partners with God in the creation itself.[25]

As the soul of the world, it is man's responsibility to turn the world into a receptacle fitting to receive God's presence, known as the *Shechinah*.[26] We are tasked with creating an environment on earth where God will feel at home, so to speak. We thereby control the amount of Godliness that is revealed in this world.[27] God's redemptive power is under the guardianship of man.

God gave man the power and the mandate to be able to complete the world that He had begun.

In what is known as *tikkun ha'olam*—the fixing of the world—we take God's deliberately fractured world and fix it.[28] God empowered us with all that we need to do this. Embedded in the giving of the Torah is the spiritual power necessary to do the job.[29]

This partnership allows us to have an unusually intimate relationship with God. Instead of being like a poor person receiving a handout, we

---

23 *Ramchal, Klalei Maamar Hachochmah, klal aleph.*

24 This is known from one of the names of God, *Sha-dai*, which means, "the One who told the world to stop" (*Mi She'amar Le'Olamo 'Dai'*). This means that God did not let the world reach the ultimate state of perfection but rather stopped it in the middle, leaving it to man to do the final fixing of the world.

25 *Ramchal, Daat Tevunot* 158 (p. 188). The *Zohar* (1:5) points out that the word *ami* (my nation) is spelled the same as the word *imi* (with me), i.e., My nation is with me as my partner.

26 *Tanya*, chap. 36.

27 Ibid.

28 It is also known as the *tikkun ha'klali*—"the general fixing."

29 *Daat Tevunot* 158 (p. 170).

are able to sit across the table with God, so to speak, as a fellow contributor to the world.[30]

This is the ultimate parenting model: nurturance of the child to make his own unique contribution to the world. How disappointing it is if we remain a perpetual child for God to look after, refusing to grow up and become fully what we are meant to and have the power to be![31]

A remarkable encounter between a Roman General and a great rabbi illustrates this. Turnus Rufus, a Roman General, once asked Rabbi Akiva, "Whose deeds are greater, God's or man's?" Surprisingly, Rabbi Akiva answered that man's deeds are greater. Rabbi Akiva showed Turnus Rufus some wheat, indicating that while God created the wheat, it is inedible in its raw form. We cannot eat it in the form that God made it! For wheat to be useful, we have to reap it, grind it into flour, and bake the flour into bread. God could have created a world where wheat stalks grew ready-to-use flour or even loaves of bread, but He didn't so that we can make our contribution to the world. Then Rabbi Akiva gave a second example: A newborn male has an extra piece of foreskin on its organ that we remove through circumcision. If God wanted the male human to be circumcised, why was he not born that way? God created the male deliberately deficient to empower man with completing His creation.[32]

THE RADICAL JEWISH AGENDA

Alfred North Whitehead stated that, "It is the business of the future to be dangerous...The major advances in civilizations...all but wreck the societies in which they occur."[33] Indeed, civilizations rise, peak, and fade into so much dust, as Mark Twain pointed out.[34] But there is a line that goes through history that has an exceptionally optimistic ending.

---

30 Ibid., p. 188, based on the Talmud *Yerushalmi*, Tractate *Peah* 1:3, which states: "Not like one who eats from food that is not his own, who is embarrassed to look in the face of he [who gives him the handout]."

31 Based on a written communication from Mrs. Yehudit Leah Feld.

32 *Midrash Tanchuma*, Leviticus, *Parashat Tazria* 5.

33 Alfred North Whitehead, *Science and the Modern World*.

34 Mark Twain, "Concerning the Jews," *Harper's Magazine*, March 1898.

Jews have a radical optimistic vision that sees the healing and completion of the world as built on the cumulative efforts of humankind.

When God finished the creation, the Torah says, "*Va'yechulu*—and He completed" the heavens and the earth.[35] This word, *va'yechulu*, comes from the word *kli*, a vessel or utensil. This allows for another interpretation of the verse: "And God turned the world into a vessel"—a vessel for man to use and complete. Hence, the Sages say, "A person who recites *Va'yechulu* on Friday night is considered as if he were a partner with God in the work of creation."[36] Such is the spiritual grandeur of man!

Each individual and each generation has its own unique contribution to the *tikkun ha'klali*—the general fixing of the world.[37] Each day, mankind is assigned to complete one aspect of the total *tikkun*.[38] God, our partner, takes all these contributions and weaves them into a fabric that reveals the complete picture of creation.[39] When complete, the Messianic Era will dawn. Woven into the whole, every aspect produces a new sustenance, each contributing to a revelation of God's glory.[40] The hues and rays of light all recombine to produce a pure white light as the entire creation moves over to eternity.

---

35 Genesis 2:1. *Chizkuni*, ibid., shows how this means that God created the entire cosmos.

36 Talmud, Tractate *Shabbat* 119b. The Gemara brings a proof for this: As it is stated: "And the heavens and the earth were finished [*va'yechulu*]." Do not read it as, "were finished [*va'yechulu*]"; rather as, "they finished [*va'yechalu*]." It is considered as though the Holy One, blessed be He, and the individual who says this become partners and completed the work together.

37 *Daat Tevunot* 128.

38 *Rashash*, introduction to *Nahar Shalom*.

39 *Daat Tevunot*, ibid.

40 Ibid.

11

IMITATING THE CREATOR

What is the proper path that a man should pursue? Whatever is of intrinsic value to himself and also earns him the esteem of his fellow men.[1]

Ethics of our Fathers (2:1)

ABRAHAM KEEPS GOD WAITING

If you had to choose between chatting with God Himself and conversing with a mere mortal, what would you do? Most people might say, "How could you possibly turn down a conversation with God?" Yet, Abraham's actions demonstrate otherwise. In the midst of talking with God—"And God appeared to him in the Plains of Mamre"[2]—Abraham noticed three travelers in idolater's garb.[3] Faced with choosing between a prophetic revelation—the greatest joy imaginable on earth[4]—and an act of hospitality to idolaters, Abraham astonishingly asks God to please wait so he could tend to the travelers' needs.[5]

---

1 The translation is according to the *Ran*, *Nedarim* 23a.

2 Genesis 18:1.

3 Ibid., v. 2.

4 *Chochmah U'Mussar*, vol. 1, no. 155.

5 Genesis 18:2–3: "And he (Abraham) said: 'Lord, if I have found favor in your eyes, do not pass

What is most surprising about this incident is that God actually listens to Abraham and waits while Abraham scurries off to invite the travelers in, only to continue their prophetic conversation afterward.[6]

How could Abraham be so brazen as to leave God waiting? And why would God agree to this? Furthermore, the Torah is known for its conciseness; as a rule, it gives tenets or examples and leaves us to determine how to apply the principle to our life.[7] For instance, the Torah instructs us to take care of our physical health.[8] It doesn't tell us the details of brushing our teeth, what diet to follow, or how to exercise.

But here, the Torah goes into great detail. We see how Abraham fussed over his guests. He washed their feet,[9] hurried to order cakes made of fine flour,[10] and ran to select a choice calf from his herd for their meal.[11] Why does the Torah, normally so concise, go into such detail with Abraham?

On the face of it, the Torah details Abraham's hospitality to emphasize the importance of kindness and hospitality, declaring that an act of hospitality is greater than receiving the face of the *Shechinah* (God's presence on earth).[12] Abraham was therefore right to interrupt his prophecy with God to tend to his guests. How can such a thing be true?

Understanding this requires a radical reformulating of what we define as being spiritual.

GIVING IS HOLIER THAN PROPHECY

We are used to thinking of giving as a humanistic trait, while prophecy is something uber-spiritual. But this is wrong.

It is not only hospitality alone that is greater than prophecy. The fulfillment of any commandment is a greater level of spirituality than

---

over (i.e., leave) your servant.'" See the *Malbim* on this verse. The word used here for God can also mean "my master," in which case it can also refer to the leading of the three guests.

6 Genesis 18:22, as per *Rashi*.

7 *Ramban*, Deuteronomy 6:18.

8 Deuteronomy 4:9.

9 Genesis 18:4.

10 Ibid., v. 6.

11 Ibid., v. 7. We will explore this in greater depth in Chapter 46.

12 Tractate *Shabbat* 127a; Tractate *Shevuot* 35b.

having a private meditation with God.[13] For the latter is a gift, and therefore never really becomes a part of the person, while the former is an acquisition and internalization of a real God-like quality.[14] "It is not abstract contemplation but fresh pulsating faithful-to-God active life that attains proximity to God."[15]

SELF-TRANSCENDENCE

The American novelist, Louis L'Amour, pointed out, "There will come the time when you believe everything is finished. That will be the beginning."[16] The reason for that is that man was created to actualize himself by reaching beyond himself through self-transcendence.

How do we self-transcend? By imitating God. One of the words related to the word *adam*, is the word *adameh*, "I will be like." *Adameh le'Elyon*—"I will be like the Above." Man should be God-like.[17] We are literally meant to imitate the way we see God manifest Himself in this world.[18]

The word *adameh* comes from the word *dimyon*,[19] which means imagination. It is our imagination that *allows* us to leap beyond ourselves and to become more God-like. The ability to see beyond oneself and to have a vision and goals opens endless opportunities for man's growth and, by the same measure, for massive self-deception.[20] It can be used for all kinds of fantasies, such as lusting after power or sensual encounters, or to dream of being rich and famous as secrets to happiness.[21] But it is that same power that gives us a vision of ourselves as holy.

---

13 Rabbi Eliyahu Dessler, *Michtav Me'Eliyahu*, vol. 2, p. 80.

14 Ibid., vol. 1, p. 140.

15 Rabbi Shimshon Raphael Hirsch, Genesis 18:2–3.

16 Louis L'Amour, *Lonely on the Mountain*.

17 Rabbi Tzadok HaKohen, *Machashavot Charutz*, no. 3. In Hebrew, *adameh le'Elyon*, "I will be like He who is above."

18 See Chapter 11.

19 Rabbi Tzadok HaKohen, *Machashavot Charutz*, no. 3.

20 Ibid.

21 See Chapter 8 for the use of imagination in activating our *yetzer hara*—our negative inclination.

The human soul is capable of "contraction" (*tzimtzum*), to form an ego that draws its boundaries tightly around the self, excluding the rest of the world. Some *tzimtzum* is essential, for otherwise we have no sense of self, no individuation. But, too tightly drawn, it tragically excludes anything beyond the self, including a relationship with God and one's fellow man. This reduces man to a pathetic and diminished egotistical self.

To find God and to connect to man requires *hitpashtut*, "expansion of the soul." Such a soul adventures beyond its self-made walls to apprehend God. That expansion can begin in different ways, either by accessing our deepest inner spirituality—called *ha'sechel ha'neelam*, "the unknowable mind" in the Kabbalistic literature—or by connecting beyond ourselves through action—most clearly by engaging the Commandments.

To find God and to connect to man requires hitpashtut, *"expansion of the soul."*

EMULATING GOD

God in His essence will always be beyond reach: "And God said: 'You cannot see My face, for no man can see me and live.'"[22] The essence of God remains an ineffable mystery. Hence, the Torah is not a book about the thoughts of man about God. Rather, it contains the thoughts of God on humanity. The Torah is our guide for understanding human conditions from God's point of view,[23] thereby demonstrating the proper approach to our fellow men.

We still can have a close relationship with God, even though we can't fully understand Him. It is not necessary to comprehend the Supernal Being for the moral behavior of man in this world.[24] When we study God's Torah, do His commandments, or pray to Him, we are relating *to* God.

---

22 Exodus 33:20.

23 Rabbi Shimshon Raphael Hirsch, ibid.

24 Rabbi Shimshon Raphael Hirsch, *Collected Writings*, vol. 3.

There is another type of relationship that we can have with God. Although we cannot understand God in His essence, we can understand how God interacts with us, i.e., His actions in the world.

God's actions in this world are acts of giving.[25] When we emulate Him by giving as well, we draw ourselves closer to Him by harmonizing ourselves with His actions. We become God-like when we choose to bestow good on others.[26] Just like He creates good, so do we. "And you should walk in His ways."[27] That is what creates our connection with God. That connection is a deep and satisfying experience.[28]

This explains why Abraham prioritized his guests over his prophetic conversation with God. Prophecy is a passive process in which the prophet receives a gift from God. Kindness, on the other hand, is a proactive deed. It is to act in this world, to participate in fixing the world, and to become a partner in the creation process itself.[29]

We are not being asked to serve God and man. God makes it clear that we serve Him when we honor our fellow.

WALKING IN HIS WAYS

The Sages gave examples of what it means to "walk in His ways":

- Just as God clothed the naked as he did with Adam and Eve after their sin,[30] we should clothe the naked.
- Just as God visited the sick when He conversed in a prophetic vision with Abraham on the third day of his circumcision,[31] we should visit the sick.
- Just as God comforted the mourning as he did with Isaac on the death of his father, Abraham,[32] we should comfort mourners.

---

25 *Maharal, Chiddushei Aggadata,* Tractate *Sotah* 14a.

26 *Ramchal, Derech Hashem* 1:2:2.

27 Deuteronomy 28:8–9, 10:12.

28 *Ramchal, Daat Tevunot* 24.

29 See the *Netziv, Haamek Davar* ad loc.

30 Genesis 3:21, "And God made for the man and for his wife coats of leather, and He dressed them."

31 Ibid. 18:1, "And God appeared to him in the plains of Mamre."

32 Ibid. 25:11, "And it was after the death of Abraham that God blessed Isaac his son."

- Just as God buried the dead as He did with Moses,[33] we should bury the dead.

And so, we are not just being good; we are being holy when we are being kind.[34] When we honor our fellow, we serve Him. If we love Him, we will love His creations.

ABRAHAM SACRIFICES HIS KABBALISTIC KNOWLEDGE

Abraham didn't just discover the existence of God; he discovered the way of God. Therefore, when initiating his spiritual lineage, Abraham chose *chessed*—giving and kindness—as the trait that he would develop to the nth degree.[35] Indeed, *chessed* has become the hallmark of the Jewish People.

In order for Abraham to become a perfected giving personality, he had to forgo some aspects of spirituality. Abraham did not achieve the exalted heights in Kabbalistic wisdom as some of those who preceded him, people like Shem, Chanoch (Hanoch), or Ever.[36] Washing idolatrous dust from the feet of strangers is just not compatible with these Kabbalistic heights.

But Abraham was aware of the sacrifice that he was making. "God has enough angels in the heavens," Abraham reasoned. "What good am I as Angel Number One-million-and-one, leaving the rest of the world in need and despair? God created me as a human to engage with this world, not to remove myself from it."[37] And despite this sacrifice, it was Abraham who became the forefather of the Jewish People—not the holy Shem, Chanoch, or Ever.

This is Abraham's legacy to us. Giving is holy.

---

33 Deuteronomy 34:6: "And He buried him (Moses) in the valley."

34 *Maharal, Netiv Hachessed*, chap. 1. The *Maharal* explains why other qualities of God that are mentioned in the Torah are not included in this commandment.

35 Genesis 18:19, where God says that He knows that Abraham will command also future generations to walk in the way of God.

36 Despite this, the oldest Kabbalistic work extant is a work written by Abraham called *Sefer Hayetzirah* (The Book of Formation).

37 *Chatam Sofer, Pituchei Chotam*, found in his introduction to Responsa, p. i.

12

BELIEF AS TRUTH

KNOW YOURSELF TO KNOW GOD

Knowledge of the self perforce precedes knowledge of God. If I don't understand myself, I cannot understand the ultimate Being beyond myself. We learn this from the story of the prophet Balaam, who was asked by King Balak to curse the Jewish People.[1] As he was riding along, Balaam's donkey kept on stopping. Thinking that it was just the obstinacy of a donkey, he hit the animal.[2] But what was really happening was that the donkey was seeing an angel of God blocking his path—an angel that Balaam did not see.[3]

This is astonishing. Balaam was a prophet,[4] matched only by Moses.[5] He was the greatest and most honored of the non-Jews in his time.[6] In fact, Moses was but the scribe to copy Balaam's prophecy into the

1 Numbers 22:9–11.

2 Ibid., v. 27.

3 Ibid., v. 23.

4 According to the *Ramban* (ibid., v. 31), Balaam's elevated level of prophecy was only for that particular episode.

5 In Deuteronomy 34:10, we read: "And there never arose another prophet in Israel like Moses who knew God face to face." The Sages (*Sifri* ad loc.) say, "In Israel [no such prophet] arose, but amongst the nations of the world, there did arise, i.e., Balaam."

6 Rabbi Meir Simchah of Dvinsk, *Meshech Chochmah*, Deuteronomy 34.

Torah.[7] Yet, when God sent Balaam a message through his donkey, Balaam could not see.

The Sages ask: "How could Balaam claim to understand God if he could not even understand his own donkey?"[8] But why does Balaam have to understand his donkey in order to understand God? Because Balaam's donkey is a parable for his own physical self. In Hebrew, the word for donkey is *chamor* (חמור). The same letters make up the word *chomer* (חומר)—the material world. Balaam's donkey—his body and materialistic self—were stronger than his soul. In the end, Balaam was so ravenously sensual that he could no longer understand even the wisdom of his own body. He was totally alienated from himself.

If we don't first understand who we are—if we are so out of touch with our soul and our physical selves—we will not be able to connect to God. On the other hand, at a certain point we need to connect to God to fully appreciate ourselves. As someone once put it, "If you really believe there is no God, then you should believe that you are insignificant."

THE REVELATION OF NATURE AND THE REVELATION OF TORAH

Abraham first discovered what I will call the God of the scientist. Everywhere he looked, he saw incredible order, demanding a higher intelligence overseeing and guiding the whole process.[9] This is Einstein's God, a God that "does not play dice," a God of beauty and order, of wonderment at the astonishing complexity of the world. A world this complex with such order and beauty must surely be the handwork of God.[10]

Nature was the first of two revelations given to us; the other was the Torah.[11] The revelation of nature—the world of physics, genetics, or

---

7 Talmud, Tractate *Bava Batra* 14b: "And Moses wrote his own book and the portion of Balaam and the Book of *Iyov* (Job)." See *Ohr Gedalyahu*, beginning of *Parashat Balak*, for a deeper understanding.

8 Tractate *Berachot* 7.

9 *Midrash Rabbah*, Genesis, beg. of *Parashat Lech Lecha* 39a.

10 Walter Isaacson, *Einstein: His Life and Universe*: "His [religious] beliefs seemed to arise from the sense of awe and transcendent order that he discovered through his scientific work." On another occasion, Einstein stated, "What separates me from most so-called atheists is a feeling of utter humility toward the unattainable secrets of the harmony of the cosmos."

11 Note at end of 18th letter in the *Nineteen Letters*.

anatomy—is a ladder that we can climb to reach the higher realms of Torah.[12] By discovering one, Abraham was able to reach the other.[13]

Rabbi Shimshon Raphael Hirsch once commented: "What will I answer when asked, 'Raphael, did you see my beautiful Alps?'" God wants us to experience the natural beauties of the world. He wants us to hear the birds sing, to see the trees blossom, and to be in awe.[14] He wants us to see the mundane and sense the sublime. And He wants us to feel His guiding presence behind all of this. This kind of God-connection was Abraham's first gift to the world.[15]

Two revelations are given to us—nature and the Torah.

BELIEF THAT—BELIEF IN

To experience the revelation of God in nature is to reach the level of "belief that"—belief *that* God exists. Abraham does not rest with just that discovery. He moved from a level of "belief that" to a level of "belief in." He provided a radically different model of how God acts and how we, in turn, must act toward Him. The gods of his contemporaries had no interest in lowly man, but Abraham concluded that this can't be true. God's whole purpose in creating man was to share His goodness—not only with mankind in general, but with each person in particular.[16] And so, Abraham's big discovery was that God is interested in each human—that God is happy to lower Himself, so to speak, into the nitty-gritty of man and his needs.[17] And this must mean that God continuously challenges us to grow by tailor-making the universe

---

12 *Maharal, Netiv HaTorah*, chap. 14. The *Maharal* continues: "And from this we can conclude that we should study everything that can lead us to an underlying understanding of the nature of the world; [and indeed] one is obligated to do so, for all is the act of God, and through this understanding one will come to understand one's Creator."

13 Even though the Torah had yet to be given to mankind, Abraham discovered the entire Torah for himself through this method.

14 Psalms 148.

15 Maimonides, *Mishneh Torah*, Laws of the Foundations of Torah 2:2.

16 *Ramchal, Daat Tevunot* 18.

17 Rabbi Shlomo Wolbe, *Alei Shur*, vol. 1, p. 307.

to perfectly fit the growth needs of every human at each and every moment. This is the principle of Divine Providence.[18]

God comes down to us because He wants to have a relationship with us. He wants to model behavior for us. He wants us to walk in His ways.[19] The redemptive power of God is bound up in the personal mystery and journey of each one of us.

The Torah introduces Abraham when he is already seventy-five years old. God tells him to leave everything and go to an unknown destination. Abraham listens because his belief in God has led to trusting in Him. He has graduated from belief that—the God of the scientists—to belief in—the God of a relationship.[20]

Judaism does not teach us about the God of the scientist—not because it is not important, but because it presumes we can get that information elsewhere. The Torah is a book that teaches us how to live; it is not a book of proofs. We don't need Torah to teach us the God of Einstein. We need it to teach us how to connect to Him.

FAITH VS. PROOF

Judaism never claimed to prove itself at the level demanded by the skeptic, for the skeptic often demands a level of proof that does not exist. The skeptic asks that Judaism be presented as the only possible explanation to its claims, but that is impossible. It is always possible to give another explanation for a given set of phenomena. What we can conclude, though, is that God and His Torah is the best possible explanation for the world we see amongst all the competing alternatives. No scientist can do better than that—or claims to—when proposing any scientific theory.[21]

Judaism does have back up, lots of it. Archeology, internal logic, codes, rational arguments, and the sheer profundity and relevance

---

18 This idea is included in Principles Nine and Ten of the Thirteen Principles of Faith.

19 Talmud, Tractate *Shabbat* 133b.

20 See next chapter.

21 In fact, according to Sir Karl Popper (*The Open Society and Its Enemies*), the best a scientific proof can do is to claim that it has not yet been disproven. Quantum physics goes much further in claiming the essential unknowability of the world.

of the Torah—they all add up to a remarkable claim of Judaism's authenticity. There is no religion that even begins to make a claim of an involved God who gave His laws to an entire people. There simply is no competing explanation that comes close to accounting for the entire sweep of what Judaism is claiming.

At some point, the cumulative observations and experiences of a person lead to an internal resonance with the Torah. The faith of the Jew is but a rational extension of what he can see and test. His faith is but a stretching of his spiritual self to the horizon that he can see and beyond.

As with the individual, so with the nation. When Moses sent the spies into the land of Israel, ten of them returned reporting that the Jewish People didn't stand a chance against the well-armed and fortified Canaanites.[22] Caleb and Joshua, the other two spies, stood in opposition.[23] Caleb pointed the Jewish People to a faith in God that places the Jewish People above the normal laws of history.[24] This is not to be irrational; it is to transcend oneself.[25]

God revealed to Elijah one of the secrets of how to do this: God tells Elijah that He is not found in the mighty wind nor the raging fire, but rather in the soft, thin voice.[26]

There are people—entire generations—who will not find God through dramatic proofs and loud noises declaring the truth of the Torah, but they will respond to the still, quiet voice of exemplary figures modeling the Torah personality. They will respond to the flavor of its festivals, and to the intellectual challenge of its wisdom. Judaism is not a loud religion. It does not solicit converts (though it welcomes them). It is not a religion whose legitimacy rests in the numbers of its adherents.[27] It is found in the still, quiet voice.

---

22 Numbers 13:27–29.

23 Ibid., v. 30; 14:6–9.

24 Ibid. 14:9.

25 *Aish Kodesh, Parashat Shekalim.*

26 Kings I 19:11–12.

27 The current world Jewish population is in the region of 14.5 million.

13

THE UNITY THEME OF THE UNIVERSE

THE HISTORY OF MAN AND THE HISTORY OF EACH MAN

We are, as the British-American poet W.H. Auden once said, "history making creatures."[1] We make this history together with our God. As Jews, we cannot allow ourselves to be passive observers, swept along by the events that others make. We are a history-making people! To make history is to build. It is to take a three-thousand-year-old legacy and to move it consciously forward. To be Jewish is to feel the pulse of the past, harness it, and leave the world a better place for the next generation.

Elisha Wiesel, son of Holocaust survivor and Nobel laureate Elie Wiesel, put it like this:

> *When I said Kaddish [for my father] for eleven months, I was not just connecting with him; I felt connected with his forebears as well. I had a real sense of history, going back thousands of years, of what it meant to be part of a lineage with certain traditions, rituals, and values. For almost 2,000 years, when a parent has passed away, the Jewish child has said Kaddish. There*

1 W.H. Auden, *The Dyer's Hand* (London: Faber and Faber, 1963), pp. 278–79.

is something profound about that. As I prepare my own son for his bar mitzvah and watch my daughter learning Hebrew, despite this crazy modern life with all of its distractions, I have this same sense of history and continuity. I think about where I came from, where I am, and where my Jewish children will go in the future. That's deeply meaningful and very grounding.

A NEW DEFINITION OF INDIVIDUALISM

Contemporary society believes that each individual needs to reinvent himself from scratch. The alternative, it is presumed, is to be stuck with outdated and irrelevant traditions, where everyone is forced to be the same.

But Judaism takes a different position. Not only is our starting point Divine and sublime, but there are well over a hundred generations of Jewish genius to build on! We begin our journey perched on the shoulders of giants. It is then up to each individual to create their own personal legacy and become someone entirely unique.

We have the gift of Sinai and 3,000 years of Jewish genius on which to build our own personal legacy.

This leads to a profound idea on the meaning of individualism.

The Western concept of individualism is that each person gets to invent himself, provided that he or she does not harm anyone else in the process.

The Jewish idea of individualism is that each individual provides his or her unique contribution to the ultimate perfection of mankind.

In other words:

- In the Western world, it is "live and let live."
- In the Jewish world, it is "I *need* your contribution, and you *need* mine. I need you to be you, and you need me to be me. I need to find ways to help you fulfill your potential, and you need to help me fulfill mine."

In the course of this book, we will see that this approach, far from limiting innovation or dampening man's entrepreneurial spirit, is actually a great enabler for these things and much more. Our highest aspirations as individuals use the same exalted guidelines as our aspirations as a global community. They reinforce rather than undermine each other.

The history of mankind is intertwined with the history of its most remarkable people, i.e., the Jews. In that history, every individual is irreplaceable.

As we weave our threads of understanding throughout this section into a whole fabric, what will emerge is that we—as humans and as Jews—are not only active participants in history, but that God created a deliberately incomplete world and empowered us to complete it.

THE UNITY THEME OF THE UNIVERSE

Quantum physics has shown that two particles can be entangled or, to use an alternative word, coupled.[2] These particles may be on two sides of the universe, yet a change in the properties of one of them—say, their spin—will lead to an instantaneous change in the other particle. Einstein called this "spooky action at a distance."[3] Since nothing can travel faster than the speed of light (not even information), these particles cannot be communicating with each other. The only explanation is they must be the same particle, separated into two expressions. This tells us that the entire universe is, in fact, a grand unity.[4]

Four basic forces underline this universe: the strong force, the weak force, the electromagnetic force, and the force of gravity.[5] Scientists

---

2 Entanglement was first discovered by the Austrian-Irish physicist Erwin Schrödinger in the early 20th century.

3 The physicist Lawrence M. Krauss explains that actually, it is much more weird than that because quantum mechanics says that the actual spin direction of either electron is not determined in advance of the measurement; the only thing that's certain is that the spins of the two atoms are anti-aligned, i.e., that their spin is pointing in opposite directions. Even stranger, until they have been measured, both electrons are actually spinning up and down at the same time. Because the two electrons are in a single quantum state—because they are entangled—the moment I measure the spin of one electron, I fix the direction of spin of the other electron. It's as though, by flipping one coin and coming up "heads," I force another coin to come up "tails."

4 Scientists have actually entangled many particles in the laboratory, and there is nothing to prevent all of matter from being in a state of entanglement.

5 The strong force holds the nucleus of an atom together. The weak force creates radiation. The other two forces are well-known. They are the force of gravity and the electromagnetic force.

believe that these four forces are really one force. They believe that only one force emerged from the Big Bang but at a very early stage (around one thirty-seventh of a second), the universe had cooled sufficiently for this one force to divide into four different expressions—the four forces we have today.

Since the 1980s, thousands of scientists dedicated their lives (and many tens of billions of dollars) to prove this. Smashing sub-atomic particles together at very high speeds, they hope to recreate the super-hot conditions that existed soon after the Big Bang when the forces were still united. In fact, they have managed to combine three of the four forces,[6] and are now working on showing that the last one (gravity) is also a part of this grand unity.[7] Scientists believe that by showing that these four forces are one, they will produce a TOE—a theory of everything.

But why set out on such a search to begin with? Why not just accept that there are four forces? The answer is that it is an axiom of science that correlates unity and truth. They believe that the deepest truth is unity. Why do scientists believe in unity so deeply? It is because they are sensing the secret behind the structure of the world.

Entanglement and combining the four forces are nature's way of revealing a second overarching theme of this section, indeed the whole book. It is the unity-theme of the universe. Let us explain this in Torah terms.

THE THREE "TENS"

In Judaism, ten symbolizes a thing in its entirety. It is the first unit of one after one itself. Only God can be one. Only God is a pure unity.

---

6 At first, scientists combined the weak force with the electromagnetic force into the electroweak force. Then they combined this force with the strong force into a GUT—a grand unified theory. Although scientists can only see these combinations for micro-seconds when they smash particles together and briefly create very high temperatures, they predicted the existence of new particles, which they were then able to measure.

7 Gravity is more difficult to combine with the others because the others are forces within the atom; they operate at a quantum level, whereas gravity is a macro-force. Scientists believe that their best shot at a breakthrough on this is to translate the idea of gravity into quantum terms—quantum gravity.

Before creation, there was only God. After He created the world, there was multiplicity—the Creator and the created. Each created being, in turn, had its own identity.

The events of the Torah unfold into a listing of ten events exactly three times.[8] Nothing is coincidental in God's gifts to mankind. So, this curious fact must mean something:

- The first "ten" happened when God created the world. There were Ten Sayings of Creation.[9]
- The second "ten" was in Egypt—the Ten Plagues.[10]
- Finally, at Sinai, we received the Ten Commandments.[11]

We cannot create one, but we can create the next unit of one. We can unify the multiple parts into a new gestalt, i.e., a whole that is more than the sum of its parts. We can, as the physicists have shown, entangle all of reality to show that they really all connect to one source. In Judaism, this new unity is expressed by the number ten. So, whenever we see ten of something, we are seeing a whole process—every angle—combined to create a new reality.[12] We are seeing the first unit of one in the creation itself.[13]

In other words, the Ten Sayings of Creation tell us that the world had a beginning, and that beginning must therefore have been for a

---

8 There are two other important "tens"—the Ten Tests of Abraham (*Ethics of Our Fathers* 5:3) which, according to the *Maharal* (ibid.), means that Abraham was challenged from every angle; his entire personality had to be actualized to pass these tests. In addition there are the ten times the Jewish people tested God (Numbers 14:22). However, the tests of Abraham are not clearly listed as such in the Torah, while the ten times that the Jewish people tested God (enumerated in the Talmud, Tractate *Arachin* 15a) were generated by the Jewish people, not God. Hence I only count three times in the text. According to the *Maharal* (ibid.), what this means is that Abraham was challenged from every angle; his entire personality had to be actualized to pass these tests.

9 Genesis, chap. 1, as per *Ethics of Our Fathers* 5:1. The first verse, "In the beginning, God created the heavens and the earth," is the first of these ten. See Chapter 20, "The Holiness of the Ten Commandments," fn 19, for the verse numbers where all Ten Sayings appear.

10 Exodus, chaps. 7–12.

11 Ibid. 20:1–14.

12 *Maharal, Derech Chaim on Ethics of Our Fathers* 5:2–3.

13 Ibid. 5:1.

purpose, for it would contradict God's absolute perfection to create something without any purpose.

The Ten Commandments represent the inner, spiritual content, the purpose of the Ten Sayings of Creation.

The Ten Plagues confirmed that God not only created the world at the beginning of time but that He continues to play an active role in the running of the world—the idea of Divine Providence. He is involved in our lives. It matters not whether this is in the form of the open miracles of the plagues, or the form of the hidden daily miracles of nature. To Him, it is all the same.[14] He is the God of history, unfolding His radical Divine plan.[15]

The Ten Commandments represent the inner, spiritual content—the purpose of the Ten Sayings of Creation. The outer, physical garments are the laws of nature. The natural world may be a thing of wonder, but it reveals no purpose. The inner, spiritual form of this world of nature is the spiritual world of the Ten Commandments. They give meaning and content to the world.

Moreover, the Ten Commandments began the process whereby the Torah entered the physical world,[16] giving the world not only its purpose but a means of achieving it. Without this, man as a physical being would have no way of cleaving to God in this world.[17] The spiritual and the physical realms would have remained totally separate. After the Torah was given, a mechanism was provided where the body could soar together with the soul, and the two were united once again.[18] So did King David put it: "The Torah of God is pure, it restores the soul."[19]

Ten, ten, and ten. God created the world; He continues to be involved in it; and He gave it its moral and spiritual purpose. The long road to human understanding begins with these three "tens."

---

14 *Ramban*, Exodus 13:16.

15 Deuteronomy 32:7 urges us to notice the Divine plan of history as it has unfolded through the generations.

16 *Sefat Emet*, *Parashat Yitro*, Year 5632.

17 Ibid.

18 Ibid.

19 Ibid.

MAN THE RESPONDER AND MAN THE INITIATOR

We, as mortal and limited humans, had no part in the Ten Sayings of Creation. In fact, we were created without the involvement of our choice, just like the rest of creation. The Ten Plagues were also completely beyond our control.

On the other hand, the final "ten," the Ten Commandments, are truly ours. The Torah was offered to man, and it was up to us to accept it.[20] We were and are given the autonomy to determine what our own inner spiritual and moral reality will be.

The Ten Commandments represent the inner, spiritual content—the purpose of the Ten Sayings of Creation.

At Sinai, the Jewish nation "bought into" core spirituality by entering a covenantal relationship with God and accepting the Torah, which was the expression of that covenant. We accepted the Torah.

The word "Torah" has two meanings:

- It is connected to the root word *harah* (הרה), which means to become pregnant or fertilized. The Torah is God's means of implanting the seeds of spirituality and morality in man.[21]
- It also means a book of teaching, from the root of *hora'ah* (הוראה); from which *moreh* (מורה), a teacher, is also derived. If God has a purpose for man, He has to have a way of communicating this. This is the Torah. Without it, the Jews would not have made history. They would not even have survived.

This book, the Torah, came not only to teach us wisdom—the subject of Section 3—but also holiness, the subject of our next section. That holiness and that wisdom translate into a practical plan of perfection of the human personality. That is the subject of the final section of this book.

---

20 Exodus 24:7.

21 Rabbi Shimshon Raphael Hirsch, Genesis 26:5; Leviticus 18:4; and *Horeb*, para. 327. Rabbi Hirsch points out that Torah is in the causative (*hiphil*) form—to plant a seed in someone else.

SECTION 2

HOLINESS

14

INNER VS. OUTER DIRECTEDNESS

And what does God demand of you except to do kindness and justice and to walk modestly with your God.

Micah (6:8)

IN THE IMAGE OF GOD

R. H. Tawney stated that "the essence of all morality is this: to believe that every human being is of infinite importance, and therefore that no consideration of expediency can justify the oppression of one by another. But to believe this, it is necessary to believe in God."[1]

Tawney is right, but he doesn't explain why. He misses the key phrase, "the sanctity of human life." For we can only consider the worth of man to be infinite if he was created in the image of an Infinite God (*tzelem Elokim*).[2] It is only when we contemplate the spiritual grandeur of man that we can begin to appreciate his worth.

God "blew" the spirit of life into man.[3] In the words of the Kabbalists, "He who blew, blew from within Himself." And so, man's essence is holy and sacred. We don't have to do anything to deserve our lives. God has already made our lives intrinsically worthwhile. Incredibly, we break the

1 See Michael Perry, *The Idea of Human Rights*.

2 Genesis 1:27.

3 Ibid. 2:7.

Shabbat to save a life even if we are certain the person will only live a few seconds longer.[4] We do not measure how much life makes it worth it. Every second of life is of infinite worth. Life itself is holy.

We don't have to do anything to deserve our lives. God blew the spirit of life into man, and hence, God has already made our lives intrinsically worthwhile.

From this idea emerged universal human rights—that every human has certain rights just by virtue of being human. All democratic countries adhere to this idea today, as if it is something that should be obvious to all. (And, in fact, the idea of democracy itself is dependent on this assumption.) But, for thousands of years the Jews stood alone on this, proclaiming their truth until the rest of the world was ready to hear it.[5] For they were dealing in a strange currency—the currency of holiness.

THE INNER-DIRECTED SELF

If I am in the image of God, and my life is therefore intrinsically worthwhile, I must draw my own feelings of self-worth from that idea. I am OK not because of what I have done or because of what I have, but because of what I am. I am OK not because of the recognition that others bestow upon me but because of my own inner sense of dignity. In other words, I am an inner-directed rather than an outer-directed person.

In *Ethics of Our Fathers*, we read, "Who is a wise man? He who learns from every man...Who is a strong man? He who conquers his desire to do evil...Who is a wealthy man? He who is happy with his lot...Who is honored? He who honors other beings."[6]

The common denominator of these qualities is that they reflect inner-directedness. We learn from every person when we are secure, have a good self-image, and do not need to be reflexively right.

---

4 Talmud, Tractate *Yoma,* 84b; *Shulchan Aruch, Orach Chaim,* 329:4.

5 The Universal Declaration of Human Rights dates back only to the UN General Assembly on December 10, 1948.

6 *Ethics of Our Fathers* 4:1.

We are strong when we have the inner strength to control our own urges.

We are wealthy when we are filled up from the inside and don't have a need to try and fill ourselves up with money and material goods, for we know that these will never fill us up and that we will be condemned to trying to fill up with more and more and more.

We are honored when we overcome the need to be honored and have enough dignity to honor others.[7]

We need to internally generate our spiritual and emotional state, independent of external influences.

By filling ourselves up by our inner strength, we liberate ourselves. We liberate ourselves because we are no longer subject to the changing values of whichever society or era we happen to be in. We liberate ourselves because we are willing to take moral stands that are not popular. We become true Abrahamic Jews. Abraham was called the *Ivri* (Hebrew), "the one who stood on the other side of the river"; so too, we become his authentic descendants. Society usually focuses on externals. We are *Ivrim*, inner-directed people,[8] the people willing to stand on the far side.

When we liberate ourselves, we sanctify ourselves. We sanctify ourselves by opening ourselves to being filled up with the only thing that really ever will fill us up—a spiritually meaningful life.

We also change the direction of our relationship with others. Instead of being needy and dependent, we generate our own internal peace. Instead of competing with others, we see how we can give to them. Instead of peaking at a certain age, we can continue to become great at any age.[9] This is the lesson of *Ethics of our Fathers*.

---

7 *Maharal*, ibid.

8 See Rabbi Jonathan Sacks, *Parashat Lech Lecha*: The Lord said to Abraham, "Go forth from your land, your birthplace and your father's house to the land that I will show you" (Genesis 12:1). Abraham was commanded to leave behind the sources of both tradition-directedness ("your father's house") and other-directness ("your land, your birthplace"). He was about to become *the father of an inner-directed people*.

9 *Maharal*, ibid.

THE DIFFERENCE BETWEEN PLENTY AND EVERYTHING

Esau hated his brother Jacob for stealing his birthright—his right to be the firstborn and hence the leader.[10] When they met as adults, Esau had a mini-army of 400 people, and Jacob felt his life was threatened.[11] Jacob prepared elaborately for his encounter with Esau. He prayed to God. He prepared gifts of animals for Esau, carefully grouped and spaced when presented. Just in case, he prepared for war.[12] When the two brothers do meet, the meeting is tense, but it goes well.

Esau at first turns down Jacob's gifts. "I have plenty," he says.[13]

Jacob persists, saying, "I have everything,"[14] so take from me.

What is the difference between Esau's "plenty" and Jacob's "everything"?

Esau was wealthier than Jacob, but Esau felt only that he had a lot, implying that he could have more. And indeed, he accepts Jacob's gifts.[15]

For Jacob, it was different. Early on in his life, Jacob asks for God to give him bread to eat and clothes to wear.[16] The body requires certain necessities, and that is all that Jacob wants. After that, he felt that nothing from the outside could add to his happiness.

In other words:

- Esau was outer-directed, and he thought that the gifts would do something for him.
- Jacob was full from the inside. Therefore, he had everything.

When we bless God after eating a meal with bread, we repeat Jacob's words, expressing the hope that God will bless us with *kol*—with

10 See Numbers 3:13, where the firstborn has a certain holiness and—prior to the sin of the golden calf—were originally the ones designated to serve in the Temple. See also Deuteronomy 21:17 with respect to inheritance.

11 Genesis, chaps. 32–33.

12 Ibid. 32:8–23.

13 Ibid. 32:9, "*Yesh li rav*"—יש לי רב.

14 Ibid., v. 11, "*Yesh li kol*"—יש לי כל.

15 Ibid.

16 Genesis 28:1: "And Jacob made an oath saying: 'If the Lord God will be with me, and will guard me on this path on which I am walking, and will give me bread to eat and clothes to wear.'"

everything.[17] We pray that we will realize that what we have *is* already *everything*. We long to be blessed in this way—to always retain the capacity to feel full from the inside.

HOLINESS AND ROOTEDNESS

The Hebrew word for "secular" or "profane" is *chol*, which means "empty." To profane something is to empty it of content. But the word *chol* also means "sand"—that which can be blown away by the wind. A huge sand dune in the Sahara can be there one day and gone the next. Hence, "profane" also means rootless and unanchored.

The righteous have roots. They are not driven by the winds of changing morality, or by sudden political or social swings. They stand firm. They grow. They bear fruit. They flourish. They do so because they follow their inner voice, not the changing vicissitudes of their environment. This is why Jews are still here, proclaiming their mission when so many other civilizations disappeared along the way.

PEERING BELOW THE SURFACE

In Hebrew, the word for "world" is *olam*. *Olam* (עולם) comes in turn from the word "hidden"—*he'elem* (העלם). This world is the world where spirituality and holiness are hidden below the surface. Someone whose entire life is lived according to an external definition of self—the world of achievements, of "likes" on social media, of competition and honor and wealth—will not develop the capacity to connect to spirituality because he is living on the surface of reality while spirituality is hidden below the surface. The challenge given to us by *Ethics of our Fathers* is to look deep into ourselves, to find our core, and to draw all our self-worth from there. This entire section has to do with how to identify and to generate that spirituality.

---

17 Toward the end of the *benching*, we say the words, "*Ba'kol, mi'kol, kol.*" The last word refers to Jacob's statement.

15

WHAT DOES IT MEAN TO BE HOLY?

Be a kingdom of priests and a holy nation.

Exodus (19:6)

THE SWEEPING BREADTH OF HOLINESS

Leviticus 19 is one of those chapters that totally changes our perspective on how to live our lives. Moses gathers the entire nation together,[1] and he transmits God's instruction: "Be holy, because I, the Lord your God, am holy."[2]

Before the Jews could receive the Torah at Sinai, they made a covenant with God. God says to the Jews, "Be a kingdom of priests (*mamlechet kohanim*) and a holy nation (*goy kadosh*)."[3] This, then, is who we are—or try to be. We are not trying to be the most brilliant, get the most Nobel prizes, or be the wealthiest. To be a Jew is to try to be holy.

The command to be holy is not counted as one of the 613 commandments. This is because it is not limited to one act.[4] It is a facet of all

1 Leviticus 19:1.

2 Ibid., v. 2.

3 Exodus 19:6.

4 This is in line with the fourth principle in the introduction of Maimonides to his *Book of*

of the other commandments. But it goes further. It spreads its canopy over all of Judaism. The [illegible] tity are inseparably woven into the fa[illegible]ce.[5] To be holy is an attitude—an appr[illegible]ur very being.[6]

With this mitzvah, th[illegible] ourselves and to the world is dramati[illegible]o discover holiness where none is ob[illegible]rly directed by halachah. We have to re[illegible]g as incapable of being infused with holiness.[7] The Jew sees everything as having "sanctity potential"—every smile, every thought, every morsel of food, every gesture honoring our fellow man.

Following the command to be holy, the Torah proceeds to give us specific examples: We are enjoined to keep the Shabbat[8] and to revere God's sanctuary.[9] We are ordered to remain strictly monotheistic and not to abuse God's name.[10] This makes sense. We cannot be holy if we don't relate properly to our God.

But the rest of the list is full of surprises. The laws of holiness span the full gamut regulating our relationships with our fellow man, with the environment, and with ourselves.

One cannot be truly good if one is not also holy.

It is here—and not within the Ten Commandments—that we are commanded to "love your neighbor like yourself."[11] We are told to uphold the rights and dignity of others and to save their lives.[12] We are enjoined to honor our parents[13] and to rise in front of the old and the

---

Commandments—that a command that has no specific expression but rather multiple expressions is not counted as one of the 613 commandments.

5 *Ramban*, Leviticus 12:2.

6 *Netivot Shalom*, Leviticus, p. 87.

7 *Ohr Gedalyahu*, Leviticus, p. 51b.

8 Leviticus 19:3, 30.

9 Ibid., v. 30.

10 Ibid., v. 4, 12, 26.

11 Ibid., v. 18.

12 Ibid., v. 16.

13 Ibid., v. 3.

wise.[14] We are told to treat and love the convert like one born among ourselves[15] and to do no wrong to a non-Jewish stranger living in our land.[16] We are told to be charitable[17] and not to hate,[18] slander,[19] or take revenge.[20] Apparently, there is no holiness if we are not caring of our fellow humans.

The holy Jew is the person who pays his employees on time, does not steal, cheat, or pressure his neighbor to make a sale.[21]

While we normally associate these things with being good, we don't normally think of these things as being holy. The innovation the Torah is making here is that one cannot be truly good if one is not also holy.[22]

We also have to be concerned with our fellow's spiritual wellbeing. We may not cause someone else to sin.[23] We have to engage those who have lost their sensitivity to this or that aspect of Judaism.[24]

The message is clear. The highest of moral sensitivities to our fellow man are expressions of holiness as much as prayer or Torah study or keeping the Shabbat is.

But that is not all. The list continues.

It extends to sensitivity to the environment: not to cross-breed different species;[25] not to mix flax and linen in clothing;[26] and not to sow our fields with mixed seed.[27] All of these tell us to respect the order of the universe and not to destroy the world we live in.[28] Maintaining the environment is a holy mission.

---

14 Ibid., v. 32.
15 Ibid., v. 34.
16 Ibid., v. 33.
17 E.g., to leave the corner of our fields and leftover grapes for the poor; ibid., v. 9–10.
18 Ibid., v. 17.
19 Ibid., v. 16.
20 Ibid., v. 18.
21 Ibid., v. 11, 13.
22 *Netivot Shalom*, Leviticus, p. 84.
23 "Don't put a stumbling block before the blind"; Leviticus 19:14.
24 Leviticus 19:17.
25 Ibid., v. 19.
26 Ibid.
27 Ibid.
28 Rabbi Shimshon Raphael Hirsch ad loc.; *Horeb*.

The command to be holy appears three times.[29] This is to include the sanctification of sexuality and the sanctification of food, i.e., our most basic urges.[30]

We are told about forbidden sexual relations,[31] about the impurity of non-kosher food,[32] as well as the prohibition not to make any cuttings in our flesh out of excessive mourning for the dead.[33] These are types of holiness that come through separation from impurity.[34]

Seeing the list, we see the potential for holiness everywhere. To adapt the Kotzker Rebbe's question: "Where is holiness? Wherever it is allowed in."[35]

A NEW PARADIGM OF HOLINESS

If we will try to define holiness as something removed from the physical and the mundane, this definition won't fit a fraction of the examples given here. We need to create a totally new paradigm of holiness.

If we look at this list, we will see that there are two levels of holiness. The first level is *taharah*—purity. It is a state of spiritual and moral fitness and life.[36] In this sense, the word *kedushah* (holiness) means to be set aside and be dedicated to something.[37] The loss of that state is *tumah*—impurity; it is that which debases and degrades.[38] *Tumah* can only come about when there was a potential for holiness to begin with.[39]

Our stereotypical definitions of holiness don't work. We need a totally new paradigm.

We become impure when we breach the boundaries of the ethical and the spiritual. The laws not

29 Leviticus 19:1; 21:26; 22:22.

30 Rabbeinu Bachya, Leviticus 19:2; *Netivot Shalom*, Leviticus, pp. 83–84.

31 Leviticus 19:29; 20:10–21.

32 Ibid. 20:26.

33 Ibid. 19:28.

34 *Rashi*, Leviticus 19:2.

35 The Kotzker Rebbe asked, "Where is God?"

36 Rabbi Tzadok HaKohen, *Likutei Maamarim* (at the end of *Divrei Sofrim*), p. 228.

37 *Tosafot*, Talmud, Tractate *Kiddushin* 2a.

38 Vilna Gaon, *Tikkunei Zohar* 41a.

39 Ibid. §71.

to hate, take revenge, damage property, and slander[40] fit into this. So do the laws of eating unkosher food[41] and adulterous relationships.[42] They are all expressed as don'ts—laws of abstinence—to avoid defiling our world. "And do not make the earth impure."[43] *Tumah* literally means a blockage, a type of spiritual contraction. It is related to *timtum ha'lev*, which means a blocked heart—blocked from purity or clarity, a contraction of the soul.[44]

The second, higher level of holiness is *kedushah*, the active creation of holiness in the world. Included in this is to keep the Shabbat, to love our neighbors and save their lives, to honor our parents and to rise in front of the old and the wise, to treat and love the convert, to give charity, and to pay wages on time.

THERE IS NO MUNDANE

What we will see in the unfolding narrative of the following chapters is that holiness extends its mandate to all areas of our life. For Judaism, nothing is just mundane. The food we eat, the love we create, the homes we set up, and our professional lives—they all have the potential to be infused with purity and holiness.[45]

The paradigm of this is the Shabbat, on which we do seemingly very physical things. We eat, sleep, and dress at a higher level than the weekday, and yet the holiness of the day elevates and spiritualizes all these activities.[46] Such a person is like a Tabernacle, and any food he eats is

---

40 Slandering (*lashon hara*) leads to a form of impurity called *tzaraat*.

41 See, for example, Leviticus 11, where verses 4–8 all end with the words, "It is impure to you." Verses 44–47 end with the general idea, "and you should not impurify your souls...and you should be holy, for I am holy, to discriminate between the impure and the pure, between the animal that is eaten and that which is not."

42 Leviticus 18:25–30.

43 *Meshech Chochmah*, Genesis 18:27.

44 Leviticus 11:13; see also *Targum Onkelos*, 14:15.

45 *Ramchal, Mesilat Yesharim*, chap. 26.

46 *Netivot Shalom*, Leviticus, pp. 84–85.

like a sacrifice brought on an altar.[47] But even during the week, we can take each meal and turn it into a holy act.[48]

God gives a reason for His demand that we be holy—"for I am holy,"[49] and you are made in My image. Therefore, the way that My holiness is reflected in this world is through you.[50] More than that, God says that He will actively help us.

The verse says, "Be holy, because I the Lord your God am holy." God assures us that He has given us the power to reach into the physical world and raise it up.[51] If we will take the first steps, He will do the rest.[52] God shadows us,[53] waiting for us to initiate so that He can respond.[54]

---

47 *Mesilat Yesharim*, chap. 26.

48 *Ohr Gedalyahu*, p. 55.

49 Leviticus 19:2.

50 *Ohr Hachaim*, ibid.

51 *Sefat Emet*, Leviticus, 5631; *Ohr Gedalyahu*, Leviticus, p. 53.

52 *Mesilat Yesharim*, chap. 26; Rabbi Tzadok HaKohen, *Resisei Laylah* 42.

53 Rabbi Chaim of Volozhin, *Nefesh Hachaim* 1:1.

54 *Daat Tevunot* calls this הנהגת המשפט.

16
HOW DOES HOLINESS WORK?

The heavens will always remain heavens.
But the earth we can elevate and make heavenly.

Kotzker Rebbe[1]

HOLINESS AS A MORAL IMPERATIVE

God gave us 613 commandments. These are precise activators of holiness. In addition, God created man with physical and other needs—taking care of our health or earning a living, for example. Since God created that world which demands of us these actions, it is as if God commanded us to do them.[2] We are doing His Will, and doing His Will generates holiness.[3] We are holier because we breathe. We are holier because we eat. We are simply asked to think that all of our bodily necessities are there to serve the soul and not the other way around.[4]

If we eat food with the intention of using the strength and health it gives us to do good, then we have sanctified the food. The table we use to serve that food, or to host guests, or to beautify our lives with a flower vase on top of the table, all achieve this idea. We use our cars

1 Quoted by Menachem Posner, Chabad.org, based on *Kochav Hashachar*, by Simcha Raz.

2 *Ramchal, Derech Hashem* 1:4:7.

3 Ibid.

4 *Derech Hashem*, ibid.

not only to get ourselves to work so we can support our family (a huge mitzvah in itself), but to give people rides, to deliver food packages, and to drive to the synagogue to pray. We see a glorious site of nature and use that inspiration to connect to God. We can harness almost anything to serve as a means for elevation and thereby sanctify it, and by failing to do this we drag the world down with our own failure.[5]

The Sages say, "Man is destined to give accounting (to God) on everything that his eyes saw and that was permissible, and of which he did not partake."[6]

There is no such thing as a neutral act.

From this, it emerges that there is no such thing as a neutral act. All of our actions—the subway ride to work, the coffee we buy along the way, our daily interactions on the job, our relationship with significant others, and how we spend our leisure-time—have the potential to be sanctified. All are agents for the achievement of perfection. Moreover, it is precisely through the physical world that such perfection is achieved. God demands that we understand the profound spiritual consequences of everything we do.[7] Even when we don't clearly see the impact of our actions, they ripple through the universe.

CONTROLLING THE PERMISSIBLE TO SANCTIFY IT

Not all holiness (*kedushah*) is accessible to us. The Torah therefore prohibits certain things and permits others—to guide us on a path of sanctifying that which we are able and to avoid engaging things where the holiness is so hidden that were we to engage in these things, we would only produce impurity (*tumah*).[8] Since we cannot release the holiness embedded in these things, our engagement with them is restricted to the unholiness that remains accessible to us.

Even those things that are permissible can be degraded. If we are controlled by the food we eat, or we buy things just because of material

5 *Ramchal, Mesilat Yesharim*, chap. 1.

6 Talmud Yerushalmi, Tractate *Kiddushin*, chap. 4.

7 *Derech Hashem* 1:4:4.

8 We will deal with this in greater depth in Chapter 7, on the positive and negative mitzvot.

urges, or exercise just so we can outdo our neighbor, we are doing the very opposite of being holy. We need to know that the world we engage in does not control us. If we wanted to, we could walk away. Then, our encounter can be with the full force of sanctity.[9]

SANCTIFYING THE WORLD THROUGH SANCTIFYING OURSELVES

What is the mechanism that allows us to make the world holy? This happens because all physical objects can ultimately be traced back to God, and hence they all have sparks of holiness.[10] Engaging the physical world in a positive manner releases these sparks of holiness, strengthens them, and connects them back to God. This is known in Kabbalistic literature as "redeeming the sparks."[11]

Jacob taught us this principle when he forgot some small utensils and went through enormous trouble to go and get them.[12] He understood that if these had been in his possession, it must be that God had intended for him to be responsible for their spiritual elevation.[13]

Where did Jacob learn this lesson? When he was fleeing Esau, he encountered "the place"[14]; he literally bumped into the material world of space.[15] Jacob placed the seat of his soul—his head—on a bunch of stones to sleep. Because of Jacob's elevated level, the stones became one stone.[16] Jacob raised the stones above the level of fragmentation of the individual stones to a level where things are combined into a higher unity.[17]

Engaging the physical world in a positive manner releases sparks of holiness, strengthens them, and connects them back to God.

9 *Mesilat Yesharim*, chap. 13.

10 In Hebrew, *nitzotzot kedushah*.

11 The *Arizal*, as quoted in the *Kedushat Levi*, "Kedushah LePurim 4," and in Rabbi Chaim Vital, *Shaar Hagilgulim* 15.

12 *Rashi*, Genesis 32:25, quoting the Talmud, Tractate *Chullin* 91.

13 Rabbi Eliyahu Dessler, *Michtav Me'Eliyahu*.

14 Genesis 28:11: "He bumped into (i.e., encountered) the place," as per *Netivot Shalom*, *Vayeitzei*, p. 173.

15 Ibid.

16 *Rashi*, Genesis 28:11.

17 *Maharal*, *Gur Aryeh*, Genesis 28:11.

While sleeping, Jacob had his famous dream of the ladder.[18] This was God's answer of how to engage the world—a ladder rooted on the ground that beckoned Jacob to rise up to the heavens.[19] But Jacob was not alone. He also saw angels going up and down the ladder.[20] This was a message to the generations. When we go up the ladder, we take everything with us, including the angels. When we go down into impurity, we drag the entire world down.[21] Man, the sinner, loses not only his internal world. He affects the world around him.[22]

GIVING THE WORLD ITS FORM

The Genesis story reports that Adam named each one of the animals.[23] The name of something refers to the essence of its being.[24] Hence, in Hebrew, the word for "name"—*shem*, has the same letters as the word for "there"—*sham*; both are שם with different vowels. The name of something is its "there-ness," its quintessential reality.

Man looked into each species on earth and understood what it was there for, what its purpose was. He gave it its name by identifying its form and hence its spiritual grandeur.[25] As humans, we all inherited this innate capacity—the ability to understand the essence of something and, consequently, to relate to it in a way that redeems its holiness.

Man looked into each species on earth and understood what it was there for, what its purpose was. He gave it its name—its form.

18 Genesis 28:12.

19 *Netivot Shalom*, ibid.

20 Ibid.

21 *Degel Machaneh Ephraim, Parashat Re'eh.*

22 Genesis 7:21, as per *Midrash Rabbah* Genesis 6:7. See also *Mimaamakim*, Genesis, pp. 46–47.

23 Genesis 2:19: "And he brought to the man to see what he would call it [each one of the animals], and whatever man called [each] living being, that was its name."

24 *Maharal, Netzach Yisrael*, chap. 57.

25 As with everything, God began the process and man completed. Hence, Genesis 2:19 states that God's creation of the animals included the word ויצר (*va'yitzer*). The word *va'yitzer* is related to the word *tzurah*, which means "form"; *Gur Aryeh* ad loc. God gave the animals their form. This was God's part of the process.

MAN—THE JOINER OF ALL WORLDS

We saw previously that our world is complemented by higher, parallel worlds of spirituality.[26] All these worlds are linked so that an effect in one of these worlds will transmit that effect to the worlds above and below it. Sometimes God begins the process—a top-down effect—and sometimes, we initiate the action—a bottom-up effect. When the latter happens, we impact the world above, which in turn transmits it to the world above that, and so on.[27] This means that there is no such thing as a trivial human act.

When God invited man to become His partner in completing creation,[28] it was not just this earthly reality that God intended. Astonishingly, God's invitation extended to our completing the entire universe! Far from being an insignificant speck in the cosmos, man is really its primary mover and shaker.

In the creation of man, we read: "And He breathed into him the spirit of life and man became a living soul."[29] But that translation is wrong, for the verse does not say *be'adam*[30]—"and *in* man there was a living soul." It says *ha'adam*[31]—"man became a living soul." Man became the living soul of the world.[32]

Man became the living soul not only of himself but of the entire world outside of himself.

What are we supposed to do with this enormous power? While it is worthy to connect all that we use back to God, as described above, our responsibility goes further.[33] We are expected to move the world forwards and upwards to its final *tikkun*.[34]

---

26 See Chapter 10.
27 Ibid., as per Rabbi Chaim of Volozhin, *Nefesh Hachaim* 1:1 and throughout the book.
28 Ibid.
29 Genesis 2:9: "*Va'yipach be'apav nishmat chaim, va'yehi ha'adam le'nefesh chayah.*"
30 באדם.
31 האדם.
32 *Nefesh Hachaim* 1:4.
33 Ibid., chap. 12.
34 *Ramchal, Daat Tevunot* throughout the book.

THE WORLD OF ENGAGEMENT

It should be clear from the above that getting "out there" and making the world a better place is central to our ability to generate holiness.[35] We need to be inner-directed to our sense of self-worth and inner-work, but outer-directed to our concerns.

In one of the grand narratives of the Torah, Jacob is left alone one night and ends up fighting with an angel of evil until dawn.[36] The angel wounds Jacob in the thigh, but Jacob defeats it and demands a blessing.[37] In response, the angel changes his name from Jacob to Israel.[38] But unlike Abraham, whose name-change from Abram was permanent,[39] Jacob afterwards would be called by either name—Jacob or Israel.[40]

Each one of these names reflect a different aspect of our engagement with the world. The name "Jacob" reflects his engagement with the messy world. In Hebrew, *Yaakov* comes from the word *ekev*, a heel.[41] This is because Jacob was supposed to be born before Esau and was clutching his heel in an attempt to come out first.[42] Jacob was born into adversity, clutching at heels in an attempt to stay honest and upright in a world of manipulation and falsehood.

Sometimes, like the weekday, we engage the world by plunging into its details and sanctifying them; we are Jacob. And sometimes, like the Shabbat, we take a step back to get the big picture; we are Israel.

---

35 See, for example, Chapter 11, where we discuss how man is empowered and obligated to imitate God by doing actions of kindness and mercy in this world.

36 Genesis 32:25.

37 Ibid., v. 26–27.

38 Ibid., v. 29. The angel was predicting the additional name that God would give to Jacob in Genesis 35:10.

39 Genesis 17: 5

40 Talmud, Tractate *Berachot* 13b. In Genesis 36, the Torah itself calls Yaakov by that name after God called him Yisrael.

41 Genesis 27:36.

42 Hence, there is a verb form of "heel," which means "to fool." Jacob says of Esau, "He [lit.] heeled me twice," which means that he outwitted him twice, as *Rashi* translates it. Rabbi Aryeh Kaplan translates, "He went behind my back twice."

But Jacob is also now Israel. *Yisrael* comes from the words "*yashar E-l*—straight with God." Jacob's legacy to us is that we need both approaches to holiness. Sometimes, like the weekday, we engage the world by plunging into its details and sanctifying them; we are Jacob. And sometimes, like the Shabbat, we take a step back to get the big picture; we are Israel.

The mission of the Jew is not an easy one. To be Jewish is to take responsibility. It is to engage. It is to make a difference—however small—so that we edge forwards toward final redemption.

17

SANCTIFICATION AS PURITY

Amongst Jews, genius is found only in the holy man.

Ludwig Wittgenstein (notebook, 1931)

There are two types of *kedushah* (holiness). The first is the active generating of holiness through doing the commandments and through sanctifying the material. However, there is another type of sanctity—purity (*taharah*).[1] Simply stated, purity is achieved through separating ourselves from that which is immoral, impure, and forbidden.[2]

Purity allows us to avoid the blockages that prevent us from connecting with our deeper, spiritual selves. Purity, in this sense, is a release from the baggage holding us back and from the layers of impurity that build up plaque around our holy soul.

The opposite of purity—impurity (*tumah*)—never means something physical. It is a purely spiritual concept. The word *tumah* is related to the word *timtum*, which means a spiritual blockage. *Timtum ha'lev* means a blockage of the heart—blocked from purity or clarity. In Hebrew, the ט (*tet*) and the צ (*tzaddi*) often interchange to form weaker and stronger forms of the same thing. Thus, the word *tameh* is related to the word *tzameh*—thirsty, indicating that *tumah* is a spiritual thirst. So too,

---

1 *Reishit Chochmah, Shaar Hakedushah*, chap. 1.

2 *Rashi*, Leviticus 19:2, explains that *kedushah* (holiness) means "separateness."

timtum—spiritual blockage, is related to *tzimtzum*—a contraction. All these "t" words have similarities for the deepest of reasons.

In the events that lead up to the story of Chanukah, the Greeks made the Holy Temple's oils impure. This means that they blocked the paths of wisdom and prevented spiritual access to clarity.[3]

Tumah, therefore, has its source in a spiritual contraction, leading to distancing and subsequent thirst. Kosher animals are called pure,[4] and unkosher ones are called impure.[5] When we eat non-kosher foods, we increase the layers around our soul and make ourselves less sensitive to spirituality.[6] The sin here is the *he'eder*[7]—the vacuum inside of ourselves devoid of spirituality because it is filled up with something else.[8] Similarly, illicit intimate relationships are also called impure.[9]

By contrast, *tahor*—to be pure—is related to *tzahor* (again the *tet -tzaddi* exchange), which means clarity or brightness. (Hence, *tzaharayim*—afternoon, the time when the sun is brightest.)

THE HOLIER THE BEING, THE MORE IMPURITY IT GENERATES

The commentators point out a fascinating thing:

- Plant life is higher than the mineral and non-living world, but if one uproots a plant, it not only dies but quickly withers and has less reality than even stones and minerals.
- Animals are higher than plants in turn, but dead animals are worse than dead plants—their rotting bodies testimony to their once-elevated status.
- Humans are higher than animals; a human has not only physical but spiritual life as well. Consequently, a person can be

---

3 *Sefer Hachinuch* 362.

4 Genesis 7:2.

5 Levitcus 11:5,29; see *Rashi* on v. 29.

6 The words "*ve'nitmeitem bam*—you will become impure through them" (Leviticus 11:43) are interpreted by the Sages as "*ve'nitamtem bam*—you will be blocked through them." In Hebrew, these two words are the same letters with different vowalization—ונטמתם.

7 העדר.

8 *Maharal*, in many places.

9 Leviticus 18:24; Numbers 5:14; Deuteronomy 24:4.

> spiritually dead even while alive, and this will be reflected by a lack of radiance on the face.[10]

This translates into purity and impurity as well. To be impure, an object must first have had some spiritual potential. Impurity draws on purity for its power.[11]

The greater the potential for purity, the greater the potential for impurity, for *tumah* is the exact opposite of purity and holiness.[12] Holiness is a spiritual force that can just as easily be turned in the opposite direction into impurity. Nothing in this world is intrinsically holy or unholy. It starts out as raw potential—a potential that can go either way. Hence, impurity draws on the same power as holiness does for its power and is in fact its exact opposite.[13] This is why the laws of human impurity come after the laws of impure animals.[14] The pure human soars above the animal; hence, the impure human sinks far lower than the impure animal.

God made a covenant with the Jews which committed them to being a holy nation.

In the past, when we were spiritually more sensitive, a person who spoke *lashon hara* (bad speech)[15] and subsequently became a *metzora*[16] would be sent out of the city and would have to undergo a whole process of purification.[17] His negative speech reduced someone else's life value, which needed to be rectified.

The *metzora* had to leave the camp and meditate in isolation. He underwent a whole series of steps and returned to society, greatly strengthened. The *tzaraat* (the disease of the *metzora*) he had been inflicted with was not just a sign of a problem but the beginning of the cure. The fact that a person found the impurity on his body was

---

10 *Netziv*, introduction to *Shir Hashirim.*

11 *Ohr Hachaim*, Genesis 1:1.

12 *Kuzari* 3:49.

13 *Ohr Hachaim*, Genesis 1:1: "For it is known that the outer shell (the impurity) draws its sustenance from the holiness."

14 Leviticus 11:39–40, as interpreted by the *Midrash Rabbah*, Leviticus 14:1.

15 Unnecessary negative speech about one's fellow.

16 A type of physical disease that resulted directly from speaking *lashon hara*. It is often mistranslated as leprosy.

17 Leviticus 14:1–30.

an indication that he had already began to get the bad out of his inner being. Hence, *tzaraat* is a combination of the words *motzi ra*—"get the evil out."[18]

THE PURIFYING WATERS OF THE MIKVEH

A menstruating woman is regarded as impure until she dips in the purifying waters of the *mikveh*.[19] During this period, husband and wife don't engage in intimate relations,[20] for her menstruation signals the loss of her egg cell (and the shedding of the lining of the uterus that was enriched for its nurture), which can now no longer be fertilized with male sperm. Hence, a potential for a new life has been lost.[21] It is that potential for life that signals the need for a period of abstinence from intimate relations between spouses. However, we will see below how this state is not just a period of abstinence.[22] There are other benefits too, including the positive dynamic of allowing the couple to focus on certain aspects of the relationship that otherwise might not be given attention.[23] When the couple returns to each other, they possess the potential to conceive a child in absolute purity. "The waters [of the *mikveh*] offer the possibility of a magnificent beginning for human life in love with life."[24]

So too, a man who has a nocturnal emission of semen is also impure for certain things and needs to go to the *mikveh*.[25] He too, has lost life-potential.[26]

---

18 Talmud, Tractate *Eruvin* 15b, as explained by the *Shelah*, *Parashat Metzora*.
19 We will explain this idea in Chapter 24.
20 Leviticus 18:19; 20:18.
21 *Kuzari* 2:60.
22 See Chapter 24.
23 See Chapter 23.
24 Rabbi Norman Lamm, *Hedge of Roses*, pp. 92–93.
25 Leviticus 15:16; Deuteronomy 23:11–12.
26 *Kuzari* 2:60.

DEATH—ULTIMATE IMPURITY

One source of *tumah* is a dead corpse.[27] The death of a human is the greatest loss of potential, and therefore the *tumah* of a dead body is the most powerful impurity of them all.[28] Death is caused by the soul separating from the body; the body then becomes a raw, material object, for the body is merely the outer casting of the soul, which continues to contain the real nucleus of his personality.[29] Bereft of all his spiritual beauty, the body is but a lump of pure physicality.[30] The empty body is now impure and imparts this to others.[31] Animals, on the other hand, lacking the holiness of humans, are never described as being intrinsically impure. Rather, they are discussed as "impure *for you*."[32]

Remarkably, the body of a totally righteous person does not transmit impurity, for his body has been completely purified by the soul.[33] Thus, when the great Rabbi Yehudah HaNasi died, even the Kohanim participated in his burial, even though this is normally forbidden.[34]

OUR DEFAULT STATE IS PURITY

Purity is our natural state.[35] It is only the empty shells that generate impurity, the body devoid of soul. But to the degree that we turn the body into an envelope for the soul, it too remains pure. Because of this, Adam and Eve saw no need to cover their naked bodies.[36] So too,

---

27 Someone who had touched a dead body, even that of an animal or an insect, was not allowed to come within the confines of the Holy Temple until he had purified himself.

28 *Sefer Hachinuch* 263. See Maimonides, Commentary to the Mishneh, Introduction to *Seder Taharah*, where he elucidates 11 different sources of impurity. However, only contact with a dead body is called "*avi avot ha'tumah*"—"the father of father's of impurity" (See *Rashi*, Numbers, 19:22).

29 Rabbi Shimshon Raphael Hirsch, Numbers 3:4.

30 *Sefer Hachinuch*, ibid.

31 Rabbi Hirsch, Numbers 5:3–4.

32 Leviticus 11:4, as pointed out by the *Kuzari* 2:60.

33 *Sefer Hachinuch*, ibid.

34 Talmud Yerushalmi, Tractate *Berachot* 3:1.

35 Rabbi Tzadok HaKohen.

36 *Ohr Gedalyahu*, *Parashat Tazria-Metzora*.

Moses' body was infused by his soul, which produced his glowing face after he came down from the mountain.[37]

Purification returns the connection of the soul to the body so that the former can permeate life into the latter. Purification is always associated with a new spirit of life.[38] Did not Moses' face begin to glow after he came down from the mountain, a radiance that we will share in the Messianic Era?[39] So too, the original "naked" bodies of Adam and Eve looked a lot less physical than our bodies look today.[40]

The death of a human is the greatest loss of potential and therefore the most powerful impurity of them all.

Jacob totally purified his soul, restoring for us the first man's pre-sin soul and left this as a legacy for all future generations.[41] This is the guarantee that the impure Jew will always be able to find his way back to holiness and purity. Our core remains holy, and hence God remains connected to us even in the midst of our impurity.[42] Our natural being never resonates with impurity; it is always on the side of purity.

37 Exodus 34:30.

38 Ezekiel 36:25–26.

39 *Sefat Emet, Ki Tisa* 5654.

40 *Ohr Gedalyahu.*

41 *Ohr Hachaim*, Deuteronomy 32:8.

42 Rabbi Tzadok HaKohen, *Resisei Laylah*, no. 19, p. 21.

18

THE HOLINESS OF THE COMMANDMENTS

Every commandment of the Torah is a basic principle of Judaism...Every detail of the commandments must be related to the great themes of man's life.

Dayan Grunfeld, Introduction to Horeb, p. 45

THE COMMANDMENTS—PRECISION INSTRUMENTS

The Torah is first and foremost a book of mitzvot, of commandments.[1] When the Jews came to Mt. Sinai, God first made a covenant with them which, on the Jewish people's side, involved commitment to all of the Commandments.[2] Only after this covenant did the revelation of the Ten Commandments take place.[3]

---

1 *Rashi*, Genesis 1:1; *Ramban* and others.

2 In Exodus 24:7 which, according to *Rashi*, happened on the fourth day after their arrival to Sinai, the Jews said the famous words, "We will do, and we will hear." But how can you do, if you havn't heard yet what it is you have to do. However, the verse means, "We are fully committed to fulfilling all of your commands. The only thing holding us back is the knowledge itself."

3 However, see the *Ramban*, that Exodus 24 took place after Sinai. Nevertheless, the Covenant described in Exodus 19:3–8 certainly took place prior to the Revelation.

Why is this so? Because the commandments are sure things. They are precision instruments that activate our inner spirituality. They are our safe-zone—our guarantee that we can become more spiritual.

LAWS OF NATURE AND LAWS OF THE SPIRIT

God looked into the Torah and created the world.[4] Two revelations emerged from this: the laws of nature and the laws of the spirit.[5]

Laws of the spirit are built into the fabric of the universe, just as the laws of nature are.[6] There is the natural order, and above it there is a spiritual order. Every time we do a mitzvah, we place ourselves in this spiritual order.[7] We create a resonance with holiness at every level of our being.[8] We activate the deepest part of ourselves that was in essential harmony with that mitzvah to begin with.[9]

God looked into the Torah and created the world. Two revelations emerged from this—the laws of nature and the laws of the spirit.

To actualize this harmony, we must act.[10] Only *doing* actualizes every aspect of our being. Therefore, we make Kiddush on Friday night,[11] we blow the shofar on Rosh Hashanah,[12] we affix a mezuzah on our doorways,[13] and we give money to charity.[14] We use our tongue, pallet, larynx, and lips to produce the words of the *Shema*—"Hear, O Israel..."

---

4 Rabbeinu Bachya, introduction of Chumash: "All the mitzvot...benefit the body as a whole in this world and benefit the soul in the World to Come."

5 Rabbi Shimshon Raphael Hirsch, *The Nineteen Letters*, letter 18.

6 *Maharal, Tiferet Yisrael*, chap. 4.

7 Numbers 15:40; Rabbi Shimshon Raphael Hirsch. Technically, the word *chukim* refers to only a specific set of mitzvot.

8 *Maharal*, ibid.

9 *Maharal, Tiferet Yisrael*, chap. 2.

10 Negative mitzvot (the don'ts) are fulfilled by abstention—by not acting. We will explain these in Chapter 21. There are some positive mitzvot that are fulfilled not by acting but by mindfulness, for example, four of the six continuous mitzvot that have to do either with remembering certain things or with belief in God.

11 Exodus 20:8.

12 Numbers 29:1.

13 Deuteronomy 6:9.

14 Ibid. 15:8.

THE COMMANDMENTS HELP BOTH SOUL AND BODY

The mitzvot don't just sanctify the body; they also strengthen the soul.[15] Even though the soul is already pure,[16] there is a difference between a soul in a state of potential and one that has been actualized to express itself fully.[17] Moreover, without soul activation, the body will drag the soul down.[18] The mitzvot purify the body sufficiently to allow the soul to be the dominant expression in the body-soul partnership.[19] We begin to identify with our soul,[20] with being a spiritual being, hence removing the primary barrier between us and our God.[21]

SEARCHING FOR REASONS

Should we look for explanations of commandments? Can we understand God's mind?

Rav said: The mitzvot were only given to purify us.

Yes and no. We can and should look for the benefits that the mitzvot give us without thinking that we have grasped the whole picture.[22]

We can, for example, understand that doing the commandments is a way of improving our world.[23] Commandments like charity, kindness, honesty, and equality before the law clearly advance the general goodwill and the well-being of society.[24]

---

15 *Tiferet Yisrael*, chaps. 7–8.

16 "God, the soul that you have put in me is pure"; morning blessings.

17 *Tiferet Yisrael*, chap. 7.

18 *Ramchal, Derech Hashem* 1:3:3.

19 *Tiferet Yisrael*, chap. 7.

20 Ibid., chap. 2.

21 *Ramchal, Derech Hashem* 1:4:5.

22 This is the opinion of the majority of the Rishonim (11th–16th cent.), including Maimonides (Laws of Meilah 8:8), the *Ramban* (Deuteronomy 22: 6), Rabbeinu Bachya, the *Sefer Hachinuch* and others. The surprising exception is the *Kuzari* (2:26 at the end), whose book is full of reasons for the mitzvot.

23 *Peah* 1:1. These benefits are called the "fruit" of the mitzvah (in contrast to the tree itself), and we list them every morning after the blessings of the Torah.

24 Maimonides, commentary on the Mishnah, *Peah* 1:1. See also the Talmud, Tractate *Berachot* 15a–b, concerning saying the *Shema*.

Other commandments teach us how to correct one of our character traits.[25]

Take a series of commandments that relate to treating animals properly:

- We have to help an animal owner unload a burden from his animal.[26]
- We have to feed our pets before we feed ourselves.[27]
- We are not allowed to slaughter a mother and child on the same day.[28]
- We are not allowed to harness together animals of different species, say an ox and a donkey, as different species may feel acute discomfort next to each other.[29]
- We are not allowed to muzzle an animal on the threshing floor as it is creuly to have him thresh the wheat and not eat some of it.[30]

In truth, though, the Torah cannot legislate every single possible act of cruelty to animals. It gives us just enough examples to get our character developed in this area. God then expects us to know of our own accord what to do.[31]

Yet, other commandments—prominently the Shabbat and the festivals—contribute to the collective character of the Jewish People. Shabbat and the festivals are our national testimony to God as creator and guide of history—including the Exodus and Sinai until its resolution in the Messianic Era. They are testimonies to our covenant with

---

25 *Ramban*, Deuteronomy 22:6.

26 Exodus 23:5; Deuteronomy 22:4.

27 *Magen Avraham*, *Orach Chaim* 167:18 and 271:12. However, the *Mishnah Berurah* (*Biur Halachah* 167:56, and *Mishnah Berurah*, ibid. §40), *Chayei Adam* 45:1, and others hold that this is only a Rabbinic command. See also *Mishneh Torah*, Laws of Slaves 9:8, that this is a *minhag chassidut*—a custom of the very righteous and not a law.

28 Leviticus 22:28.

29 Deuteronomy 22:10, as explained by the *Chinuch*, mitzvah 550.

30 Deuteronomy 25:4. The verse refers specifically to an ox, but the Mishnah in Tractate *Bava Kama* 5:7 says that it applies to any animal.

31 We will develop this theme more extensively in Chapter 44.

God as much as mezuzot on our doorposts and tefillin against our heart and mind do the same.[32]

JUSTICE, LOVE, AND EDUCATION

Three overarching themes are reflected in the mitzvot: justice, love, and education.[33] The principle of **justice** is divided into two, *mishpatim* and *chukim*. *Mishpatim* is justice toward our fellow human beings.[34] "Justice, justice you shall pursue," God tells His people.[35] We must be totally honest and outraged by injustices anywhere and especially fight for the rights of the weaker segments of the population, as it says, "Grant justice to the orphan, stand up for the widow."[36] "Let justice roll down like water and charity like a mighty stream."[37]

By perfecting our moral character, the mitzvot contribute to the collective character of the Jewish People.

The second expression of justice is the *chukim*. *Chukim* are the commandments of justice toward the earth, plants, and animals, i.e., things subordinated to ourselves including our own body. These include the dietary laws and the laws of sexual immorality. They also include the principle of *l'mino* ("according to its species"). When God created the plant and animal world, it is repeatedly stated that He created each one *l'mino*.[38] The message to man as the readers of the Torah is that we should maintain these species; neither should we allow any species to go extinct nor should we interfere with the order and harmony of creation.[39] There are several commandments that sensitize us to this idea.[40]

---

32 Rabbi Shimshon Raphael Hirsch, *Horeb 11, Edoth* (pronounced "*eidot*").

33 Rabbi Shimshon Raphael Hirsch, *The Nineteen Letters*, p. 105.

34 *Horeb* 321.

35 Deuteronomy 16:20.

36 Isaiah 1:18.

37 Amos 5:24.

38 Genesis 1:11, 21, 24. See also Leviticus 11:15, 22.

39 Genesis 3:2–3, 26:5; Leviticus 2.

40 Examples are the laws not to mix wool and linen in one garment (known as *shaatnez*), not to grow certain species in the same field together (known as *kilayim*), and not to cross-breed different species; Leviticus 19:19.

The second great arm of the mitzvot is the principle of **love**. Our love of our fellow man and God's love for us are both included. So is our love for our spouse.

Finally, there is the principle of **education**. This includes historically revealed ideas concerning God, the world, the mission of humanity, and the mission of Israel. We testify to these truths in the form of the Shabbat, the festivals, prayer, and putting mezuzot on our doors.

THE MYSTERY OF TASTE

Although we can understand a lot about the mitzvot, we nevertheless cannot fully understand the reasoning of even a single mitzvah.[41] God's mind is much deeper than anything we can fathom. Even on the physical plane, we can perhaps explain what we see, but we can never know, for example, why God created a giraffe with one neck rather than two.[42] We know gravity as an attractive force, but it could just as easily have been the opposite—gravity could have been repulsive (as it may have been during the inflationary stage of the Big Bang). We have no clue why time only moves in one direction.

Understanding the mitzvot is not a zero-sum game. We have some access to the logic of spirituality, and we can peel away the outer layer of meaning contained within each mitzvah.[43] The greater we are spiritually, the more we will understand. Moses understood the reasons for the most esoteric command—that of the Red Heifer,[44] a mitzvah that stumped even the wise Solomon.[45] But we will always get to a point when we find ourselves limited.

We embrace the limitations of our understanding happily, for if we were to understand everything, we would be reducing God's intelligence

---

41 *Maharal, Gur Aryeh*, Leviticus, beg. *Parashat Bechukotai.*

42 *Maharal, Tiferet Yisrael*, chap. 7.

43 *Gur Aryeh*, beg. *Parashat Bechukotai*, and *Tiferet Yisrael*, chap. 8.

44 *Midrash Rabbah*, Numbers 19:6. The ashes of the Red Heifer purified someone who has the impurity of having touched a dead body. Yet, paradoxically, the Kohen sprinkling the ashes became impure by doing so.

45 Ecclesiastes 7:23: "I thought I would get wise, but it [the reasoning behind the Red Heifer] remains far from me."

to our own, and that would be a very sad thing indeed.[46] It is not just one of degree; God's logic exists on an entirely different plane.[47] It is for this reason that the Torah reveals the reasons for the mitzvot only in rare instances.[48]

Judaism prides itself in being a rational religion, but we cannot take this too far. We trust that God wants our good, and that what He has commanded us to do is in our best interest.[49] What we can understand is deep, relevant, profound, rational, and good, and hence our trust in the goodness of these or those details is not a blind one but rather a natural extension of what we know.

For this reason, we call the explanations for the commandments *taamim*—tastes. When we taste food, we get its flavor. We may not yet have eaten the food, but we get an idea what we are in for. On the other hand, the taste per se will not sustain us.[50] Its purpose is to make us passionate about eating.

Our leap of faith is not a blind one but rather a natural and rational extension of what we know.

Similarly, the *taamim* of the mitzvot generate our excitement to connect with them. We can never plumb the depths of God's mind, but we can at least discern that the mitzvot are "tasty."

TO UNDERSTAND IS TO DO

To taste is to experience. It is to engage. A purely intellectual understanding of the commandments is sure to be still-born. For by their very nature, the mitzvot require our engagement to be meaningful. Imagine trying to explain to someone who has never tasted ice cream what it tastes like. You tell her that ice-cream has some milk, a little vanilla essence, etc., but she will not have a clue what the ice cream tastes like.

---

46 Based on Rebbe Nachman of Breslov.

47 *Tiferet Yisrael*, chap. 9.

48 Talmud, Tractate *Sanhedrin* 21b, with respect to Solomon's wives and horses.

49 Maimonides, *Mishneh Torah*, end of the laws of *Temurah*.

50 In fact, Proverbs 30:8 refers to the basic portion of food necessary for minimal human survival as לחם חוקי—*lechem chuki*—the bread of necessity, but literally "the bread of *chok*," from the same word that we use to explain the mitzvot.

So too, we might give a profound lesson on the Shabbat to someone who has never kept it. She may walk away with a sense that this is something profound, but until that person sits around the Friday night table—with the aura of the candles, the sanctity of the Kiddush, the family together, the meaningful conversations, the songs, and the food—she is not going to taste the flavor of the Shabbat. As King David put it, "Taste and you will see."[51]

We are called on by God to operate in this world not only to fulfill our own potential, but also to move the world forward to its final completion.[52] The single most effective way of doing this is by engaging in the mitzvot.[53] Quintessential man is the mitzvah-keeping species.[54]

---

51 The Hebrew reads, "*taamu u'reu.*"

52 *Ramchal, Daat Tevunot,* throughout the book.

53 Ibid., no.40; and in Vol II, no. 62.

54 *Ramchal, Sefer Kinat HaShem Tzevakot* (p. 78 in the *sefer Ginzei Ramchal*) states that man is comprised of 613 components in parallel with the 613 Commandments, and that in fact the world as a whole is comprised of 613 facets. Hence, when man does the Commandments, he harmonizes all elements of himself with holiness and simulataneously harmonizes the world outside of himself in a like manner. In the *Daat Tevunot,* Vol II, no. 67, the *Ramchal* shows how the higher spiritual realms (the *Sefirot)* are also composed of 613 units. In the *Ramchal's Klalei Pitchei Chochmah Ve'Daat,* the third *Klal,* he states further that the *me'orot* (spiritual lights) are divided into 613 parts.

19

WHEN GOD REDEEMS THE SPARKS

I have brought two doves from [the Moabites and from the Amonites]: Ruth the Moabitess and Naamah the Ammonitess.

Talmud, Bava Kama 38b

THE FLOW OF HISTORY TOWARD PERFECTION

We Jews have a radical vision of the future. We project a horizon that scripts God's revelation totally changing the order of the world as we know it. Then will begin a new and more spiritually profound process called the Messianic Era.

The Messianic Era doesn't suddenly emerge out of nowhere. Rather, every day contributes toward achieving its end.[1] The soul behind the world is God Himself, Who operates at all times to ensure that none of our actions get lost. Nothing goes to waste. Mostly unseen by us, it is all contributing to the perfection of the world.[2] God takes all that we do and winds it into the fabric of history so that, at the end of time, a complete design—a whole picture—will emerge.[3]

---

1 *Ramchal, Klalim Rishonim* 66.

2 *Ramchal, Daat Tevunot* 48.

3 This is the theme of the *Ramchal*'s book, *Daat Tevunot*.

Often, we see God's hand in the ironies of history, unfolding so differently from the plans of man. Pharaoh, who heard that the savior of the Jewish People will somehow be afflicted by water,[4] decreed that all boys should be thrown into the river.[5] That very action brought baby Moses right into Pharaoh's palace by Pharaoh's own daughter.[6] Moses gets taught politics, state management, and other necessary skills by the very person who wants him dead.[7]

And so, not only are the evil powerless to prevent redemption, they often unwittingly contribute toward it.[8]

In the Scroll of Esther (which deals with the story of Purim), Haman advises the king to kill his queen, Vashti, for refusing to appear before him, and his very own action produces Esther as queen, who becomes central to saving the Jews from that very Haman.[9] The gallows that he builds on which to hang the Jewish sage, Mordechai, are the same ones that he gets hanged on himself.[10] The whole Book of Esther is full of such ironies.[11]

Every day contributes to turning the great wheels of history toward their end.

If God uses the bad people as his unwitting instruments, then he certainly uses the righteous in the same way. Hence, the brothers of Joseph wanted to deny his prophetic dreams by selling him. This is exactly what caused his dreams to come true.[12]

Balaam wants to curse the Jews, but is forced by God to bless them instead.[13] History is replete with thousands of such cases where man thought to achieve one thing but God produced another.

---

4 As he indeed was when he hit the rock to bring forth water instead of speaking to it and, as a result, was denied entry into the Land of Israel.

5 Exodus 1:22.

6 Ibid. 2:1–10.

7 Rav Simcha Zisel Ziv Broida, the Alter of Kelm, *Chochmah U'Mussar*.

8 *Daat Tevunot* 48. In §158, the *Ramchal* goes further, stating that, at the end of days, the evil will be turned into good.

9 Rabbi Simcha Zissel of Kelm.

10 Book of Esther 7:9.

11 See, for example, Book of Esther, chap. 6.

12 *Iyunim* of Rabbi Chaim Friedlander on *Daat Tevunot* 14.

13 Numbers 23:24.

THE HIDDEN HAND OF GOD

Sometimes God's hand is so hidden that we scarcely notice what is unfolding. The great principle is that no holiness gets lost. Even the holiness bound up in prohibited things gets redeemed by God and becomes a part of the great *tikkun*—correction of the world.[14]

One of the most fascinating examples of this is the lineage of the Messiah. The Messiah, we are told, will come from the house of King David. But David's lineage on both his mother's and his father's sides have murky roots.

On his father's side, David is a descendant of Yehudah (Judah), one of the twelve tribes. Yehudah's descendant, Boaz, married Ruth, a Moabitess convert, and this led, three generations later, to King David.[15]

Both Yehudah and Ruth, though, had quite unusual stories.

Yehudah's son, Er, married Tamar.[16] He died with no offspring.[17] Tamar then married Onan, Er's brother.[18] He too died, again with no children.[19] Tamar was bound by the Levirite (*yibum*) laws to marry Yehudah's last son, but Yehudah, seeing two sons die in marriage with Tamar, was worried that his third and last son would reach a similar end and held off the wedding indefinitely.[20]

Tamar was now stuck; Levirite marriage bound her to the family of her first husband. So, she hatched a plan. She dressed as a harlot and managed to seduce the holy Yehudah, falling pregnant by him.[21] The "harlot" then disappeared.[22] When Tamar's pregnancy became known, Yehudah condemned her for breaching the Levirite laws and having relations with someone else.[23]

---

14 *Daat Tevunot* 40.

15 Boaz and Ruth's son was Oved, who was the father of Yishai (Jesse), who was the father of David.

16 Genesis 38:6.

17 Ibid., v. 7.

18 Ibid., v. 8.

19 Ibid., v. 10.

20 Ibid., v. 11.

21 Ibid., v. 12–18.

22 Ibid., v. 20–23.

23 Ibid., v. 24.

But Tamar, when "acting as a prostitute," had asked Yehudah to give her certain collateral,[24] and at this time stated in public that the person to whom those items belonged was the father of the child.[25] Yehudah immediately admitted his guilt,[26] and a whole cycle of goodness was launched, as we shall see.[27]

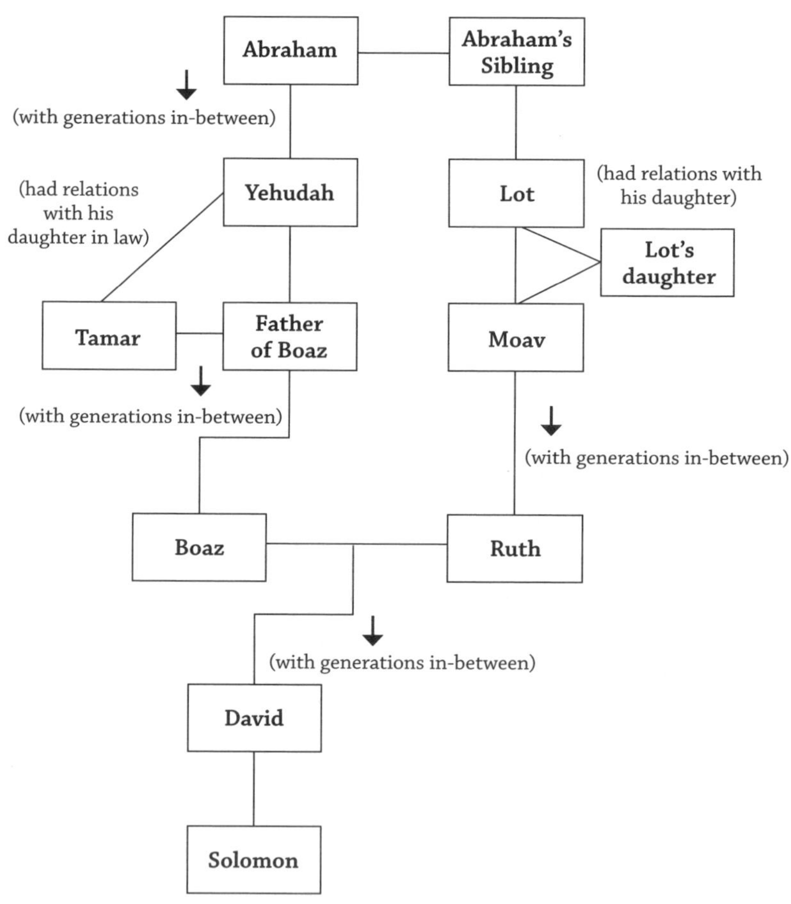

24 Ibid., v. 16–18.

25 Ibid., v. 25.

26 Ibid., v. 26.

27 *Zohar*, *Parashat Vayeishev*.

Ruth, who married Yehudah's descendant Boaz, also had a seemingly troublesome past. Her nation originated in an incestuous relationship from Lot, Abraham's nephew, and his daughter.[28] So proud was Lot's daughter of this event (she thought she was saving the world![29]) that she called her child Moab, which literally means "from my father."[30] She enshrined her incestuous act in the name of her descendants forever, the great Moabite nation.[31]

Ruth the Moabitess was a part of the royal family. She had within her the kernel of holiness that Lot, her original forefather, had absorbed from Abraham, his uncle.[32] Lot, who was brought up by Abraham, retained a spark of Abraham's kindness, as witnessed by his risking his life to host the angels (whom he thought to be people) who came to tell him of Sodom's pending destruction.[33] Although Moav's national values were the opposite of kindness,[34] the flicker of holiness imbedded through Lot went all the way down to Ruth, when her conversion to Judaism brought it back into the Jewish People.

Ruth and Boaz were married for one night before Boaz died, but this was enough to produce the lineage of King David—all the way down to the future Messiah![35]

THE TZADDIK AND THE BAAL TESHUVAH

Yehudah was seduced by a harlot, or so he thought, and succumbed. Joseph, Yehudah's brother, was nearly seduced by the wife of Potiphar, but he held fast, earning him the title Yosef Hatzaddik—Joseph the Righteous One.[36]

---

28 Genesis 19:31–38.

29 See ibid., v. 30–31, as explained by Tractate *Horiyot*, p. 10b, and the *Maharsha* ad locum.

30 Genesis 19:37, as per Tractate *Horiyot*, ibid. Perhaps she did not realize that the numerical value of Moav (מואב) amounts to 49—representative of the 49 levels of impurity.

31 See Chapter 46.

32 Lot's father had died (Genesis 11:28), and Abraham, his uncle, had brought him up (Genesis 12:4).

33 Genesis 10:1–19.

34 Deuteronomy 23:4.

35 *Zohar, Parashat Vayeishev*.

36 Genesis 39:7–20.

By all accounts, Joseph seemed to be a more obvious forefather of the Messianic lineage. Joseph had been chosen by his father Jacob to gather all the holiness of the forefathers and pass them on to his brothers and the future Jewish nation.[37] Besides for that, Joseph played a major role in the future of the Jewish People by supervising their settlement in Egypt, the seed of their future birth as a nation.[38] Joseph's descendant, Joshua, took us into Israel.[39] The Ark containing the Tablets of the Ten Commandments rested in the tribe of Joseph (Ephraim) for over three and a half centuries.[40] Joseph, after all, is the eldest child of Rachel, who was the wife whom Jacob originally wanted to marry.[41]

And yet, the Messiah has to come from Yehudah,[42] and even today, we call ourselves Jews, *Yehudim*, after Yehudah.[43]

Why? Because Yehudah went where he shouldn't go. He fell off the ladder, but then he returned.[44] When he repented, he brought that broad swath of this worldly sensuality into holiness.[45] By so doing he made holy even the darkest part of the world. He surpassed Joseph's achievement because he covered not only Joseph's narrow spectrum of the ladder (the safe spaces that are the rungs of the ladder themselves), but also all that was to the right and left of the ladder where if you step initially you will fall. So too, the Messiah's coming will be when spirituality will also be brought into the world's worst corners. For that to happen, the Messiah's soul has to be big—very big. It has to encompass every kind of spirituality in the world—a universal soul. To do this, the

---

37 Rabbi Tzadok HaKohen, *Takanat Hashavim* 6. See *Rashi*, Genesis 37:2.

38 Genesis 46:29–34.

39 The whole book of Joshua essentially deals with this.

40 Joshua 18:1. The *Mishkan* stayed in Shiloh for 369 years.

41 Genesis 29:18.

42 *Ramban*, Genesis 49:10; Maimonides, commentary on the Mishnah, *Sanhedrin*, intro to last chap. As per Samuel II 22:51; Psalms 132:17; Habakkuk 3:13, and many more.

43 The name Yehudah was coined by his mother, who stated upon his birth, "This time I will thank God"; Genesis 29:35. To be a Jew is to be grateful for the opportunity to engage in spiritual passion.

44 Genesis 38:26.

45 Rabbi Tzadok HaKohen, *Takanat Hashavim*.

Messiah has to come from the lineage of those who have been there and emerged, i.e. the *baalei teshuvah*—"those who return."

THE TWISTS OF HISTORY CONTINUE

Ruth came from Moab. Boaz himself was a descendant of Yehudah's forbidden union with Tamar. David and his son Solomon were their descendants.[46]

We surely could imagine a more glorious lineage for the Messiah, but the Messiah must draw from every corner of mankind and must redeem all the scattered sparks of holiness. He must have a universal soul. He will be tasked with teaching the non-Jews spirituality and ethics.[47] He will be tasked with uniting all the Jews of our fractious and discordant nation and bringing them home.[48]

DAVID—WHAT THE WORLD COULDN'T SEE

Let's look at one more twist in this story. When Samuel the prophet went to the house of Jesse (Yishai) to anoint the future king,[49] Samuel instructed Jesse to gather all of his children from which one will be chosen.[50] Jesse, a totally righteous man,[51] gathered all of his children except David.[52] David was so obviously not the candidate, that Jesse left him out. Even after Samuel anointed David in front of all the others,[53] the holy Jesse continued to insist that he remain the family shepherd.[54]

---

46 Solomon married Naamah, who came from Ammon, the descendant of Lot's incestuous relationship with his younger daughter, through which the Messianic lineage continued. (Lot's younger daughter called her son born of incest *Ben Ami*—"The son of my nation", a more humble name than the name Lot's elder daughter gave, and hence she was rewarded for this [Talmud, *Bava Kama* 38b].) Naamah gave birth to Rechavam who became King.

47 Rabbi Tzadok HaKohen, *Resisei Laylah*. He states that Jews will not need the Messiah to teach them Torah. They will manage this on their own, as the verse states, "No longer will a man teach his neighbor, saying, 'Know God!'" (Jeremiah 31:33). Rather, he will teach the non-Jews their obligations.

48 Maimonides, *Mishneh Torah*, Laws of Kings 11:4.

49 Samuel I 16:1.

50 Ibid., v. 5.

51 Talmud, Tractate *Shabbat* 55b.

52 Samuel I 16:11.

53 Ibid, v. 13.

54 Eliyahu Ki Tov, *Book of Our Heritage*, chap. 29 (Heb. ed.).

And why was this? For David had been born with more than a whiff of a scandal, for the night that his father, Yishai, thought that he was secluding himself with his concubine (*shifcha*), she had instead arranged that David's mother secretly replace her. When David's mother fell pregnant, she was suspected of adultery. And when David was born reddish—a result of Yishai's focus on his concubine that night—it was apparent to David's father, but not to others, what had happened.[55]

David first became famous for killing Goliath, but he was only sent to the war front to find out how his brothers were doing. He was the simple shepherd—not cut out for war![56] Moreover, he was shrouded by a new wave of whispers of a scandal when Doeg, one of the great sages of the generation, accused him of being descended of an illicit union to a Moabitess—Ruth, his great-grandmother.[57]

THE GUIDING HAND OF HISTORY

See how the world turns with the light of the Messiah winding its sinuous way through Moab to Ruth, through Yehudah and Tamar to Boaz, and then onto King David, whom no one was capable of recognizing as king even after he was anointed!

Can we imagine for a moment that all of this just "happened"? How do we explain the inexplicable? As Job put it, who but God could draw such purity from impurity?[58] While we glide and bump through history, God works to tie up all the loose ends to ensure that His vision for mankind will one day come about.

"The tribes were busy with the selling of Joseph, and Jacob was busy with his sackcloth and fasting, and Yehudah (Judah) was busy with taking a wife; and God was busy with the light of the Messiah."[59]

---

55 *Yalkut Hamakiri*, Samuel 1:16.

56 Ibid.

57 Talmud, Tractate *Yevamot* 76b.

58 Iyov (Job) 14:3. *Ramchal* (*Megilat Setarim*) uses *Bamidbar Rabbah* 19:1 to say that this is referring to the Messiah's murky roots.

59 *Midrash Rabbah* Genesis 75.

20

THE HOLINESS OF THE TEN COMMANDMENTS

If the angel Gabriel came to me and said, "Look, I'm willing to take your soul now and give it back to you at any period of time in the history of the nation of Israel, from the very beginning to this very day," I think I would not think of any other time except for when Moses brought down the Ten Commandments from Mount Sinai.

Yitzchak Navon, former President of Israel

Nothing evokes the grand universalism of Judaism more than the Ten Commandments. Surprisingly, as individual mitzvot, the "Ten Commandments" are not more important or holier than any other commandment in the Torah. "God clearly and expressly proclaimed them as being merely a preparatory introduction to the whole...giving of the Law."[1] In order that we should not give more importance to the Ten Commandments than others, the Sages decided *not* to include the Ten Commandments in the morning prayers.[2]

1 Rabbi Shimshon Raphael Hirsch, Exodus 20:14.

2 Talmud, Tractate *Berachot* 12a.

However, as principles, the Ten Commandments hold pride of place. On Mount Sinai, the Jews engaged God and received a set of principles that nourishes and nurtures the world to this day. At that grand revelation, the Jews reached such an exalted spiritual level that they were able to understand the entire Torah in a highly contracted form. God only spoke the Ten Commandments, but for the Jews it was as if they had heard the entire Torah.[3] They were at such a high level that they were able to understand from these Ten Commandments all the other commandments.[4] When the commandments were put in a written form on the Tablets, the Jews were able to hold, in a contracted form, all of the Torah.[5]

The Ten Commandments are really ten broad categories under which all 613 mitzvot can be subsumed. They are the roots and fundamentals, the essence of the whole Torah.[6] "The Ten Commandments…contain the main principles necessary for the survival of the Jewish People, both religiously and ethically."[7] Throughout the forty years in the desert thereafter, the Jews heard in detail the unfolding of the Torah that they had already heard, in a contracted form, at Sinai.[8]

At Sinai, the Jews were able to understand the entire Torah in a highly contracted form.

When we received the Torah, we made a *brit*—a covenant with God. A *brit* is a mutual pact; both parties commit to each other. We committed to God's Torah, and He committed to look after us.[9] We became the obligated people, and as part of that obligation we

3 In truth, they only heard the first two commandments from God before requesting that Moses deliver the rest. However, the Oral Law tells us that prior to this, God spoke the entire Ten Commandments in one saying, something the Jews could not understand at an intellectual level. Nonetheless their souls absorbed it.

4 Hence, the Ten Commandments are general sayings that subsume all of the 613 mitzvot.

5 *Ralbag, Avodat Hakodesh* 4:34; Kings I 8:9; *Ha'ketav V'Hakabbalah*, Exodus 32:16. See also next note.

6 Rabbi Saadyah Gaon, Maimonides, and others show how all the 613 commandments fit under one of the ten headings that are the Ten Commandments; see also *Rashi*, Exodus 24:12.

7 Rabbi Aryeh Kaplan, *Handbook of Jewish Thought* 5:24.

8 The Torah itself provides the timeline that we can piece together, over which Moses taught the Jewish People the Torah.

9 This included the commitment to relate to us on a plane of reality that would not follow

committed to ensure that society continues to define itself as one that is under God.

The Tablets on which He wrote the Ten Commandments are called the Tablets of the Covenant—"*Luchot Habrit*."[10] The Ark that contained the Tablets is called the Ark of the Covenant.[11] The entry portal by the Jews to be a Torah-keeping nation was done through the Ten Commandments.

TWO EQUAL TABLETS

The Ten Commandments are divided into two separate Tablets.[12] The first one deals with laws between man and God,[13] while the second one deals with laws between man and man.[14] Each of the Ten Commandments correlates with its "twin" on the other tablet. Hence, "I am the Lord your God" is twinned with "You shall not murder,"[15] for we cannot divorce the command against murder from that of believing in God without compromising the value of life. After all, the inherent value of every person lies just in that he or she was created in the image of God. Hence, there can be no vision of man without the God who is the source of that vision. Similarly, we cannot believe in God if we do not believe in the sanctity of His creatures.[16] Monotheism and morality

---

normal historical rules. If we don't keep to our part of the deal, we place ourselves in the historical reality that other nations live—with slim survival chances.

10 Deuteronomy 9:9, 11, 15.

11 Exodus 24:22, 26:33.

12 Exodus 31:18, 32:15, and in several other places.

13 Ibid. 20:2–12. On the first tablets, we find the commandment to believe in God, not to worship idols, not to swear falsely using God's name, keep the Shabbat, and honor one's parents. This last command to honor one's parents seems to be out of place—being an interpersonal command. The commentators, in fact, show that this is also a man-God command, because if we fail to honor our parents, this leads to breakdown in the tradition, in society, and its values—in effect, an erosion of the Torah.

14 Ibid. 20:13–14. On the second tablets, we find the prohibitions against murdering, forbidden sexual relations, kidnapping, perjuring as a witness, and coveting. Concerning kidnapping: Although the commandment is in the form of not stealing, the commentators show how the wording—and the fact that the prohibition against stealing appears elsewhere—determines that this is a prohibition of stealing a person, i.e., kidnapping.

15 *Mechilta*, Exodus, chap. 20.

16 *Midrash Rabbah* Genesis, end of chap. 24.

go hand in hand. Belief in God allowed us, for the first time, to believe that life has transcendent value.[17]

The interesting thing is that the man-to-man commandments are much briefer in their formulation than the man-to-God commandments. And this fact meant that the size of the letters of these commandments were larger. This larger message came to compensate for our tendency to neglect the interpersonal commandments and to ensure that we regard them with equal gravity as the man-to-God commandments.[18]

THREE GROUPS OF TEN

As we saw, there are Ten Sayings of Creation, Ten Plagues, and Ten Commandments.

The Ten Sayings of Creation appear in the first chapter of Genesis.[19] They formed the world of nature—the outer garment of the world. The natural world is so unfathomably deep that for thousands of years, scientists have been discovering hundreds, if not thousands, of new things about it every day.

The next group of ten was the Ten Plagues. Each one of the plagues came to show God's ongoing involvement with a different level of the creation. Each one peeled away another mask that hid God's Providence in the world of nature. God did not just create the world and then withdraw, leaving the world entirely to man to do with it as he pleases. Rather, He remains actively involved, sustaining the world, directing it, and guaranteeing that it would achieve its purpose. The lesson was well-learned—not only by the Jews, but by the Egyptians as well.

The Ten Commandments began the process whereby the Torah entered the physical world, giving the world not only its purpose but a means of achieving it.[20] The Ten Sayings of Creation were but the outer physical body for the Ten Commandments, which were their inner spiritual content, its spiritual life-blood.[21] Without this inner content, the

---

17 Rabbi Jonathan Sacks, *The Great Partnership*.

18 Mabit, *Beit Elokim*, *Shaar Hayesodot*, chap. 12.

19 1:1, 3, 6, 9, 11, 14, 20, 24, 26, 28. (For 1:1 see Tractate *Rosh Hashanah* 32a.)

20 *Sefat Emet*, Exodus 5632.

21 *Pachad Yitzchak*.

world would have remained as formless a mass as it was at the beginning of creation.[22] Hence, all the creation is reconstituted in a spiritual form in the Tablets.[23]

This is similar to how a child is created: In the beginning, he is totally egocentric and self-absorbed, all sensual and not spiritual. He develops a spiritual and moral sense later on in life.[24] The Ten Commandments indicated that it was time for the world to grow up.

The Ten Sayings of Creation formed the outer garment of the world. The Ten Commandments gave the world its purpose.

Prior to the giving of the Ten Commandments, the spiritual and the physical realms remained totally separate. In those days, man could only become spiritual by separating from the world.[25] The Ten Commandments gave man the tools to be spiritual in this world—to cleave to God in this world and to take the world with him as he rose in spirituality.[26]

For this to happen, man had to take ownership of the Torah. The Ten Sayings of Creation use the term "*maamar*—saying" (they are the Ten *Maamarot* of Creation).[27] However, the Ten Commandments use the stronger term "*dibbur*—speaking" (they are the Ten *Dibrot*).[28] A *maamar* is something that is said; it is put out there as a reality. Creation was imposed upon the world as a reality. *Dibbur*, on the other hand, is said *to* someone. It is a moral imperative. It requires a recipient, a reaction from us. We were no longer innocent. We had spoken with our God, and He revealed what He wanted from us.[29] Body and soul could now

---

22 *Sefat Emet*, Exodus 5632. One of the words used to describe the world at the beginning is *tohu* (Genesis 1:2), which means "undifferentiated mass."

23 Rabbi Tzadok HaKohen, *Resisei Laylah*, pp. 139–45.

24 Ibid.

25 The forefathers—Abraham, Isaac, and Jacob—tried to reverse this. They were all about engagement of the world. However, even they were not able to transmit sanctity to the world itself.

26 *Sefat Emet*, ibid.: "[The Torah was given] so that man could cleave to God even in This World."

27 In Hebrew, we call them the *Asarah Maamarot shel Maaseh Bereishit*.

28 In Hebrew, we call them the *Aseret HaDibrot*.

29 Rabbi Moshe Shapiro.

soar together.[30] This is what King David meant when he so beautifully stated: "The Torah of God is pure; it restores the soul [to the body]."[31]

At Sinai, the Jews took a risk and stepped into the truth. They overcame their vulnerability of losing themselves, and history was changed forever.

30 *Sefat Emet*, ibid.

31 Ibid.

21

THE POSITIVE AND THE NEGATIVE COMMANDMENTS

Who is the person who seeks life…
Stay away from negativity and do good.

King David, Psalms (34:13–15)

BOUND AND UNBOUND

There are 613 mitzvot, including 248 positive ones and 365 negative ones.[1] Just as there are 613 commands, so too, the soul has 613 components.[2] Each mitzvah was crafted to add a dimension of purity and holiness to a different part of our soul. Together, these 613 form a complete whole that is more than the sum of the parts.[3] A person fulfilling all the 613 commandments would find his entire soul bathed in spiritual energy.[4]

---

1 Talmud, Tractate *Makkot* 23b–24a.

2 *Ramchal, Daat Tevunot* 2:7 (beg. of p 24); *Klalei Pitchei Chochmah V'Daat* 3, p. 295.

3 *Sefer Chareidim*, "Conditions for Fulfilling the Mitzvot."

4 *Tanya* 4:23. In practice, it is impossible for any one person to keep all 613 commandments, for some are specific to the Kohanim, some to specific situations, and some require the presence of the Holy Temple. However, for those we can gain their holiness through: a) study of those commandments, or b) helping those who are commanded to fulfill them; *Kiryat Sefer*, commentary on the *Rambam*, intro.

The two types of mitzvot work together:

- The positive mitzvot tell us to do something active, such as give charity, be kind, or believe in God.
- The negative commandments tell us to refrain from doing something, such as not eating nonkosher food, not stealing, and not killing.

In essence, the first expands our spiritual horizons, while the second provides its boundaries.[5]

The Hebrew word for forbidden is *assur*. The opposite, permitted, is *mutar*. These words actually mean "bound" and "unbound" and are applied to what is permissible and forbidden for Kabbalistic reasons. When something is forbidden, the holy sparks are bound up in that particular object, making them spiritually inaccessible to us.[6] Something that is unbound means that we can release its holiness, and hence it is permissible.[7]

Even something forbidden like pork is ultimately connected to God, for otherwise it would not exist, and therefore it must contain some spark of holiness. But we cannot release the pork's holiness by eating it, no matter how noble our intentions. The holiness of the pork is bound too tightly by shells of impurity.[8]

When something is forbidden, the holy sparks are bound up in that particular object, making them inaccessible to us. Something that is unbound means that we can release its holiness, and hence it is permissible.

God therefore guides us to maximize our spirituality through keeping us away from things that are inaccessible to us. He gives us negative mitzvot that provide us with the parameters in which we may operate. By contrast, the positive mitzvot have a greater power than just ensuring that we

5 *Pachad Yitzchak*, based on the *Ramban*, Exodus 20:8.
6 *Tanya*, chap. 8.
7 *Tanya*, chap. 6–7.
8 Ibid.

keep within the parameters of that which is permissible; they take us up the spiritual ladder in the most effective way possible.[9]

GET ON THE HIGHWAY AND DRIVE

Let's say that I want to drive from Los Angeles to Santa Barbara. First, I have to get on the right highway. The wrong highway will never get me there, no matter how fast I drive. Once I am on the right highway, though, I still can't just park on the side. I have to move.

This is a parable to the mitzvot. The negative mitzvot represent the right highway, while the positive mitzvot represent the movement on that highway.

Alternatively, imagine that our spiritual climb is up a ladder. The negative mitzvot are the vertical frame of the ladder. If we step outside of the frame, we will fall, no matter how noble the step. The positive mitzvot represent the actual steps of the ladder—the climb itself.[10]

WE ENTER JUDAISM THROUGH THE POSITIVE MITZVOT

If we want to know the essence of something, we must look at the first place that it appears in the Torah. Hence, if we wish to know the relationship between the positive and the negative mitzvot, we need to look at the very first place God commands something to man. This is when God told Adam and Eve: "From all the trees of the garden you should eat, but from the tree of knowledge of good and evil you should not eat."[11] The positive precedes the negative.

Again, when God commands Adam and Eve to look after the garden (to work it) and yet to preserve it, the positive comes before the negative.[12]

Similarly, the first of the Ten Commandments is positive—"I am the Lord your God..."—whereas the Second Commandment is negative, telling us not to serve any other gods. God tells us first to believe and pray to Him before He has even commanded us to throw our idols out.

---

9 *Maharal, Tiferet Yisrael,* chap. 8.

10 *Tiferet Yisrael,* chap. 4.

11 Genesis 1:29.

12 Ibid. 2:15.

But this doesn't make sense. Surely, one needs to get into the framework of things before one can grow and develop as one wishes. Do we not know from the mitzvah of *teshuvah* that you first have to leave your sins before you can repent?[13] Do we not know from the highway example above that it is useless to be moving to your destination until you are on the right highway?

There is, however, a difference between our first approach to Torah and the way we must act after full commitment.

If we had to first purify ourselves before we started to serve God, we might never do it. The challenge of throwing out all of our idols might just be too much for us. So, He allows us to approach Him with all of our baggage, our negative behaviors, and our flawed character traits. He allows us to start keeping the Shabbat by lighting candles, having two bread-challot, and making Kiddush—even before we switch our iPhones off! Taste, embrace, and grow![14]

> *God allows us to approach Him with all of our baggage, our negative behaviors, and our flawed character traits.*

In fact, we start every Shabbat with the positive action of lighting the candles and only afterward cease from work (*melacha*). In addition, straight after the prayer service we first make Kiddush—a positive sanctification of the day on wine. Only then do we purify ourselves by washing our hands over bread—purification from the impure.[15]

The bottom line of God's message to man is: "Don't wait until you are pure before you start your Jewish journey, for you might never start. So, come as you are and begin."

---

13 Maimonides compares someone who repents while he is still sinning to someone who immerses himself in a *mikveh* to purify himself while holding an impure object in his hand!

14 Rabbi Tzadok HaKohen, *Machashavot Charutz*.

15 *Shem MiShmuel*, Haggadah of Pesach, why *Kadesh* comes before *Urchatz*.

LIMBS OF THE BODY—DAYS OF THE YEAR

What is the mystery of the number of commandments—613? Why are there 365 negative and 248 positive commandments?[16] What is so special about those numbers?

The Sages tell us that the 248 positive commandments reflect the 248 limbs of the body, whereas the 365 negative commandments reflect the days of the year.[17]

We can be sure that when the Sages tell us something like this, it is not just a mnemonic device or something purely symbolic.[18] Rather, there is something about the positive mitzvot that are fundamentally parallel with the human structure, while the negative mitzvot are similarly connected with the sun and its annual cycle.[19]

The sun represents the order of nature. Whenever the term "everything under the sun" is used in the Scriptures,[20] it implies everything within the natural order of the world.[21] We disobey the laws of nature at our peril. Gravity and other forces of nature are the givens within which we must operate. They will not suspend themselves simply because we have a quirk to defy them. So too, the negative commands are the natural spiritual framework of reality in which we must operate. 365 days of the year—365 negative commandments.

The negative commandments reflect the spiritual order in which we must operate. The positive commandments reflect our spiritual form.

By obeying the "don'ts," we harmonize ourselves with the deeper spiritual order that exists below the surface of the world.[22] Staying

---

16 Talmud, Tractate *Makkot* 23b.

17 Ibid. Many Kabbalists, however, understand that the 365 negative commandments reflect the number of sinews in a person, so that both positive and negative commandments combined are reflective of the human form. (Rabbi Chaim Vital, Shaarei Kedusha, 1:1.)

18 If it were just some device to remember, then the reverse would do just as well, and then there would be no meaning to the number of positive and negative mitzvot itself. But, surely, this cannot be, for every aspect of something Godly has to be intrinsic.

19 *Tiferet Yisrael*, chap. 4.

20 Ecclesiastes 1:3, 14.

21 *Tiferet Yisrael*, chap. 4.

22 *Tiferet Yisrael*, chap. 9.

within bounds stimulates our strength of character, e.g., the discipline of not engaging in forbidden sexual relations or the mercy involved in not being cruel to animals.

THE BODY—COVERING OF A SPIRITUAL FORM

The 248 positive commands parallel the limbs of the body. The body is physical, but its form is shaped by our spiritual souls. We were created "in the image of God."[23] The form of man—with the intellect on top, and below it the center of emotions [i.e., the heart], and below that the sensual and physical aspects—is an indication of his spiritual form. Man walks upright; his face reflects his inner spirituality.[24] Man is a spiritual being coated in 248 outer limbs. In fact, if man's body were a natural thing, man's body would belong to the same category as the days of the year—in which case there should have been 365 limbs.

All the elevated and exalted ideas of Judaism are positive commands.[25] These include the fundamentals of our relationship with God: to believe in Him,[26] love Him,[27] to walk in His ways,[28] and to cleave to Him.[29] They also embrace our core interpersonal relationships: to do acts of kindness,[30] honor the old and the wise,[31] judge our fellow man favorably,[32] give charity,[33] and honor our parents.[34]

The negative commandments achieve purity, whereas the positive commandments achieve holiness.[35] The commands to choose life it-

---

23 Genesis 1:27.
24 "The Wisdom of Man lights up his face"; Ecclesiastes 8:1.
25 Rabbeinu Yonah, *Shaarei Teshuvah* 3:17.
26 Exodus 20:2.
27 Deuteronomy 6:5.
28 Ibid. 28:9.
29 Ibid. 6:5.
30 Leviticus 19:18; Exodus 18:20.
31 Leviticus 19:32.
32 Exodus 18:20; see Tractate *Bava Metzia* 30b.
33 Deuteronomy 15:7–11.
34 Exodus 20:12.
35 *Reishit Chochmah*, the Gates of Holiness 1:17 (last paragraph).

self,[36] be holy,[37]and study the Torah that explains us how to do this[38] are all positive commands.

THE BODY AND SPIRITUALITY

The body functions with amazing precision and intricacy. Judaism states that behind every physical effect lies a spiritual cause.[39] The staggering sophistication and wisdom of the body is but a hint to the spiritual forces that moves this system—the reasons behind the reasons.

Man has an eye, say the Kabbalists, because there is a spiritual concept of an eye—of seeing above.

Man has an eye, say the Kabbalists, because there is a spiritual concept of an eye—of seeing above.[40] Man has two of everything because he is reflecting the right-Mercy side and the left-Justice side of God.[41]

What this means is that whereas 365 is the unit of the basic order of the world (days of the year; negative commands), 248 becomes the unit of wholeness in the world (limbs of the body; positive commands). The limbs are 248 pieces of potential. The 248 mitzvot are the actualizers of that potential. No Jew can hope to become spiritual without the mitzvot.

---

36 Deuteronomy 30:19: "And choose life..."

37 Leviticus 11:44, 19:2.

38 Deuteronomy 6:7: "And you should speak of them."

39 *Maharal, Beer Hagolah* 6.

40 *Ramchal, Daat Tevunot*; *Shelah, Parashat Matot-Masei.*

41 *Maharal, derash* on the Shabbat. The mouth of man is one because speech is the core of man—he is "the being that speaks"—and if he would have two mouths, there would be two of men; *Maharal*, ibid.

22

THE HOLINESS OF THE SHABBAT—PART I

A human being without a day to himself once a week
is not a human being.

COMPLETION AND WHOLENESS

There was never a generation so starving for a day of rest more than ours. We desperately need a day where we have permission to unplug and recover moments to reflect. The Shabbat provides a framework to deepen relationships, and hence it is a key to our emotional and relational health. It is the gateway to our making space for all those things that give us dignity as a human—to take a step back and see the big picture of our lives.

During the weekday, we say, "How *manifold* is Your creation!" (*Ma rabu ma'asecha*),[1] but on the Shabbat, we say, "How *great* is Your creation!" (*Ma gadlu ma'asecha*).[2] "Manifold" reflects the exquisite details

---

1 Psalms 104:24. This is said in the first of the Blessings of the *Shema*.

2 Ibid. 92:6. This is the Psalm for the Shabbat day. We say it three times on the Shabbat: once at the end of the *Kabbalat Shabbat* ("Welcoming the Shabbat") service; once in the extra psalms of *Pesukei D'zimrah* in the morning, and once at the end of *Musaf* as the Psalm of the day.

of the universe. We go deeper and deeper and see amazing complexity. This is our weekday service. But on the Shabbat, we see the gestalt of how all of that comes together. It is the perspective of "how *great* is Your creation!"[3] We take all the fragments of our lives and connect them together into one integrated person.

Shabbat is the gateway to our making space for all those things that give us human dignity—of making us whole and integrated.

Every Shabbat we become whole people again. We gain an extra soul (*neshamah yeteirah*—an extra spiritual capacity).[4] We light candles and make Kiddush over wine.[5] We sit down to meals with family, friends, and often strangers; we talk, we sing, we experience the radiance of the Shabbat table. We take all our fragmented roles—mother, professional, friend—and combine them to become one integrated human. As we silence the noise around us and create the necessary stillness and quiet, we are able to get in touch with the still, small voice inside of us and get to know ourselves again.[6] By doing that, we get to understand how we are supposed to connect to the world outside of ourselves as well. We turn the world into being humanly significant.

ACTIVE REST

The joy of the Shabbat is not simply the joy of having a day off with which to sleep off the tiredness of the week. In fact, if one would sleep right through the Shabbat, one would miss the whole point of keeping it. The Shabbat needs to be an active force in our lives, not just a passive switching off and out. The Shabbat is not a vacation from life but an embrace of it.

---

3 Rabbi Yitzchak Hutner, *Pachad Yitzchak*, Shabbat 1.

4 Talmud, Tractate *Taanit* 27b. On Saturday night, we smell spices as a type of revival from the loss of this extra *neshamah*.

5 *Shulchan Aruch*, *Orach Chaim* 261–62.

6 See Kings I 19:11–12, which refers to the still, small voice of God. *Targum* says it was the soft praise of the angels. This voice is also inside of our spiritual depths.

We don't have to create the holiness of Shabbat. God does that for us. He initiates this relationship.[7] We just have to tune into it.[8] Because it comes from God, it is the purest type of holiness imaginable.[9] Hence, the easiest way to connect to God is through the Shabbat.[10]

We don't rest on the Shabbat because we are tired. We rest because it is holy. And it is holy because God rested on the Shabbat. What does it mean for God to rest? God does not get tired. The clue to this lies in a contradiction in the verses. The Torah tells us: "And there was evening and there was morning [on] the sixth day.[11] Thus the heavens and earth were finished, and their entire array."[12] So God created the world in six days. But the very next verse reads: "On the seventh day, God completed His work that He had done."[13] Seemingly, God created something on the seventh day as well. So, were there six or seven days of creation?

The resolution to this lies in the end of the last-quoted verse, which reads: "And He abstained from all His work that He had done."[14] God's abstention from work was the creation on the seventh day. God didn't rest. He created rest (*menuchah*). The abstention from work was specifically from the type of creative activity of the other six days. So too, our Shabbat rest must be an active force in its own right.

When God was creating, He was hiding himself in the natural order. We need to look below the surface to see Him. But on the Shabbat, God rested from hiding Himself in the world. More accurately, God caused the world to rest from hiding Himself. This was the vital ingredient

---

7 Rabbi Tzadok HaKohen, *Resisei Laylah*.

8 Rabbi Tzadok HaKohen, *Pri Tzaddik*, Genesis 2, interpreting the Talmud, Tractate *Pesachim* 117b.

9 *Netivot Shalom*, festivals, sect. 2, Shabbat 3. For this reason, it is the source of all types of holiness; *Reishit Chochmah*, Gates of Holiness 2.

10 *Netivot Shalom*, ibid.

11 Genesis 1:31.

12 Ibid. 2:1.

13 Ibid., v. 2.

14 Exodus 20:8–11; Genesis 2:3.

that was lacking in the creation, and hence, with this, God completed the world.[15]

Because new things were not being created, one could now see how the whole picture fits together. The grand design of the universe was revealed and with it the Designer himself. As a result, the Shabbat is the day par excellence for connecting with God. All the barriers are gone.[16]

CONTRACTED AND EXPANDED TIME

As long as things are incomplete, they are subject to change—to wear and tear and be affected by outside forces. It is only when something is complete that it is no longer subject to change.[17] The universe now gained a certain degree of permanence. Indeed, when we gather the fragmented sparks of our weekday holiness and consolidate them on the Shabbat, we too give a certain sense of permanence and continuity to our lives.

The Shabbat is only meaningful because we have the weekday.

Why do we greet people on the Shabbat with the words, "*Shabbat Shalom*"? The word *shalom*—peace—comes from the word *sheleimut*—completion. *Shabbat Shalom*—the Shabbat of wholeness and completion. *Shalom* in fact is one of the names of God.[18] Hence, "Shabbat of that name of God, which is *Shalom*." This expresses our experience of feeling whole and completely integrated on that day.

The Shabbat is so central to being Jewish that it is the only mitzvah that appears in every book of the Torah.[19] The sanctification of Kiddush over wine at the beginning of the Shabbat is completed by sanctification of Havdalah over wine at the end of the Shabbat. *Havdalah* means

---

15 *Rashi*, Genesis 2:2, quoting a midrash.

16 Rabbi Shimshon Pincus, *Shabbat Malketa*, introduction.

17 *Maharal, Chiddushei Aggadata* on the Talmud, Tractate *Shabbat* 118.

18 Hence, we don't greet each other with "*Shalom*" in the bathroom; *Shulchan Aruch, Orach Chaim* 74.

19
- Genesis 2:3.
- Exodus 16:23, 20:8–11, 23:12, 31:13–17, 34:21, 35:2–3.
- Leviticus 19:3, 30, 23:3.
- Numbers 15:32–36, 28:9.
- Deuteronomy 5:12–15.

"making a distinction"; we separate the holy Shabbat from the weekday we are about to enter. It is hard to come back—to enter the weekday, but God wanted us to sanctify the weekdays with the spirit of the Shabbat. Havdalah is not therefore a note of regret that the holy Shabbat is over. It is an announcement that our week will now be a different week because of the Shabbat we just had.[20]

This is not just because we have been inspired. Every week, God contracts six days of weekday time into the Shabbat and then unfolds it again by spreading the time and infusing the holiness of Shabbat over the next weekdays.[21] The expanded time of the weekday is the concentrated time of the Shabbat, and vice versa. Hence, when we unpack the Shabbat into the weekdays, how spiritual a week it will be is determined by what kind of a Shabbat preceded them.

The opposite is also true. The Shabbat is only meaningful because we have the weekday. Just like God's original Shabbat was only meaningful at the end of the six days of creation,[22] so our Shabbat is only produced by our weekday: "For six days you should work and do all of your labor and on the seventh, it should be the Shabbat."[23] We are not really Shabbat observers. We are weekday-Shabbat observers, imitating God in His creation of the world. We create our part of the world in six days and celebrate its completion on the seventh.[24] Unplugged from the world, we are totally present, and what we enjoy is far, far richer than just a dose of digital detox.

---

20 Rabbi J.B. Soloveitchik, "Catharsis," *Tradition* 17 (1978): 2.

21 *Netivot Shalom*, festivals, sect. 2, Shabbat 3. Hence when it says (Exodus 31): "You should keep the Shabbat because it is holy to you," it really means, "because it is the source of holiness to you."

22 "For six days He did...and He rested on the seventh."

23 Rabbi Tzadok HaKohen, *Pri Tzaddik*, Genesis, *aleph*. The verse is from the Ten Commandments, Exodus 20:8–11; similar verses appear in several places in the Torah, e.g., Exodus 31:15 and 34: 21. See Talmud, Tractate *Shabbat*—that the first man first went into the Shabbat and then kept the six weekdays.

24 Rabbi Tzadok HaKohen, ibid.

23

THE HOLINESS OF THE SHABBAT–PART II

ONE NATION ALONE SANCTIFIED THE SHABBAT

In 1982, Israeli Prime Minister Menachem Begin addressed the Knesset (the Israeli parliament), an address that led to the government decision not to fly El AL flights—then the national airline carrier—on the Shabbat:

> *Shabbat enshrines a social-ethical principle without peer. Shabbat is one of the loftiest values in all of humanity. It originated with us, the Jews. It is all ours. No other civilization in history knew a day of rest. Ancient Egypt had a great culture whose treasures are on view to this day, yet the Egypt of antiquity did not know a day of rest. The Greeks of old excelled in philosophy and the arts, yet they did not know a day of rest. Rome established mighty empires and instituted a system of law that is relevant to this day, yet they did not know a day of rest. Neither did the civilizations of Assyria, Babylon, Persia, India, China—not one of them knew a day of rest.*
>
> *One nation alone sanctified the Shabbat, a small nation, the nation that heard the Voice at Sinai, "so that your manservant and your maidservant may rest as well as you." Ours is*

> *the nation that bequeathed to humanity the imperative of a day of rest to apply to the most humble of beings. Ours is the nation that gave the laborers the dignity equal to that of their employers—that both are equal in the eyes of God. Ours is the nation that bequeathed this gift to other faiths: Christianity—Sunday; Islam—Friday. Ours is the nation that enthroned Shabbat as sovereign Queen.*
>
> *So, are we, in our own reborn Jewish State, to allow our blue and white El Al planes to fly to and fro, as if to broadcast to the world that there is no Shabbat in Israel?...I shudder at the thought that the aircraft of our national carrier have been taking off the world over on the seventh day over these many years, in full view of Jews and Gentiles alike.*
>
> *There is no way of assessing the religious, national, social, historical, and ethical values of the Shabbat day by the yardstick of financial loss or gain. In our revived Jewish State, we simply cannot engage in such calculations. If it were not for the Shabbat that restored the souls and revived the spiritual lives, week by week, of our long-suffering nation, our trials and vicissitudes would have pulled us down to the lowest levels of materialism and moral and intellectual decay...More than the Jews have kept the Shabbat, the Shabbat has kept the Jews!*

Menachem Begin felt that the secret of the Shabbat is that it restored our souls, that it is an active force, as we saw in the last chapter. Let's go a little deeper and show that even the prohibitions on the Shabbat are a part of this.

SHABBAT AND THE UNITY THEME

On Friday night, we welcome the Shabbat with the song: "Come my friend, to meet the bride" ("*Lecha dodi likrat kallah*").[1] The first stanza begins: "'Keep (the Shabbat)' and 'remember (the Shabbat)' were said

---

1 This song is sung during the *Kabbalat Shabbat* service. It was composed by the Kabbalist, Rabbi Shlomo HaLevi Alkabetz, in the sixteenth century.

in **one utterance**…" "Keep" and "remember" refer to the two places in which Shabbat is mentioned in the Ten Commandments. There is a change from the wording in Exodus, ("*Remember* the Shabbat day"),[2] to the wording in Deuteronomy ("*Keep* the Shabbat day")[3]:

- *Remember* is a positive act. We need to make Kiddush, to enjoy three meals, and to make Havdalah at the end of the Shabbat.[4] We include in this marital relations between husband and wife, spending the day in Torah study, contemplation, connecting to God, and any positive enjoyment one may have on the Shabbat, such as reading, talking, or taking walks. This is known as the mitzvah of *oneg Shabbat*.[5]
- *Keeping* the Shabbat, on the other hand, refers to the thirty-nine prohibited categories of labor.

Since God only said the Ten Commandments once,[6] it must be that God said both words—*remember* and *keep*—in one utterance. This is exactly what the first stanza of the *Lecha Dodi* song quoted above describes. This is also why we light two candles—one for *remembering* and one for *keeping*.[7]

Remembering and *keeping*. If these two were said in the same utterance at Sinai, it must be that the thirty-nine prohibitions of work and the positive commandments are two faces of the same thing. To understand this, we need to understand the definition of work that we refrain from on Shabbat.

---

2 Exodus 20:8.

3 Deuteronomy 5:15.

4 According to Maimonides (*Sefer Hamitzvot*, positive mitzvah 155), Kiddush and Havdalah are part of the same mitzvah.

5 Isaiah 58:13.

6 Although He gave the tablets twice, since the first tablets were broken by Moses.

7 *Shulchan Aruch*, *Orach Chaim* 263:1; *Mishnah Berurah*, ibid. 5.

WORK AS A CREATIVE ACT

The Hebrew word for physical work or labor is *avodah*,[8] but the category of work prohibited on the Shabbat is called *melachah*.[9] Work is not defined as physical labor but rather as doing anything creative or productive. We withdraw from driving and using electronic goods and switching on and off lights—all of which hardly are going to work up a sweat. On the other hand, the Torah did not prohibit us from carrying a heavy weight up and down fifty stories.[10] Clearly, then, we need a new definition of what a *melachah* on Shabbat is.

Melachah—Shabbat work—is very much a function of our state of mind—a spiritual state.

We will see that *melachah* is very much a function of our state of mind—a spiritual state.

The Oral Law teaches us that the thirty-nine prohibited categories of creative labor are learned from the same categories that were used in the building of the *Mishkan*—the portable Tabernacle, in the desert, the precursor of the Temple in Jerusalem.[11]

The *Mishkan* was like a map showing each person how he himself was put together; it was a model of a perfect human, so to speak.[12] Like man, the *Mishkan* comprised all the elements and forces in the world.[13] It was a whole world. As such, it was a symbolic model of spiritual-man, who is also a whole world.[14] When a person would see that the exact components of the *Mishkan* came together to bring the presence of

---

8 Leviticus 25:40.

9 Exodus 20:1; Deuteronomy 5:14.

10 See the *Ramban*, Leviticus 23:24. Although the rabbis did limit the amount of sheer physical exertion we may do on the Sabbath.

11 Talmud, Tractate *Shabbat* 49b. This is why the Torah juxtaposes the keeping of the Shabbat to the building of the *Mishkan* in Exodus, chap. 35 (*Rashi*, ibid.). The listing of these thirty-nine *melachot* is brought in Tractate *Shabbat* 73a.

12 The *Netziv*, *Haamek Davar*, Exodus 25:8; see also *Ohr Gedalyahu*, *Tetzaveh* 2; *Nefesh Hachaim* 1:12.

13 Rabbi Chaim of Volozhin, *Nefesh Hachaim*, chap. 4.

14 Ibid.

God—the *Shechinah*—into it, he would understand how to construct himself to bring the presence of God into himself.[15]

Hence, the verse reads, "And they will make for Me a *Mikdash* [i.e. the Tabernacle] and I will dwell in **them**."[16] It does not say that God will dwell in the *Mikdash*; rather it says that He will dwell in man. The end-goal of the Tabernacle (the *Mishkan*) was that mankind should learn how to be holy inside of himself—how to become a human *Mishkan*.[17]

But, for the *Mishkan* to exist, man had to build. Man initiated and God responded. The thirty-nine categories of labor that were used in building the *Mishkan* reflect the full range of man's creative activities—the ability to produce a whole mini-world of holiness.

Man builds the Tabernacle and God responds, but God initiates the holines of the Shabbat and challenges man to respond.

SHABBAT—A TABERNACLE IN TIME

The Shabbat is the exact opposite of the *Mishkan*. God initiates the sanctity, and we respond. The Shabbat is holy whether we keep it or not. On the Shabbat, we sanctify our creativity—not by expressing it, but rather by withdrawing it in the face of God's higher creativity. We thereby show that all of our weekday activity is guided by a higher purpose.

God, however, did not want the type of withdrawal that deadens the mind. He wanted a cessation of creative *activity* while maintaining an active understanding of all that we are withdrawing from. He wanted not only our spirit but also our minds to be engaged. To this end, the Torah introduces a novel concept: *m'lechet machshevet*, literally, "thought work."[18] It is *m'lechet machshevet* that is prohibited on Shabbat.

M'lechet machshevet means that what is going on in my mind when I do an activity actually determines the definition of the activity. For example, making a furrow is an act of plowing—one of the thirty-nine

---

15 *Malbim*, Exodus 35:21; see Rabbeinu Bachya, ibid., on how different aspects of the *Mishkan* modeled different aspects of greatness; *Nefesh Hachaim*, ibid.

16 Exodus 28:8.

17 *Nefesh Hachaim* 1:4.

18 Talmud, Tractate *Beitzah* 13b, based on Exodus 35:33.

prohibited categories of work on the Sabbath. Say I dragged a bench over the ground, thereby creating a furrow. If I simply wanted to move the bench, then I have done an act of transferring an object from one place to another, and it is permitted within the confines of a private domain.[19] If, however, I wanted to use the bench as a primitive plowing device, then I have transgressed by creating a furrow.

Let's say that my cat dies on the Shabbat and I am only allowed to bury it after the Shabbat goes out. In the meantime, I don't want to keep it in the house, and so I carry it into a secure but public area. Have I transgressed the prohibition of carrying on the Shabbat? No, because my interest is not in the cat being in the public domain but merely that I want it removed from my house.[20] (This action, however, was not allowed by the Sages.[21])

This is unique in Jewish law. A man takes his friend's object. Regardless of whether he did so deliberately, negligently, or accidentally, the money has to be returned to its owner. An act was done and it has to be corrected. By Shabbat, however, one is not considered to have done anything unless it was done intentionally. Only on the Shabbat does my intention determine the definition of the action itself.[22]

On the Shabbat, my intention is not superimposed on the action; it is a part of the action itself. The action must be productive,[23] and the desired result must resemble the same creative category as the building of the *Mishkan*.[24] These thirty-nine acts reflect the totality of our creative abilities. We must *not* do on the Shabbat exactly what we *must* do when building the *Mishkan*.

The significance of this is that, on the Shabbat, I must retain my awareness of what I am thinking and how I am relating to my environment. For the Shabbat is not an escape from life but rather an opportunity to

---

19 *Shulchan Aruch*, *Orach Chaim* 337:4.
20 *Meiri*, Tractate *Shabbat* 93b.
21 *Mishnah Berurah* 316:34.
22 Rabbi Yitzchak Hutner, *Pachad Yitzchak*, Shabbat 1.
23 Talmud, Tractate *Shabbat* 105b.
24 Tractate *Chagigah* 10b.

reframe life. It is a chance to regain our bearings, feel close to God, and be confident that we are all under His care.

This is the resolution to the mystery of why *keep* and *remember*—the negative and the positive aspects of the Shabbat—were said simultaneously by God. For the "keeping" parts of the Shabbat—the withdrawal from creative acts—is a positive thing in its own right. I withdraw my control over the world to show that everything is connected to the Source, and by surrendering my own, limited creativity to the Almighty's creativity, I empower myself for the week to come.

24

THE HOLINESS OF HUMAN INTIMACY

Your good inclination was created for you yourself while your bad inclination (i.e., your sexual urge) was created in order to give to your spouse.

Zohar[1]

THE UNIFICATION OF SPOUSES THROUGH THE SEXUAL ACT

Sexuality is an inherent part of who we are. God put this basic urge into us so that we would neither suppress it nor express it freely. Rather, we are to channel it into our marriage. When done in the context of marriage, the sexual union is a paradigm of the Jewish approach to holiness.[2] We keep this as something special and holy between husband and wife that never gets cheapened by separating the sexual desire from the intimacy of a couple bonding for life.

Certainly, as Jews, we should want to build a family through our marital union, though that is not always possible.[3] However, we don't just

---

1 Quoted in Rabbi Moshe Cordovero, *Tomer Devorah*, in the name of the *Zohar*, *Parashat Bereishit*.

2 *Ramban*, *The Holy Letter* (*Iggeret Hakodesh*).

3 As per Genesis 1:28.

have sex because of the mitzvah of procreation.[4] Sexual relations are just as special when a woman cannot become pregnant because of her own or her husband's infertility, or if she is post-menopausal, pregnant, or nursing. In fact, marital intimacy is listed by the Torah as one of three basic things that a husband must provide to his wife.[5] The message is unquestionably to be concerned and focused on one's partner's sexual and emotional satisfaction rather than one's own.[6]

Done with the right approach, making love is so holy that the Song of Songs uses imagery of making love to reflect the relationship we have with God.[7] The Holy of Holies in the Temple was also referred to as the bedroom,[8] in which our love for God was revealed like the passion between a man and a woman.[9] And indeed, the presence of God hovers over a husband and wife making love.[10]

In fact, the greatest expression of fulfilling the mitzvah to be holy is through sexual relations.[11]

The Torah frames this act with the following words:

"Therefore, a man should leave his father and his mother, and he should cleave to his wife, and they should become as one flesh."[12]

Becoming "one flesh"—a total unity—refers to marital relations.[13] The sexual act reflects the culminating feelings of spiritual, intellectual, and emotional bonding. Through this bonding, we create a complete unity between ourselves and our spouses.[14] It is that unity down here that God finds so pleasing, so to speak.[15]

---

4 The first commandment in the Torah is "be fruitful and multiply" (Genesis 1:28).

5 Exodus 21:10. The other two are food and clothing.

6 *Midrash Rabbah*, Genesis 9:10.

7 The Song of Songs was composed by King Solomon. It is full of the imagery of two lovers, for example, "Let Him kiss me with the kisses of His mouth" (1:2).

8 Kings II 11:2.

9 Talmud, Tractate *Yoma* 54a.

10 *Zohar*, Genesis 176a.

11 Vilna Gaon, Commentary on the *Tikkunei Zohar* 53.

12 Genesis 2:24.

13 *Ramban*, ibid.

14 Talmud, Tractate *Niddah* 31a.

15 *Zohar*, Leviticus 71b.

Hence, when the Torah talks of Adam and Eve (Chavah) having relations, it says, "And Adam knew Eve."[16] The state of knowing—"*yediah*"—is called *daat*. When we know something, we no longer have knowledge in our heads; we *are* the knowledge. It infuses our being.[17] When Adam "knew" Eve, it means that at the point of sexual union, he felt totally fused with her and she with him.

SEX AS A PRIMAL URGE

Maimonides writes that getting married and having sexual relations are built into the basic needs of mankind. Like all our basic needs, we need to channel this urge and use it in the right way and with the right intention.[18] Judaism asserts that the proper place for sexual relations is within the framework of marriage. Separating the sexual act from marriage weakens marriage and debases sex. It inevitably leads to turning sex into an act of self-gratification.[19] But today's gratification is tomorrow's boredom, triggering an endless cycle of increasing needs.[20] It turns sex on its head. Instead of becoming an act of giving, it becomes an act of taking.

The Jewish ideal is to create a great desire that in turn leads our partner to want to bond.[21] The Talmud describes the special efforts that the holy Rabbi Yehudah, the son of Rabbi Chiya, used to show his wife love and affection on the eve of the Shabbat in order to create a romantic atmosphere for Friday night.[22]

The pleasure of the actual act is a reward and natural consequence of being engaged in such a holy endeavor.[23] The amazing thing is how something that, on the surface, is so sensual and physical serves this higher purpose.[24] The pleasure itself facilitates the unifying of the cou-

---

16 Genesis 4:1. This is also the wording used for Kayin and his wife in Genesis 4:17.

17 We will expand this idea in the next section.

18 Maimonides, *Mishneh Torah*, Laws of Attributes 3:2.

19 Ibid.; also *Guide to the Perplexed* 3:49, as interpreted by Rabbi Yitzchak Isaac Sher, *Kuntres Kedushat Yisrael*; *Ramban*, Leviticus 18:10.

20 Talmud, Tractate *Sukkah* 52b.

21 Tractate *Niddah* 71a; *Shulchan Aruch*, *Orach Chaim* 240.

22 Tractate *Ketuvot* 72b, as understood by the *Bach*, *Orach Chaim* 280.

23 *Duties of the Heart*, Gate of Abstention, chap. 1.

24 The Maggid of Mezeritch, *Maggid Devaro LeYaakov* 432.

ple into a feeling of total oneness. That oneness, in turn, channels the primal urge of sensuality, turning it into unparalleled holiness.[25]

Friday night is regarded as especially propitious for marital relations as it adds to the pleasure of celebrating the Shabbat, and the holiness of the Shabbat adds to the act in turn.[26]

FAMILY PURITY

Many couples feel that each time they come together after each separation, it is like their wedding night.

God created a system to keep this relationship fresh and pure. These are the laws of family purity (*taharat ha'mishpachah*), as they are known. During a woman's menstrual period and for a week of purity thereafter, a couple does not have marital relations or any physical contact and intimacies that may lead to them.[27] This is the *niddah* period. At the conclusion of this time, a woman immerses herself in a ritual pool of water called a *mikveh*, after which the husband and wife renew their physical relationship.

A woman's menstrual cycle is the result of a loss of the embryo's potential to be fertilized. A woman's bodily energies during this period are focused on preparing for a new cycle of potential. Since her bodily energies are more focused on this, she is less available for the kind of holistic, spiritual, intellectual, and emotional unity that ought to accompany relations with her husband. Hence, relations during this time would become more of a base, physical act, not in keeping with the ideals of marriage.[28]

But here we see an interesting thing, for the menstrual period is not just a period of abstinence. It is meant to have its own positive dynamic, allowing the couple to focus on certain aspects of the relationship that otherwise would not be given attention. The physical relations, if expressed without a break, can actually prevent certain dimensions of non-physical communication and bonding from maturing.[29]

---

25 *Ramban, Iggeret Hakodesh*; Shelah, *Shaar HaOtiot, Kedushah.*

26 *Shulchan Aruch, Orach Chaim* 180.

27 Leviticus 18:19.

28 *Ohel Rachel*, chap. 3.

29 See Rabbi Yirmiyahu and Tehillah Abramov, *Two Halves of a Whole*, p. 180.

During this time, the marriage bonds become strengthened through communication, as each partner learns to share thoughts and feelings verbally. The couple gets to know each other better in ways they would otherwise not have put their minds to—to take walks together or just chat. Disputes are settled through discussions, truly settling problems rather than just allowing the couple to "kiss and make up"—which will simply lead to another round of the same.

In addition, because both husband and wife are aware of the laws and restrictions of this time, neither partner feels rejected or imposed upon.

The separation keeps the sexual aspect of the relationship fresh and constantly renewed.[30] Continued openness to physical contact between the spouses would lead this aspect of the marriage to grow stale through perpetual accessibility. It would lead to desensitization to little acts of touch and other kinds of physical communication that ought to be charged with intimate meaning. Physical contact between husband and wife should be electric. The periods of separation and coming together again means that the marriage will constantly experience renewal. Many couples feel that each time they come together after each separation, it is comparable to their wedding night.

THE MIKVEH

A woman goes to the *mikveh* after her menstruation in preparation for renewing sexual relations with her husband—an experience that greatly contributes to the holiness and the anticipation of getting together again.

The *mikveh* is a ritual pool that is used when going from one spiritual state to a higher one. We immerse in the waters of a *mikveh* before the Day of Atonement,[31] as well as on our wedding day.[32] A convert goes into the *mikveh* as a non-Jew and emerges Jewish.[33]

---

30 Talmud, Tractate *Niddah* 31b.

31 *Shulchan Aruch*, *Orach Chaim* 604:4.

32 *Shulchan Aruch*, *Yoreh Deah* 192, with respect to women. For men, *Sefer Chupat Hachatanim* 6:1.

33 *Shulchan Aruch*, *Yoreh Deah* 268:1–2.

In all of these cases, one enters into the *mikveh* in one state and emerges purer. The source of this idea goes back to the beginning of creation where it says that "the spirit of God hovered over the waters."[34] We are never told when or how those waters were created. What we are told is that the earth emerged out of those waters in part by separating them and creating dry land. "Water" in Hebrew is always plural—*mayim*—because it lacks form. Water always takes on the form of whatever contains it. In the beginning, the formless earth was submerged in water. God then fashioned the world out of this. The world was given form. So, in a sense, each time we dip in a *mikveh*, we come out more created—more form than matter.[35]

The waters of the mikveh take us to a higher spiritual state as if we are being created anew.

A similar idea occurred with the flood during Noah's time. The flood was like the primordial waters coming to cover the earth and purify it once more, just as a *mikveh* of water purifies the one immersing in it.[36] During that time, the only dry land was the ark, the place where man could serve his Maker.[37] When it came time for the land to dry up, the spirit of God again hovered over the water, just as He did at the beginning of creation.[38]

THE NORM AND THE SPECIAL

Possibly no other area of Judaism has suffered so much disinformation as the area of sex (e.g., there are no sheets with holes in them). If we stand apart from contemporary sensitivities in this issue, it is because we have no intention of cheapening that which is holy. This has nothing to do with being outdated and everything to do with wanting to keep that which is special unsullied by the fashions of the age.

---

34 Genesis 1:2.

35 *Sefer Hachinuch.*

36 Rabbi Moshe Shapiro.

37 The Sages in the Talmud, Tractate *Zevachim*, 113a have a discussion about whether the Land of Israel was an exception to this.

38 Genesis 7:1, as explained by *Daat Zekeinim MiBaalei HaTosafot*.

25

THE HOLINESS OF KEEPING KOSHER

The main aim [of the kosher laws] is holiness...the moral perfection of man, and have indeed contributed largely toward molding the collective character of our nation.

Dayan Grunfeld[1]

If eating was purely a physical activity, i.e., an exercise in survival, then we would take the minimum amount, prepared in the simplest way, lock ourselves in a room, and do what we have to do.

The attitude of Judaism to food is very different from this. The introduction to the laws of keeping kosher begin with the words, "and you should be to Me a holy people."[2]

Food is a centerpiece of many of our most transcendent moments. On the Shabbat and the festivals, we make Kiddush over wine prior to the meals,[3] and use wine in our Havdalah at the end of the day.[4] The meals themselves are an integral part of the Shabbat and festivals. The

---

1 Introduction to *Horeb*, p. 48.

2 *Ramban*, Exodus 30:23, as explained by the *Kur Zahav*.

3 *Shulchan Aruch*, *Orach Chaim* 271, 473.

4 Ibid., 296.

Passover Seder involves eating matzah and drinking four cups of wine. We use wine and make meals at weddings,[5] circumcisions, bar and bat-mitzvahs, for finishing a tractate of the Talmud, and for all sorts of other special occasions.[6]

God created man with physical needs because He wanted man to sanctify them.[7] In the case of food, we don't just use it; we ingest it, and it becomes part of our system. It is no accident that we spend significant time and effort preparing the food for this.

The food that a person eats has a spark of life. God put that spark into the food when He spoke the world into existence. The Torah says: "Not on bread alone does a man exist, but on that which comes out of the mouth of God,"[8] i.e., at the time of the creation. When we make a blessing on the food prior to eating, we connect with that original life-source—that spark of life that was put into the food.[9]

God gave us many commandments relating to food so that we would sensitize ourselves to this idea that eating is a spiritual endeavor. For example, there are tithes on the food, and the first fruits of the seven species indigenous to Israel had to be brought to Jerusalem (*bikkurim*).[10]

A person's table is his altar; it has the force of purification.[11] For man's eating is intended to draw out the holy sparks that are in the food and to bring them into his soul. In this way, man provides the food with its own completion—its *tikkun*.[12] In fact, if a lifeless altar of the Temple was able to elevate food to the level of holiness, a human soul can surely do that, and more.[13]

The opposite is also true. Give food to sustain someone who is evil, and the world will suffer. Jacob fed Esau lentils and a famine befell the

---

5 Maimonides, *Mishneh Torah*, Laws of Marriage 3:23.
6 *Yam Shel Shlomo*, Tractate *Bava Kama* 87:37.
7 Rabbi Tzadok HaKohen, *Tzidkat Hatzaddik* 173.
8 Deuteronomy 8:3.
9 The Arizal, *Sefer Halikutim*, *Parashat Eikev* 8.
10 *Shelah*, *Parashat Ki Tavo*.
11 Talmud, Tractate *Berachot* 55a.
12 *Ohr Hachaim*, *Parashat Terumah*.
13 *Avodat Yisrael*, Genesis, *Parashat Toldot*.

land.[14] Disobey me, says God, and the land of Israel will not produce its yield.[15]

PROHIBITED FOODS

Every plant and every animal have sparks of holiness waiting to be released. But only those that are kosher have holiness that is accessible to us. Unkosher animals are *assur*—forbidden. As we have seen, *assur* means bound—the holiness is bound up in the animal and not accessible by us as Jews.[16] We are therefore forbidden to eat such an animal since our act could not elevate it.[17]

Forbidden foods actually affect us in a negative way. They cloud our spiritual sensitivity by layering it and blocking its expression. In short, they make us impure. And so, repeatedly, each kosher law ends with the words that "they are impure *for you*."[18] We explained above that the word for impure—*v'nitmeitem*—is written without its normal *aleph*, allowing it also to be read "*v'nitamtem*—and you will become blocked."[19] Non-kosher food turns the body into a less-perfect vehicle to hold the soul. Since the body is the instrument through which the soul expresses itself, the soul finds itself blocked.[20] If the soul is blocked, our character will be affected. We will become more like the animals we eat.[21]

Non-kosher foods block the soul and muddy the mind.

In contrast to animals, all fruits and vegetables are kosher. (Dairy products need to come from a kosher animal to be kosher.) At the bottom of the food chain, they lack the animal soul that gives

---

14 Rabbi Tzadok HaKohen, *Tzidkat Hatzaddik*, p. 180.

15 Deuteronomy 11:17.

16 See Chapter 21.

17 Rabbi Shneur Zalman of Liadi, *Tanya*, chap. 7.

18 See, for example, Leviticus 11, where v. 4–8 all end with the words, "it is impure to you." Verses 44–47 end with the general idea, "and you should not impurify your souls...and you should be holy, for I am holy, to discriminate between the impure and the pure, between the animal that is eaten and that which is not." See also v. 10–11, 43 for a variation on this language.

19 *Rashi*, Tractate *Yoma* 39a; see Chapter 17.

20 *Sefer Hachinuch* 73.

21 *Ramban*, Leviticus 11:13, Deuteronomy 14:3.

animals specific character traits that can affect man negatively. In fact, the animals permitted by the Torah all subsist on vegetative matter alone. Only carnivorous animals and birds are forbidden by the Torah, since we will become influenced by their consumption of other animals for their sustenance.[22]

KOSHER AS A HEALTH LAW

There is something to the idea that eating kosher means eating healthier. Fish with fins and scales—the signs that they are kosher—tend to swim higher up in oceans, receiving some sunlight and hence processing more toxins out of their systems.[23] All kosher animals are herbivores; none are carnivores.[24] The blood of the meat has to be drained.[25] Fruit and vegetables have to be cleaned of all insects.[26] Even animals that we are allowed to eat need to be healthy; animals that die of injury or ill health are more likely to bear diseases and are hence prohibited.[27]

It would make sense that God gave us kosher laws that were healthy, but that is not to say that it is the reason for doing the mitzvah. The Torah was not given as a guide to healthy eating. "Kosher healthy" means healthy for the spiritual side of man.[28] It means maintaining the exquisite equilibrium of body and soul.[29] Ultimately, God is the doctor of all doctors.[30] The physical diet He gives us nourishes the soul.[31]

---

22 Rabbi Shimshon Raphael Hirsch, *Horeb*, chap. 68. The Torah does not tell us what the signs of a kosher bird are. It merely brings us a list of twenty-four non-kosher birds, and we are not clear as to their identity. We need to refer to the Oral Law to find out what these signs are. One of the signs is birds that claw their prey, i.e., are predators, are non-kosher. Eagles, falcons, and the like belong to this category. Chicken, duck, and turkey are kosher.

23 *Ramban*, Leviticus 11:9.

24 Ibid. See there an additional health reason for this law.

25 Deuteronomy 12:23; Leviticus 3:17.

26 Leviticus 11:23.

27 *Ramban*, Deuteronomy 14:3.

28 *Ramban*, Exodus 23:30; *Abarbanel*, Leviticus, chap. 11.

29 *Sefer Hachinuch* 73.

30 Ibid.

31 Rabbi Tzadok HaKohen, *Machshavot Charutz*, end of 18.

THE PROHIBITION OF MIXING MEAT AND MILK

The prohibition of eating meat and milk together introduces a second major theme in the kosher laws: the sensitivity to the order of creation.[32] We see this principle expressed in *kilayim*, the prohibition of mixing species. There are separate prohibitions against growing certain products together, as well as mixing wool and linen in clothing (*shaatnez*).[33] Neither may we plow with an ox and a donkey together.[34] The Torah applies these laws to the plant and animal world, on agriculture and labor, and to our clothing. With the laws of meat and milk, it extends this idea to our food.[35]

Humans can never fully understand the delicate balance of the ecosystem, and hence we are not authorized to interfere with it.

God created a universe with a natural order of species and forces. Humans can never fully understand the delicate balance of the ecosystem, and hence we are not authorized to interfere with it. It would be presumptuous for us to assume to know more than God about His creation.[36] Hence, when God created each plant or animal, He stated that each was "according to its species."[37]

The separation of meat and milk is a part of this idea. The milk of the animal is a part of the animal's giving side—to provide nourishment for the next generation. The meat of the animal reflects its care of self—its own survival.[38]

Mixing these two is an insensitivity that is tantamount to cruelty.[39] The Hebrew word for "cruel" is *achzar*. This comes from the words *ach zar*—to be only a stranger. The source of cruelty is the alienation that one has from that person or animal. It is the inability to relate to the

---

32 Exodus 23:19; 34:26; Deuteronomy 14:21, as understood by the *Kli Yakar* and Rabbi Shimshon Raphael Hirsch, both on Exodus 23:19.

33 Leviticus 19:19; Deuteronomy 22:9, 11.

34 Deuteronomy 22:10.

35 Rabbi Hirsch, Exodus 23:19.

36 *Sefer Hachinuch* 89; see also 92.

37 Genesis 1:12, 21, 25, as explained by Rabbi Hirsch ad loc.

38 Rabbi Hirsch, Exodus 23:19.

39 *Ibn Ezra*, Exodus 19:22.

pain of others. The Torah tells us that to retain mindfulness of this issue, we should not mix meat and milk.

The actual wording used in the Torah is: "Do not cook a kid [baby goat] in its mother's milk."[40] There can be no greater insensitivity to animals than that!

THE PRICE OF KEEPING KOSHER

In the course of my work, I have traveled extensively. Often, I found myself on flights without kosher food. I often found myself staying in hotels that seemed to have the most delicious non-kosher breakfasts. Yet, I never believed that I was being a hero when I refused to eat non-kosher options. I never saw such food as belonging to me. For me, keeping kosher goes deeply into my identity as a Jew. It allows me to identify with all kinds of other Jews as well; we are all in this together. It changes eating from being a selfish act into something far more sublime. "If you keep kosher," said Lauren F. Winner, "the protagonist of your meal is not you; it is God."[41]

---

40 Exodus 23:19, 34:26; Deuteronomy 14:21.

41 Lauren F. Winner, *Mudhouse Shabbat: An Invitation to a Life of Spiritual Discipline.*

26
THE HOLINESS OF THE HEBREW LANGUAGE

In the small village I'm from, we had a very old custom. On a child's first day of school, the rabbi would give him a slate on which the first two letters of the Hebrew alphabet were written in honey. The rabbi asked the child to lick up the letters and go on to use the slate to learn to read and write on. The child would always remember that learning was sweet like honey.

Abe Opincar, Fried Butter: A Food Memoir

This ancient custom exists to this day.[1] My children in Jerusalem experienced the same excitement when they too licked off letters written in honey at the age of three.

The Hebrew language is called *lashon ha'kodesh*—the "holy language." The Torah was written in Hebrew because it is a precise language

1 The custom is based on the verse in Song of Songs (4:11), "Our lips, O my bride, distill like the honeycomb; honey and milk are under your tongue; and the scent of your garments is like the scent of Lebanon." *Shir Hashirim Rabbah* 1:3 says that just as honey and milk is sweet, so Torah is sweet, as it says in Psalms 19:11, "And they are sweeter than honey"; see also *Midrash Tanchuma*, *Ki Tisa* 9.

designed to describe all aspects of spirituality. Hebrew is exceptionally rich in words that describe different manifestations of God, different aspects of spirituality, and also its opposites—impurity and negativity. This helps us Jews to form a spiritual paradigm—a more spiritual way of viewing the world. Translated into English, these concepts are dumbed down, squeezed into far fewer words that are then less precise and not as meaningful.

But there is more. God used the Hebrew language to create the world,[2] and it continues to be the vehicle through which God influences the world to this day.[3]

When God speaks, He does so in Hebrew. He created the world through Ten Sayings of creation: "And God said, 'Let there be light,' and there was light..."[4] God is omnipotent (all powerful). Had He wanted to create the world without speech, it was certainly possible for Him to do so. He could have willed the world into being from thought alone, but God saw fit to create a hierarchy of spirituality, divided into four parallel worlds, as we discussed above.[5] Hebrew has a very important place in that hierarchy.

The world of speech exists at the level called the World of Formation—the third highest world of spirituality. Thus, when God "spoke," it meant that God's creative will devolved down from higher levels until it took the form of speech in the World of Formation. At that level, the entire world existed as words. These words then translated into the physical world that we see around us. The word, therefore, actually sustains the physical reality it produced. If we would transform the physical world into a purely spiritual form, we would again get the words.[6]

God used the Hebrew language to create the world, and it continues to be the vehicle through which God influences the world to this day.

---

2 "By the word of God, the heavens were made; and by the spirit of His mouth, [He created] all the hosts" (Psalm 33:6).

3 *Ramban*, Exodus 30:13.

4 Genesis 1:3.

5 See p. 66, "Man—a Mini-World."

6 Rabbi Tzadok HaKohen, *Machashavot Charutz* 11 (at the beginning), p. 83.

HEBREW—A LANGUAGE THAT SUSTAINS THE WORLD

In any language, the rules of grammar and the words themselves are agreed upon by convention. People agree that a certain set of sounds will signify a certain object or action. In English, we use the word "table" to represent a certain physical idea. Most tables have four legs and a top. Were we to all agree that instead of the word "table" we will henceforth use the word "klaka," then that would be just as good. The only requirement is that we all agree what words we are using for what.

Not so with Hebrew. The Hebrew word is not just a symbolic representation of the thing. It is the thing itself on a different plane of spirituality.

In Hebrew, the word for "thing" or "object" is *davar* (דבר). This has the same letters as *diber*, to speak.[7] The words for "speaking" and for "thing" have the same letters because the spoken word of God produced the reality—the thing. Hence, embedded in every object is its Hebrew word.[8]

The words for "speaking" and for "thing" have the same letters because the spoken word of God produced the reality—the thing.

Moreover, from the word we can understand the purpose of the object. Hence in Hebrew the word for "name" is *sheim* (שם), whose same letters are the word *sham*, "there." The "name" is the "there-ness" of the thing. In Hebrew, reality and word converge; the word is the reality of the object at a higher level.

We see this expressed when God brought before Adam all the animals and Adam named them.[9] The verse doesn't say that he gave them names, but rather that he "came to see"—to understand—"what to call them", i.e. what their names were.

Their names reflected their essence, for their names were their "thereness"—their "*sham*-ness."[10]

---

7 *Hu diber* would mean "he spoke."

8 Rabbi Moshe Shapiro.

9 Genesis 2:19.

10 Rabbi Hirsch.

AN INTERLINKED WEB

The physical world we see has many links and crossovers. Ecosystems are exquisitely balanced environments. The body's systems work in remarkable tandem. If the Hebrew language reflects the words behind the world, then it too should show these crossovers in the forms of interlinking words. And this is what we find.

For example, the English words to eat, to feed, and to devour have related meanings, but are etymologically completely unconnected words. There is zero connection between the letters "e-a-t," "f-e-e-d," "d-e-v-o-u-r." But in Hebrew, these words are made up of the same letters just with different vowels. (Remember, in Hebrew the letters are all consonants, and the vowels are written beneath.) The general root for "eating" comprises the three-letters of *aleph* (א), *chaf* (כ), and *lamed* (ל). So, "he ate" would be *achal*, "he consumed" would be *ikeil*,[11] and "he fed" would be *he'echil*—all from the same three-root letters (*aleph*, *chaf*, *lamed*—אכל).

---

11 The *k* sound is the *ch* sound with a dot in the letter. Although we do not find the *pi'el*—strong form in the active in the Chumash, we do find it is attested to in the passive—*pu'al* form in Exodus 3:2, where the buning bush was not consumed (*eineno ukal*). See too Isaiah 1:20.

It should be remembered that, in Hebrew, we have only a small part of the original vocabulary. In the original language each word might have existed in all four active and three passive tenses, seven in all. Nevertheless, there are several words that exist in all the declensions, for example *pakad*. Modern Hebrew also has such words, based on the biblical, such as the word *patar*.

In addition, the Kabbalistic work, *Sefer HaYetzira* (the Book of Formation) tells us that letters in the same sound categories have similar but slightly divergent meanings. So, the *aleph* and the *ayin*—both gutturals—can get interchanged. *Ikel* with an *ayin* (עכל) means to consume or digest as in a fire, or a chemical process.

To give another example the word *shalach* means to send (Exodus 4:4); the word in its stronger, *pi'el* form (*shilach*) means to let go, or to set free (Exodus 7:14). In the causative, *hif'il*, form (*mashliach*), it means to let loose (Exodus 8:17), and in the reflexive *hitpael* form it means "commissioned with" or "charged with" (*Rashi*, Genesis 32:30).

These words in English, send, let go, let loose, commissioned with—have no etymological connection one with the other. The letters S-E-N-D are completely different from the word L-O-O-S-E, for example. But in Hebrew, these variations of meaning come from the same three letters written with different vowelizations,

We could show this pattern with other words as well, such as *lavash* (לבש), to dress.

More than that, Hebrew words that end with the same letter-sound grouping are all related.[12] So, for example, the labials (letters said by closing your lips) are the *b*, *v*, *m*, and *p* sounds. These are comprised of the Hebrew letters *beit* (ב), *vav* (ו), *mem* (מ), and *peh* (פ). The gutturals (letters said at the back of your throat) are represented by the *aleph* (א), *hei* (ה), *chet* (ח), and *ayin* (ע) letters, and when interchanged modify the meaning of a given word.

To see this in action, let's take the first verb in the Torah—*bara* (ברא), "created,"[13] made up of the letters *beit*, *reish*, and *aleph*. The word *bara* means (He) "created," caused something *to break out* into existence. If we replace the guttural *aleph* at the end with a guttural *chet*, we get *barach* (ברח), which means "he fled," *broke out* of constraints." If we replace the labial *beit* with labial *peh*, we get *parach* (פרח), which means "to flower" or "to fly"[14]—also a type of breaking of constraints.

Or take the word *para* (with an *ayin*—פרע), which means "to let one's hair loose"—freed from its constraints. Similarly, the word *pere* (with an *aleph*—פרא) means "wild, savage, and unconstrained." All of these words have a specific meaning but share an underlying theme, as reflected in their shared letter-categories.

We could go through the entire Biblical Jewish vocabulary, showing hundreds of links. No other language begins to be as sophisticated and interconnected as Hebrew. No other language could be. Hebrew is God's language, the language of the angels, and in fact, until the Tower of Babel, the language of the whole world.[15]

EVERYTHING HINTED AT IN THE TORAH

The Torah is the blueprint of the world. Hence, whatever was, is, or will be until the end of time is also hinted at somewhere in the Torah.[16] In many cases, it is the specific division of the words into different

---

12 *Sefer Hayetzirah*, written by Abraham.

13 Genesis 1:1.

14 Literally, "he flowered" and "he flew." The simplest form of any verb is in the third-person past-tense.

15 *Rashi*, Genesis 11:1.

16 Commentary of the Vilna Gaon, *Safra De'tzniuta*, chap. 5.

combinations of the letters that reveal different secrets of the universe.[17] Not only that, but each of us can find our personal odyssey hinted to in the Torah as well.[18] In fact, we can find all of this in a more contracted and esoteric form in the creation story. The first verse of the Torah has seven words, the number that encompasses all of the natural order, encapsulating the essence of the world.[19]

BETZALEL—WHO UNDERSTOOD THE SECRETS OF THE LETTERS

One of the most remarkable figures in the Torah is Betzalel, who built the *Mishkan* (Tabernacle).[20] The *Mishkan* contained within it all the elements of the world. By building the Tabernacle, Betzalel was recreating the world in a miniature form.[21]

To do this, Betzalel needed to understand what letter combinations God had used in the creation of the world.[22] This was no luxury, for this mini-world required that the entire creation pass through the level of language in order to allow God's presence to contract into its space. Hence, he was granted this as a gift of wisdom from above.[23]

THE HEBREW LANGUAGE TODAY

Modern Hebrew is akin to the Biblical. An Israeli has no problem opening up the Torah and understanding what it is says, but it is not exactly the same thing.

Today, we are left with just a fragment of the original Hebrew language, the part that is used in the writing of the Torah, Prophets, and Writings (the *Tanach*). The revival of Modern Hebrew as the language of the State of Israel is truly remarkable. At the same time, it required compromises with its Biblical antecedent and a vocabulary many times the size of the vocabulary we inherited from the Bible.

---

17 Rabbi Moshe Sternbuch, *Sta"m Kehilchatan*, chap. 9.

18 See p. 187, "Each Person Brings Their Uniqueness to Torah."

19 Vilna Gaon, ibid.

20 Exodus 31:2; in 35:30, Moses echoes this message to the people.

21 Rabbi Chaim of Volozhin, *Nefesh Hachaim* 1:4.

22 Talmud, Tractate *Berachot* 55a.

23 Exodus 31:3.

Despite a noble attempt to develop the language from within, some of the replacement words reflect modern cultural sensitivities rather than the profundity presumed to exist in the original words. Purists are aghast at these insensitivities, while others marvel at the revival of the language as the spoken tongue of what is now the largest population of Jews in any one country, and the Jewish state to boot. The truth is that the language was never dead. For thousands of years, every Jewish child was taught at an early age to read and understand the Hebrew of the Torah, which Jewish scholars had so masterfully employed throughout the generations. They wrote their great works in Hebrew, and others studied and continue to study these in Hebrew. Modern Hebrew was not so much the revival of a dead language as it was the adoption of that ancient and mystical tongue by an entire state.

SECTION 3

WISDOM

27
THE LOVE OF WISDOM

The wise of heart will abandon ease and pleasures,
for in his library he will find treasures.

Rabbi Shmuel Hanagid

Some readers may question why I placed the section of holiness before the section on wisdom. This is because our attitude to wisdom is significantly affected by our attitude to holiness. Wisdom, even of the sciences, is affected by our paradigm, and the paradigm of Jewish wisdom is holiness.

Jews are the people of The Book. To be a Jew means to engage a culture of scholarship and to embrace a lifelong love for wisdom. Yehudah HaLevi expressed it so beautifully: "My pen is my harp and my lyre, my library is my garden and orchard."[1]

Even if it is true that Jews have higher average IQs than the general population, this would not be enough to account for their significant over-representation as physicists, Nobel prize–winners, and other such achievements. They achieve more because of their approach to wisdom—something deeply embedded in our culture.

1 *Collected Poems of Yehudah HaLevi*, p. 166.

As Jews, we seek not just to acquire wisdom but to acquire the love of wisdom. It is this love of learning that ensures that Jewish genius does not get lost.

The great second-century sage, Ben Zoma, said, "Who is a wise man? One who learns from all people."[2] A person who truly loves wisdom won't pick and choose who to learn from. A child can be his teacher just as an adult. Moreover, as Shakespeare put it, "A fool thinks himself to be wise, but a wise man knows himself to be a fool."[3] The wise focus on what they don't know and are driven to seek it out. A person who has this attitude to wisdom is considered wise even before he has gained the knowledge. He will surely overcome his ignorance. His is the approach of a wise man.[4]

A Torah sage is called a talmid chacham—"the student of a wise man." He is forever a student.

A Torah sage is called a *talmid chacham*—"the student of a wise man." He is never "done." He is always in process. He is always a student. Einstein got it right when he said, "The important thing is not to stop questioning."[5]

It was enough for King David to learn two laws from his counselor Achitofel to call him "my rabbi" for the rest of his days.[6] Even if we learn but one letter from someone else, we have to show him honor and respect.[7]

We live in an age where whiz kids in their twenties become overnight billionaires. They are clever, but are they wise? "At sixty, a person acquires age."[8] The Hebrew word for age is *ziknah*, which is an acronym that means "*zeh kanah chochmah*—This one has acquired wisdom."[9] Certainly, we have seen brilliant young scholars, but it takes time to come of age and be wise.

---

2 *Ethics of Our Fathers* 4:1.

3 *As You Like It*, Act 5, Scene 1.

4 Rabbeinu Yonah, *Ethics of our Fathers* ad loc.

5 "Old Man's Advice to Youth: 'Never Lose a Holy Curiosity.'" *LIFE Magazine* (May 2, 1955): p. 64.

6 *Ethics of our Fathers*, 6:3.

7 Ibid. The Sages derive this from King David himself.

8 *Ethics of our Fathers*, 5:21.

9 The first letters of each word make up the word *zaken*, the noun for *ziknah*.

Wisdom is much more than knowledge. It is the ability to understand the big picture, to see what is behind all of the details, and to understand what is primary and what is secondary. British philosopher Alfred North Whitehead stated that "Knowledge shrinks as wisdom grows, for details are swallowed up in principles." No greater example of this can be brought than the methodology of Judaism—its principles are so profound that, as the world unfolds into ever new dilemmas, we are able to clearly draw on our Judaism and feel that it is relevant, meaningful, and contemporary.

TO LEARN IS TO TEACH

A wise person who refuses to teach his Torah is a thief, for the Torah belongs to all of the Jewish People.[10]

In addition, such a person is shooting himself in the foot.[11] Rabbi Yehudah HaNasi (Rebbi) said, "I have learned a great deal from my teachers, and even more from my colleagues, but I have learned the most from my students."[12]

To teach students, one has to have absolute clarity. One has to order, prioritize, and filter. One has to anticipate all kinds of questions. All of this expands the boundaries of our wisdom. When one has enough wisdom to teach, one has reached the stage where one is about to learn the most.

But, Rebbi was also saying that someone who loves wisdom so much that he desires to pass it onto others will have a different relationship with that wisdom. Since he is not just looking to satisfy his own intellectual curiosity but really cares about the value of the information, he will achieve a level of integration and resonance with his knowledge that he otherwise could not have aspired to. It will not speak just to his head. It will speak to his core.[13]

---

10 Deuteronomy 33:4.

11 *Rishfei Aish Dat, Shaar HaTorah.*

12 Talmud, Tractate *Makkot* 10a; Tractate *Taanit* 7a.

13 We will discuss in Chapters 29–31 wisdom of the mind, heart, and action, respectively.

QUALIFICATIONS OF A TEACHER

The wise person has but one condition of his teacher—that he walks the walk or at least makes every effort to do so. The teacher must radiate all the values that the Torah stands for. The student cannot learn from someone for whom this wisdom is purely theoretical, for then the wisdom itself will come out distorted. In the inimitable word of the Sages, "If the rabbi is like an angel, one should seek Torah from him; and if he is not, one should not seek from such a person."[14] Similarly, someone who wants to study Torah with the intention of distorting it or manipulating it should not be taught.[15]

I have learned a great deal from my teachers, and even more from my colleagues. But I have learned the most from my students.

Someone whose character and observance are not sterling will introduce his own biases, even unwittingly, to his interpretation of the text. In fact, twenty-four thousand students of Rabbi Akiva died because "they did not deal respectfully with one another."[16] Their lack of character perfection—even though they were admired by those around them—created a fatal flaw in their role as transmitters of the tradition.

HUMILITY WITHOUT BASHFULNESS

A lover of wisdom must have both humility and courage—two seemingly contradictory qualities. On the one hand, "The bashful person does not learn."[17] Never should we feel burdened by the idea that we are making a fool of ourselves.[18] We must have the courage to ask, to challenge, and to probe at the edges to find new points of tension. More than that, we should be truly bothered by anything we do not understand. Great sages were known to have sleepless nights thinking about an apparent contradiction in the Talmud.

---

14 Talmud, Tractate *Chagigah* 16b.

15 Talmud, Tractate *Chullin* 133a.

16 Talmud, Tractate *Yevamot* 62b.

17 *Ethics of Our Fathers* 2:6 (in some additions, this is Mishnah 5).

18 *Rashi*, Rabbeinu Yonah, Bartenura, *Meiri*, ibid.

But there is a difference between the courage to learn and intellectual arrogance. The latter is one of the great blockages to wisdom. Its opposite, intellectual humility, opens the person to new knowledge and keeps him fresh and growing. Humility is not a lack of courage. It is simply an awareness of the gap between what we know and who we are, and our ultimate potential.

Humility keeps us honest, sharp, and learning from others. Courage makes us determined not to accept that wisdom until it makes sense. To simply cave into the opinions of others is not humility; it is a lack of belief in our own inner resources to get to the truth.[19]

TO BE CHALLENGED IS TO SHARPEN THE TRUTH

The Sage's greatest joy is to study with someone who will show him all the flaws in his argument. Aware of his fallibility, he embraces challenges to his thinking. One has only to enter the study hall of any yeshiva and witness the arguments for truth to understand this.

Reish Lakish[20] was a most distinguished student of the great Rabbi Yochanan. The Talmud relates that when Reish Lakish died, Rabbi Yochanan was plunged into a state of deep mourning.[21] The rabbis sent the brilliant Rabbi Elazar ben Pedat to be his new study partner. Whenever Rabbi Yochanan taught a sophisticated Torah idea, Rabbi Elazar ben Pedat would offer proofs to its correctness. Rabbi Yochanan was unhappy with this. "When I stated a law, Reish Lakish used to raise twenty-four objections, to which I gave twenty-four answers, which consequently led to a fuller comprehension of the law, while you say, 'Something has been taught that supports you.'" With the death of Reish Lakish, Rabbi Yochanan not only lost someone dear to him but the ability to sharpen his wisdom. Cut off from this level of truth, Rabbi Yochanan eventually died from sorrow and pain.

---

19 Maimonides, in his *Shemoneh Perakim* (introduction to *Ethics of Our Fathers*), says that *bayshan* is the balancing trait between *boshet panim* (complete shamefulness) and arrogance.

20 His real name was Rabbi Shimon ben Lakish.

21 Talmud, Tractate *Bava Metzia* 84a.

THE GIFT OF RIVALRY

In the world of academia, an intellectual rival is seen as competition for who will publish first and who will be given credit. In Judaism, an intellectual rival is a great gift from God to delve further into the truth, sharpen one's understanding of it, and deepen one's perspective.

The Academy of Hillel and the Academy of Shammai had many disagreements. Their interactions provide famous instances of each striving to determine the correctness of their positions. Yet, it would be a mistake to see this as a rivalry. The Academy of Hillel and the Academy of Shammai were known to marry spouses from the opposite community. This was what the prophet Zechariah meant when he stated, "Love truth and peace"[22]—"Love truth": Be a lion in search of clarifying the truth of the Torah, but simultaneously "love peace": respect, admire, and even marry into those who argue with you.[23] Wisdom is not the flourish of creativity by the lonely genius. The Academy of Hillel deeply appreciated that they owed their wisdom in large part to the Academy of Shammai, and vice versa.

To learn from a child; to want to share one's wisdom; to have humility yet the courage to ask; to realize that one's intellectual adversaries are one's greatest friends—these are not just approaches to Jewish wisdom but are a part of that wisdom itself. God revealed the Torah to us together with the keys to unlocking it. If we use the wrong set of keys, the Torah will not yield its secrets. Wisdom may start with man's efforts, but it must end as a gift of God: "And Moses called...every person...to which God gave wisdom into his heart."[24]

---

22 Zechariah 8:19.

23 Tractate *Yevamot* 14b.

24 Exodus 36:2.

28

THE WISDOM OF THE TORAH

And God said...eat this Scroll...and it tasted as sweet as honey to me.

Ezekiel (3:1–3)

THE TORAH—THE BLUEPRINT OF THE WORLD

The word "Torah" comes from the word "to teach." It is the Book of Guidance. But it is much more than just a self-help manual. The Torah preceded the creation of the world. God looked into the Torah to create the world.[1] The Torah is God's blueprint, His master plan for the world.[2] When we study Torah, we are akin to poring over those original plans together with God Himself! We are reconnecting to the source.

God invites us in to express our understanding of His plans, similar to how a leader of state would consult with his advisors.[3] We sit down with the Master Planner in an intimate encounter over his intentions for the world. Learning Torah is as much a conversation with God as is prayer. But the conversation of Torah is of a completely different sort.[4]

---

1 Talmud, Tractate *Pesachim* 54b.

2 *Maharal, Netivot Olam, Netivat HaTorah*, chap. 1.

3 Talmud, Tractate *Berachot* 34b, regarding the story of Rabbi Chanina ben Dosa and Rabbi Yochanan ben Zakkai.

4 Ibid.

UNIVERSALISM

Although the Torah is the book of the Jews, God wanted the wisdom of everything to be in the Torah, including the wisdom that non-Jews need to serve Him.[5] "Turn it over; turn it over, for all is in it."[6] In fact, before entering Israel, Moses translated the Torah into seventy languages.[7] Moreover, the light of the *Menorah* in the Temple—symbolic of the Oral Law—was meant to radiate outward as testimony to all the world that here lay the presence of God.[8]

In fact, in an ideal world, the whole distinction between Jew and non-Jew would not exist, and the entire Torah would have been a document for all of mankind. As it is, it contains the Seven Noahide commands that are considered universals, incumbent on all non-Jews.[9]

Almost the entire Genesis deals with the kind of wisdom that is not necessarily unique to the Jews. There are only three commandments in the entire book. The reason for this is that "the development of good character" precedes the Torah.[10] Hence, Genesis is a book of dramatic stories that highlight the failures and successes of our forefathers in dealing with their challenges on their way to establishing a permanent multi-generational connection with God.

---

5 *Sefat Emet*, as brought in *Ohr Gedalyahu*, Genesis, p. 6.

6 *Ethics of Our Fathers* 5:22.

7 *Rashi*, Deuteronomy 1:5.

8 Rabbi Mordechai Miller, *Shabbat Shiurim*, vol. 1, p. 65.

9 Talmud, Tractate *Sanhedrin* 59a finds an inference to these laws. They are:

1. Not to profane God's Oneness.
2. Not to curse God.
3. Not to murder.
4. Not to steal.
5. Not to commit adultery.
6. Not to be cruel to animals. (The actual wording is not to eat the limb of a living creature which the *Sefer Hachinuch* understands is only an example to cruelty to animals in general.)
7. To set up a just system of courts.

See also Chapter 18 for the universalism of the Ten Commandments.

10 *Yalkut Shimoni*, Genesis 3:34.

THE JEWS ARE WISE ONLY BECAUSE OF THEIR TORAH

In *A History of the Jews*, Paul Johnson writes with his usual incisiveness as follows:

The genius of the Jews is only because they took God's Torah as their guide.

> *All the great conceptual discoveries of the intellect seem obvious and inescapable once they have been revealed, but it requires a special genius to formulate them for the first time. The Jews had this gift. To them we owe the idea of equality before the law, both Divine and human; of the sanctity of life and the dignity of the human person; of the individual conscience and social responsibility; of peace as an abstract ideal and love as the foundation of justice, and many other items which constitute the basic moral furniture of the human mind. Without the Jews it might have been a much emptier place.*[11]

But it was not a special moral and spiritual genius that made the Jews so wise. Our secret was to accept God's revelation of His infinite wisdom.

Moses, in the name of God, tells us at the end of his life: "See! I have taught you laws...that you should keep...for they are your wisdom and your understanding...And where can you find a great nation who had righteous laws like this entire Torah..."[12]

"If you see wisdom residing with the nations of the world, believe it," say the Sages.[13] That refers to science, psychology, medicine, technology, and economics. The miracle of the Jewish spirit came because Torah turned us into a wise and discerning nation in ethics, spirituality, and repairing the world.[14]

---

11 Paul Johnson, *History of the Jews,* Epilogue.

12 Deuteronomy 4:5–8.

13 *Midrash Rabbah,* Lamentations, chap. 2. The end of the saying is, "But if someone were to tell you that there is Torah in the possession of the nations, do not believe this." This is for the simple reason that they did not accept it.

14 *Malbim,* Deuteronomy, ibid.

THE STUDY OF TORAH

Jews study the Torah throughout their whole lives. It is not a course, degree, or series. It is our life.[15] This process starts earlier than one might imagine. The Sages tell us that an angel teaches every child all of the Torah while still in his or her mother's womb.[16] At a conscious level, we forget that Torah when we are born, but it remains in the deepest recesses of our souls. Throughout our lives, whenever we study that Torah again, it resonates with the Torah already hidden inside of ourselves.[17]

> *At a conscious level, we forget our Torah when we are born, but it remains in the deepest recesses of our souls.*

We study the Torah not just to gain the knowledge; rather, it is an experience in and of itself. Plumbing the depths of God's wisdom purifies ourselves and generates holiness. As the second president of the United States, John Adams said, the Bible has a way of "making you wiser and more virtuous."[18]

A RELATIONSHIP WITH GOD INITIATED BY US

At Sinai, the Torah was brought from the heavens down to earth. When we study Torah, we reverse the order: We climb the ladder of Torah wisdom back up to the very heavens. In the words of the Kabbalists, it is an "arousal from the bottom to the top."[19]

There is a fascinating illusion to this in the Hebrew letter *lamed*—ל. Each of the Hebrew letters has a literal meaning. The letter *beit*—ב means a house (pronounced *bayit*). The letter *gimmel*—ג means a camel (pronounced *gamal*). The letter *kuf*—ק means a monkey (pronounced *kof*). There are Kabbalistic reasons for all of this.

The letter *lamed*—ל means to learn, specifically related to study of Torah.[20] The *lamed* has a unique property. When a Torah scroll is written

---

15 Evening prayer service, second blessing.

16 Talmud, Tractate *Niddah* 30b.

17 *B'nei Yissaschar*, month of Shevat, on the verse, "For a man is a tree of the field."

18 John Adams wrote this in 1811, in a letter to his son Quincy, the future president.

19 The concept has its origins in the *Zohar* 1:35:1.

20 In this form—*lamed*—it is the imperative form of teach—*lamed*. The words "learn" and

by a scribe, he first engraves lines on the parchment.[21] The letters start at this line and extend downwards. There is only one letter that extends above the line, and that is the *lamed*. The *lamed*, in fact, has no upper limits, for such is how our relationship with the wisdom of Torah is supposed to be. We can study Torah deeper and deeper without limit. It is up to us.[22]

EACH PERSON BRINGS THEIR UNIQUENESS TO TORAH

Every morning when we get up, we make what are called the "blessings of the Torah." We say, "And give us our portion in the Torah," referring to the unique portion each one of us has in it.[23]

The French public intellectual Bernard-Henri Lévy described the Torah as "a book immensely simple and prodigiously complex," all in one.[24] As God's word, the Torah has infinite depth. This allows for multiple perspectives and levels of understanding.[25] King Solomon was able to give three thousand parables on every concept of the Torah and five thousand reasons for each idea contained in the Oral Law.[26] And yet, a five-year old can grasp the basic storyline of the Torah.[27]

Each generation finds itself at a unique moment in history. Therefore, each will connect to the Torah in a unique way. Each must find its own relevance in this immutable law.[28]

In fact, each individual soul has its own unique portion in the Torah. This is hinted at in the word *Yisrael* (Israel), which is an acronym for

***Y**eish **S**hishim **R**ibo **O**tiot **L**a'Torah*[29]—"There are six hundred thousand letters in the Torah."

"teach" in Hebrew come from the same root—to teach is to cause someone else to learn, to facilitate their learning.

21 These lines are called *sirtut*.

22 Rabbi Tzadok HaKohen, *Machashavot Charutz*.

23 *Rishfei Aish Dat, Shaar HaTorah*.

24 Bernard-Henri Lévy, speech delivered at the Academic College of Netanya, June 18, 2018.

25 *Shulchan Aruch HaRav*, Laws of Talmud Study 1:5.

26 Talmud, Tractate *Eruvin* 21a, based on Kings I 5:12.

27 *Ethics of Our Fathers* 5:21.

28 *Michtav Me'Eliyahu, Maamar al HaTorah*.

29 *Zohar Chadash* 91a. This is clearer in the Hebrew lettering: יש שישים ריבוא אותיות לתורה. The first letters of each word spell out the word "Israel"—ישראל.

Israel, that giant collective soul, was divided into six hundred thousand root souls who stood at Sinai.[30] These souls all received the Torah according to their root, leading to many perspectives of the same thing.[31] These root souls in turn are divided into all the individual souls in all future generations.[32] God engraved the entire Torah on every Jewish soul, which later gave life to one of the Jews.[33] This allows each one of us to resonate with the Torah—a Torah that is already deep within us.[34]

Israel is a giant collective soul divided into root souls who stood at Sinai and then in turn into all the individual souls in all future generations.

Your attempt to objectively understand the Torah will connect with your personality, your cultural background, and your personal baggage. Perforce, your Torah will be different than mine, without any attempt by either of us to distort its meaning. I need your unique Torah, and you need mine. The idea that one can enter a cave and study Torah in splendid isolation is an anathema. God designed the world so that it is the combined understanding of every soul that completes the understanding of the Torah.

Can this process ever be complete? The Torah, being God's word, is far deeper and has more perspectives than any one soul could ever encompass.[35] "It is longer than the measure of [all] the land and wider than any sea."[36] As a result, there will always be room for more people to discover novel insights into the Torah.[37] Every person is responsible

---

30 The Torah gives the total number of men between the ages of twenty and sixty as six hundred thousand. Hence, there were many more that actually stood at Sinai.

31 And even though the Sages stated, "There are seventy faces to the Torah," *Sefer Hachinuch* (95) explains that these seventy divide into multiple roots, and each root into multiple branches, and ultimately into the individual fruits that reflect our integration of the Torah. See also *Ohr Hachaim*, Exodus 31:13.

32 *Michtav Me'Eliyahu*, *Maamar al HaTorah*.

33 *Meshech Chochmah*, Exodus 24:12, words beg. "and the Torah."

34 *Midrash Rabbah*, Genesis 97:5.

35 Talmud, Tractate *Eruvin* 21a.

36 Job 11:9. The Talmud (*Eruvin* 21a) interprets this as referring to the infinitude of the Torah.

37 Maimonides, intro. to his commentary on the Mishnah, par. beg. "And when Moshe died." Presumably, this is based on Tractate *Chagigah* 3b, which states, "The words of Torah continuously multiply."

for bringing his or her novel insight into the world. Only the totality of insights will give us, collectively, the broadest perspective of the Torah. God Himself rejoices in this continuous process of revelation by man, for it means that more of His ultimate purpose in creating the world has been uncovered.[38]

38 *Zohar*, brought in *Nefesh Hachaim* 4:12.

29
THE WISDOM OF THE MIND

If a man will tell you [concerning wisdom],
"I have toiled and not found," don't believe him;
"I have not toiled and found," don't believe him;
"I have toiled and found," believe him.

Talmud, Tractate Megillah 6a

THREE TYPES OF WISDOM

Jewish wisdom unfolds in a process. It begins with *chochmah*—the wisdom of the mind; it moves onto *binah*—the wisdom of the heart; and it culminates in *daat*—the wisdom of action.[1] In the Kabbalistic literature, these are known as the three mothers (*imahot*), as they are the roots of our other qualities.[2] (The famous CHABAD movement is actually made up of an acronym of the first letters of ***ch**ochmah*, ***b**inah*, and ***da**at*.)

Chochmah is the koach mah, "the power of what," the power that is still only a "what"—a potential.

Chochmah is the pure knowledge of things. The word *chochmah* (חכמה) is made up of the words *koach* and *mah* (כח מה) translating to "the power

1 Rabbi Shneur Zalman of Liadi, *Tanya*, chap. 3.

2 Ibid.

of what," the power that is still only a "what"—a potential.[3] The word *mah* has the same numerical value as *adam*. Man is quintessentially the power of what, the potential to advance continuously in his wisdom.[4]

Chochmah is the flash of inspiration. It is the surge of creativity. It is the wonder of a new insight. It is the journey of discovery. As exciting as all of this is, it is worth nothing if it will not be nurtured and developed. Pure wisdom remains "the power of what"—pure potential. It is but abstract information; it doesn't really mean anything to us. We can know without understanding; we can learn without appreciating.[5]

To be of value to us, *chochmah* must transform itself into wisdom of the heart—the level of *binah*. This is where integration takes place. *Binah* answers the question, "What does this have to do with me?" *Binah* is where we begin to resonate with the information. It creates the conditions necessary for the emotional integration of the wisdom, where a person feels comfortable with that knowledge, can relate to it personally, and therefore also understands where it is and where it is not relevant to his or her life.[6]

However, there is a further stage, which is the wisdom of action. We call this *daat*. *Daat* is total integration. It is when the information is so much a part of who we are that we no longer hold the information; we *are* the information. It is an intrinsic part of our identity. Our natural and unfiltered thoughts are in harmony with our *daat* information. This means that we automatically translate that wisdom into action for there is now complete unity between ourselves and the knowledge.[7]

Daat is when the information is so much a part of who we are that we no longer hold the information; we are the information.

3 Ibid.

4 Rabbi Tzadok HaKohen, *Machashavot Charutz*.

5 *Rashi*, Exodus 31:3, defines it as "that which a person hears from another and learned it."

6 *Binah* itself is only the first stop in this process. It does so by limiting the flow of *chochmah*, analogous of a faucet giving direction to the water stored in a tank by containing its flow. A "child" of *binah* is *tevunah*, which *Rashi*, Exodus 31:3, says is where "one understands something *from his heart* amongst the things that he has learned."

7 *Rashi* (ibid.) says that this is "*ruach ha'kodesh*"—Divine inspiration.

TWO TYPES OF SIMPLICITY

Before we start our journey in Judaism, we classically oversimplify. We think of Judaism as a bunch of customs. We know something about the Shabbat and the festivals, and about keeping kosher, but at best these are meaningful rituals—good to add some spice to our lives but hardly something by which we define ourselves. This type of simplicity does Judaism a great disservice. However, there is another level of simplicity—the simplicity of seeing the whole picture, the helicopter view.[8]

As we plunge into the Torah, it becomes a little intimidating and bewildering. It is humbling for a well-functioning adult to think of himself as child-like in his level of mastery of Judaism. However, if we persist, the pieces slowly fall into place. We begin to understand the relationship between God's Divine Providence and our choice; between the Shabbat and the weekday. The themes behind the festivals and how they all together make up the annual cycle fall into place. The Torah starts to feel like an old friend. It is still awfully complex, but we learn our way around the maze.

To be of practical benefit, knowledge needs to be personalized.

It takes a lot more knowledge to reach the final stage of the simplicity of seeing a whole picture—of understanding how all the pieces come together. It is what Leonardo da Vinci meant when he stated that simplicity is the ultimate sophistication.[9]

King David was referring to this when he stated, "When I look at all of your commandments, I will not be ashamed."[10] When King David grasped the grand sweep of all the commandments, he had a sense of the relationship between them. He understood the spirit of the laws and their inner logic. He intuited the grand principles that produced the details to begin with, and hence he understood what God wants from him in completely novel situations. He had made Jewish wisdom his home.

---

8 This is an adapted phrase from Leo Tolstoy, who stated, "There is no greatness where there is no simplicity, goodness, and truth."

9 However, see https://quoteinvestigator.com/2015/04/02/simple/, which attributes this quote to American playwright and ambassador Clare Boothe Luce. She stated: "The height of sophistication is simplicity."

10 Psalms 119:6.

PARTAKING OF GOD'S WISDOM

For the accumulation of knowledge to translate into the simplicity, depth, and coherence of wisdom, a process needs to happen.

"If you have toiled [in acquiring wisdom] and you have found, believe," say the Sages. "If you have not toiled and found, don't believe [that you have found]." This seems pretty basic. There are no handouts in life.

But there is a deeper point here. The wording here is unusual. "I have toiled and I have *found*." What he will learn will be a "find," a *metziah*. Elsewhere, the Sages tell us that one finds a *metziah*—an ownerless, lost object—*b'hesech ha'daat*—when one is distracted.[11] We toil and then, unexpectedly, we grasp what we have been striving for. This is because wisdom is ultimately a gift. It all suddenly falls into place, like finding an ownerless diamond in the street.

Three times a day we pray: "You bestow upon man *daat*, and you teach humans *binah*; bestow upon us *chochmah*, *binah*, and *daat*."[12]

We look on wisdom as our achievement. It is we who have toiled. And yet, in great humility, we turn to God and ask Him to grant us the gift of wisdom. In a sense, we are not asking God to grant us knowledge; we are requesting to partake of His knowledge.[13] We ask God for the gift of being able to make moral choices in an environment full of grays and subtleties; we ask to have clarity and see truth in a messy world. The greatest genius and the simplest Jew both use the same wording before God. On our own, we are up the creek. Connected to God, we stand a chance of becoming wise.

---

11 Talmud, Tractate *Sanhedrin* 97a: "Three things are found *b'hesech ha'daat*—the Messiah, a lost object, and a scorpion."

12 There is a slight variation in the Ashkenazi version.

13 Maimonides, *Mishneh Torah*, Laws of the Fundamentals of Torah 2:10, explains that God's wisdom is a total unity with whom He is, a part of His absolute goodness and His absolute unity.

30

THE WISDOM OF THE HEART—BINAH AND THE FEMININE

The heart is much closer than the mind
to the limbs of the body.

Rabbi Moshe Shapiro (a recent sage)

FROM ABSTRACTION TO INTEGRATION

Studying Torah is not just an intellectual exercise. When we learn God's words, we are purifying ourselves. We are connecting to Torah with the innermost sense of our being. A purely intellectual pursuit of Torah is an aberration of the Torah's intended purpose.[1] The goal is transformation of self—a rebirth of our own inner reality. The Sages say, "A person who studies Torah with the proper intention is as if he has made himself."[2] He has done so because, if studied correctly, he will not just become wiser, he will act wiser.

This level of understanding is called *binah*. *Binah* is wisdom of the heart.[3] While *binah* is an intellectual trait, it is the means through

1 *Rishfei Aish Dat*, *Shaar HaTorah*.

2 Talmud, Tractate *Sanhedrin* 99b.

3 See Chapter 29.

which *chochmah* speaks to the emotions.[4] It is the understanding that allows us to connect to knowledge and personalize it, and hence to assimilate and integrate it. It then becomes relevant to our lives, sharpening our moral compass and the way we act.

Chochmah is so high and spiritual that it is like someone else's information, and therefore it cannot be used in its raw form.[5] Just knowing about something is not likely to change us or to lead to action. *Chochmah* on its own is still-born.[6]

Because of this, *chochmah* is called *ayin*—nothingness.[7] It takes *binah* to turn *chochmah* into something of value to us. *Binah* is *yesh*—being. *Binah* is that faculty that elucidates the details of any concept, bringing it into the realm of the personal.[8] *Binah* bridges the gap between the majestic awe of abstract knowledge and our raw and vulnerable emotions. *Binah* is sometimes defined as the ability to understand one thing from another.[9] Because we understand what it means, we begin to see how it applies to all kinds of new situations in our lives. We begin to develop Torah-intuition, which is the ability to grasp our wisdom with a single act of the mind.

In the Kabbalistic wisdom, *chochmah* is placed on the male side, while *binah* is on the female side. This is because the feminine force in the world is comparable to the eternal womb—absorbing sparks and nurturing them into reality.[10] The female by nature abhors leaving something as a mere abstraction.[11] We will develop this below.

---

4 In the Kabbalistic literature, *chochmah* and *binah* are the two intellectual *sefirot* that give birth to the lower seven, which are emotive attributes.

5 *Rashi*, Exodus 31:3; it is important to note that *chochmah* is a very high spiritual source from which our *neshamot* come. (In the Kabbalistic wisdom, *chochmah* is *yud* in the Divine Name. This *yud* is really just a point, and it in turn is connected to an even higher source called *keter*.) So, the intention here of saying that it is "someone else's" is only in the sense that, at a practical level, we cannot yet use something that is so high and spiritual. It needs to come down through numerous filters before it is accessible to us.

6 Rabbi Tzadok HaKohen, *Dover Tzedek*, p. 48.

7 Job 28:12: "*Chochmah* appears from nothingness."

8 *Tanya*, chap. 3.

9 *Rashi*, Exodus 31:3.

10 *Maharal, Netivot Olam, Netiv HaAvodah*, chap. 16.

11 *Maharal, Derech Chaim on Ethics of Our Fathers* 1:5.

THE PARADIGM OF THE WOMB

Carl Jung stated that "there can be no transforming darkness into light and of apathy into movement without emotion." Intellect can determine the vision and the goals. The heart determines the desire, the passion, and the commitment. The road to the emotions is through the gateway of *binah*, as we shall see.

In Kabbalistic wisdom, *chochmah* is called *aba*, father, while *binah* is called *ima*, mother.[12] *Binah*, the mother, gives birth to action.

Previously, we described the woman's womb as that which nurtures the fetus to life.[13] Unless the female ovum absorbs a man's seminal spark, it will have no expression. Similarly, the *aba/chochmah* is a spark of inspiration that would quickly dissipate, unless the female *binah* would absorb it. In the Kabbalistic literature, *chochmah* and *binah* are called the two inseparable companions.[14] Each one without the other could not express itself.

Nurturing inspiration to a point of integration is hard work. In the case of a fetus, it takes nine months of providing a total environment in which that spark can grow into a child. Even after birth, it is the mother who nurses the baby.[15]

In the case of wisdom, we all have to call on our female side, on our *binah*, to transform *chochmah* into something that we can really feel and relate to.[16] This is *binah,* the mother, who has awakened within her a desire to join and unite with *chochmah* to create a new, sustainable, and relevant reality.

---

12 *Zohar*, Exodus, *Yitro* 5:1; *Tanya*, chap. 3.

13 See Chapter 7.

14 *Zohar Chadash* 3:4a. Rav Tzadok HaKohen, *Pri Tzaddik*, *Behar* 9 states: "And the joining of *chochmah* and *binah*—mind and heart—creates *daat*, which is deeper than all of them, as the verse (Proverbs 2:5) states, 'Then you will understand the fear of God and you will find the *daat* (knowledge) of God.'"

15 *Maharal*, *Chiddushei Aggadata*, Tractate *Shabbat* 53.

16 As mentioned above, *binah* itself is not an emotive *sefirah*, but it is the means through which intellect gets translated to the lower *sefirot*, which are emotive.

Because we now understand what our wisdom means to us individually and personally, we can apply it to all kinds of new situations.[17] We give birth to our children of wisdom.

MOTHER AND DAUGHTER IN THE HEAVENS ON HIGH

God Himself uses *binah* to influence the world. In the Kabbalistic literature, God bestows His beneficence on us through the *sefirot*, vessels that receive and transmit His will down to earth. These begin with *chochmah* and then go onto *binah*. *Binah* gives birth to the rest of the *sefirot*, which receive from it and transmit God's goodness earthwards.[18]

Binah, the mother, gives birth to the final stage of that transmission—the *bat*, daughter.[19] This is the feminine quality of *malchut* ("queenship") because it serves to reveal God's glory on this earth.[20] This revelation of God's presence on earth is called the *Shechinah*, also a feminine word. Hence, *malchut*, the daughter, is simply the completion of the process started by *binah*, the mother.[21]

These two—*binah* and *malchut*—are the two ends of what we call *nukva*, the feminine force.[22] The source of this power goes up to the highest of spiritual levels.[23] It is this feminine power that we all draw on to translate our spirituality into action.

God used this female side (*nukva*) to create the world.[24] In a way, the world is an environment—with physical and spiritual laws—just like the womb is an environment for a fetus.

---

17 *Rashi* ad loc.

18 *Chessed*, *gevurah*, *tiferet*, *netzach*, and *hod*. *Chochmah* and *binah* are known as the *arich anpin*, the long face, whereas the next five *sefirot* are known as the *zeer anpin*, the small face.

19 *Binah* is sometimes called the "higher mother," while *malchut* is called the "lower mother"; *Zohar* 1:50a. The concept "*ben*," son, refers to the lower *daat*; *Zohar* 3:290a.

20 There are ten *sefirot* that allow God's influence on the world to "chain down" from Him to us. *Malchut* is the last of these *sefirot*. Hence, it is the final filter through which all spiritual influences must ultimately go.

21 See the *Ramchal*, *Sefer Haklalim* 25: "She is the power behind reality in the lower realities (i.e., the world we live in)...which receives that which God bestows."

22 The Hebrew word for female is *nekeivah*. *Nukva* is an Aramaic form of this.

23 It is referred to in Aramaic as the "*sitra de'nukva*." See, for example, *Zohar* 3:45b, 14a.

24 *Sefer Galia Razia* (authorship unkown). Similarly, Rav Tzadok HaKohen says in *Machashavot Charutz* 3 that the world was created from *sitra de'gevurah*, which is the feminine side.

So too, when God gave us the Torah, He did so from *nukva*.[25] The Torah in heaven would be incomprehensible to us. It had to be brought down to earth from the heavens in a form that could be contained by our souls. It has to be written on a physical (albeit very holy) Torah scroll. This is the power of the female force.

Malchut is female. It serves to reveal God's presence on earth, the Shechinah.

WE ARE MIXTURES OF MALE AND FEMALE

Even though *binah* is female, there is no such thing as pure male and pure female on this earth. Both males and females have elements of maleness and femaleness within themselves and draw on this when a situation requires a *nukva* response.[26]

Friday night, for example, is a female time, and requires that we all—male and female—tune into that, as I shall now explain.

Whenever there is a transition from one environment to another, we need to draw on the female force within us to create that new environment. This is why, Friday night is female. We are now transitioning from the weekday to the holier framework of the Sabbath. Both male and female need to tap into their inner female to do this.

It is the female force which distinguishes Shabbat from the days of the week. It is the woman who lights the Friday night candles on behalf

---

However, the intention is not to say that *chochmah* was not involved, but rather that our world—with its scientific laws and its specific environmental parameters—could only be given expression if God's creative force was filtered through the female side. (That *chochmah* is also involved is indicated by the *Targum* on Genesis 1:1, "In the beginning God created..." which he translates as, "He created with his *chochmah*." Similarly, we say in the morning prayers, "You made them all with your *chochmah*." Similarly, "*Bereishis bara*" is translated in the *Targum* as "*b'choch'm'ta*," and every day in davening we say "*kulam b'chochmah asita*.")

25 Rabbi Tzadok HaKohen, *Resisei Laylah*.

26 Based on *Pardes Rimonim* 1:4, 7:2, 8:24. Hence, males are predominantly male with a good dose of female in them. Females are predominantly female with a good dose of male inside of them. The explanation of this is beyond our current scope. It has to do with the mixing and remixing of the right (male) and left (female) *sefirot* into their synthesis in the middle and then spreading out again to the male and the female side, but now each with elements of the other side.

of the men of the house as well.[27] In the famous *Lechah Dodi* song, sung during the *Kabbalat Shabbat* ("Welcoming the Shabbat") service, we call the Shabbat a bride *(kallah)*, a female. There are other signs of the "femaleness" of Friday night as well.[28]

By contrast, Shabbat in the morning is male. Now, we talk in the Shemoneh Esreh not of God's creation of the world (which He did from the female side) but of man operating in history—"Moses was happy...the Children of Israel kept the Sabbath," etc. At the end of this blessing, we now change the Shabbat to a male gender—"And they rested on *him*" and the male challah is cut. Maleness operates within the structure, once it has been created.

We see this idea expressed in many different places. Immediately below we will explain why it is that whether one is born Jewish or not is determined by the mother, but once a person is born Jewish, whether the person will be a Cohen, Levi or Yisrael will be determined by the father.

THE FEMALE—DEFINING THE IDENTITY OF THE INDIVIDUAL AND THE NATION

In Judaism, it is the mother, rather than the father, who determines whether the child is Jewish or not.[29] The Hebrew word for mother is *eim*[30] (or *ima*), which is the same word as *im*, meaning "if." The mother determines the "*if*," the conditions under which the child will express itself.[31] Furthermore, the word for female, *nekeivah*, comes from the word *nekov*, which means "to designate, articulate, or define."[32]

But it is not just individuals who are defined as Jewish or not by their mother. At two critical junctures in Jewish history, there were major

---

27 This is so even though the male is just as obligated in candle lighting as the female. On Chanuka, where the lighting of the candles is a different idea, a man lights the candles on behalf of the women of the house as well even though they are both equally obligated.

28 Hence we cut the "female" challah, and, in the last paragraph of the middle blessing of the Shemoneh Esreh, we say *Ve'yanuchu Vah*—"and they will rest on her."

29 Deuteronomy 7:3–4, as interpreted by the Talmud, Tractate *Kiddushin* 68b.

30 אם.

31 Rabbi Moshe Shapiro.

32 See, for example, Genesis 30:28.

husband-wife disputes as to what the future definition of the Jewish People would be.

- In the very first generation of Jewish history, Sarah and Abraham argued over Ishmael, the eldest son born of Hagar. Abraham wanted him as a part of the Jewish nation, but Sarah determined that Ishmael would be kicked out.[33] He would be blessed with a nation of his own.[34] God resolved the dispute by telling Abraham to listen to his wife Sarah.[35]
- In the second generation, there was a repeat of this dispute between Rebecca and Isaac with respect to their son Esau. Once again, the nascent nation-to-be—and world history with it—was at a critical juncture. Isaac was inclined to bless Esau as the firstborn, a decision to which Rebecca was utterly opposed. In the end, it was Rebecca who got to decide. She did this by dressing Jacob up as Esau to get his blessings.[36] She is never criticized for doing so. In fact, once Isaac delivered these blessings to Jacob, he recognized that he deserved them.[37]

We see that it is the woman who nurtures the spark, who produces the child, who determines its Jewishness, and who determined the very definition and parameters of the Jewish People. All of these examples are expressions of the same force of *binah*, the ability to create the appropriate environment, and, within that environment, to nurture a concept, a human being, or the Jewish nation into reality.

WOMEN'S WISDOM—SONG

For a woman, wisdom is song. King Solomon stated, "Her mouth was opened in wisdom."[38] The Midrash interprets this as the song that the Jewish People sang to God at the crossing of the Red Sea.[39] When

---

33 Genesis 21:10; see Chapter 7.

34 Genesis 21:18.

35 *Rashi*, Genesis 21:12.

36 Genesis, chap. 27.

37 Genesis 27:33.

38 Proverbs 31:26.

39 *Midrash Rabbah*, Exodus 23:4.

everything is integrated and all the pieces come together, the result is a song.

The deaf and blind American author and activist, Helen Keller, said that "the best and most beautiful things in the world cannot be seen or even touched; they must be felt with the heart." Without the power of *nukva* and its accompanying *binah* in the world, Judaism would never be a living system. We would never be able to taste the flavor of Judaism. Its books would be condemned to some obscure library—its knowledge an intellectual curiosity.

31
THE WISDOM OF ACTION

Whoever learns in order to teach, merits to learn and teach; and whoever learns in order to act, merits to learn and to teach, to keep, and to do.

Ethics of Our Fathers (4:5)

DAAT

When masculine *chochmah* combines with feminine *binah*, we get *daat*—a total connection and synthesis of the two.[1] *Daat* is therefore the knowing of something to the point where there is no separation between you and the knowledge. The knowledge becomes you, and hence you naturally speak and act according to your *daat*.

The Torah first uses the word *daat* with respect to sexual relations between a husband and a wife: "And Adam knew Eve, his wife";[2] "And Elkanah knew Chanah, his wife."[3] Marital relations are meant to be the culminating expression of a spiritual, emotional, intellectual, and physical bonding between husband and wife. At that point, they cleave

---

1 *Ramban, Iggeret Hakodesh*, chap. 1.

2 Genesis 4:1.

3 Samuel I 1:19.

to each other and are one. Hence, the verse states, "And therefore a man should...cleave to his wife, and they should be as *one* flesh."[4]

Chochmah is wisdom, *binah* is resonance with that wisdom, but true knowledge is *daat*. *Chochmah* is the wisdom of the mind; *binah* is the wisdom of the heart, the integration of *chochmah*; but *daat* is the wisdom of action, because you act out who you are.[5]

LIVING THE THOUGHTS THAT GOD HAS ABOUT MAN

Many times, we learn values or ideas and we find them interesting—e.g., a psychological study about forgiveness, an article about the state of the economy, a health alert, etc. We may be intellectually aroused (*chochmah*); we may even be gripped by the pathos of a story of someone who survived cancer, or in awe of a hero who saved someone from the tracks of the subway (*bina*). But we are not changed by the information, in part because we do not know what to do with it. We pass on, touched by the moment, but essentially unchanged.

Torah was never intended to be this. More than a book of beliefs, the Torah is a book of practice. The Torah, said Rabbi Hirsch, comes not to tell us how to understand God and the cosmos, but rather to tell us what we need to understand of ourselves in order to do God's will.[6] The Torah is not theology, "for while 'theology' contains the thoughts of man on God and things Divine, the Torah contains the thoughts of God on man and things human."[7] The Torah wants us to translate its wisdom into action—to be changed. In fact, if we don't read the Torah through the eyes of someone who wants to learn what to do, we will not understand it.[8]

If we don't read the Torah through the eyes of someone who wants to learn what to do, we will not understand it.

---

4 Genesis 2:24; see Chapter 24.

5 Rabbi Tzadok HaKohen, *Machashavot Charutz*.

6 Rabbi Shimshon Raphael Hirsch.

7 Ibid., as quoted in Dayan Grunfeld's introduction to *Horeb*, p. xlix.

8 In the words of Allan Bloom, *The Closing of the American Mind* (1987), books have to be read as their authors wish them to be read to fully understand them. So, in that sense, God asked us to read the Torah as a book of practice.

IN THE GRIP OF GOODNESS

Binah's purpose is to personalize the experience of the knowledge—to align our emotions with our thoughts. *Daat* takes this personalization and leads it to a change in character until our whole being is aligned with our values.[9] *Daat* resolves our ambiguities about good and evil.[10]

We begin to not only know and to feel the value but to be gripped by a need to live that way. *Daat* creates not only clarity but the inner will to exemplify that clarity. The *daat*-driven person not only lives with intellectual integrity but with total authenticity at every level of his being.

Most of us don't only know that murder is wrong, we live that idea. We won't pull out a knife on someone who bumps us on the subway. We won't even be tempted to. We don't have to tell ourselves that murder is wrong. We so totally identify with the value that we automatically respond to conflict or tension with murder clearly and safely off the table. The impossibility of us committing murder is a part of whom we are. This is the level of *daat*.

The wisdom of the Jews is their Torah. Yet, we don't call the Torah "the Book of Wisdom" because the Torah is not just a brilliant insight into the nature of man. It is a way to live a meaningful life. It is not wisdom only as an end but also wisdom as a means to the moral perfection of man.[11] "If there are no actions," says the *Maharal*, "there is no Torah."[12]

Certainly, someone who pours over holy texts is doing something of value in and of itself.[13] The study of Torah itself generates holiness and purifies us through our very engagement with it. But, for this to be true, we must have the end goal in mind. We need to also understand what we are supposed to *do*. We must be aiming to "walk the talk."[14]

9 *Tanya*, chap. 3.

10 Hence, at one level, *daat* is all about distinctions; Talmud, Tractate *Eruvin* 19a.

11 Dayan Grunfeld's introduction to *Horeb*, p. xlviii.

12 *Maharal, Drush al Hamitzvot*.

13 Rabbi Chaim of Volozhin, *Nefesh Hachaim*, Gate 4, chap. 1

14 Hence the name "Torah" applies also to the mitzvot (*Maharal, Drush al Hamitzvot*), as in Numbers 15:29: "There shall be one Torah for you." The word "Torah" here refers to the mitzvot. Similarly, see Exodus 12:49.

Only when we do this will the wisdom of Torah become a part of our core identity.

The action plan of the Torah is transformative. The Sages say that someone who stands for a Torah scroll but does not stand for a sage is a fool,[15] for the sage is a human Torah scroll. He is the human embodiment of that Torah—a Torah with a soul.

The Sages say that someone who stands for a Torah scroll but does not stand for a sage is a fool, for the sage is a human Torah scroll.

Upon seeing a great sage, we say a blessing: "Blessed be He who *shares* His wisdom with those who are in awe of Him." God shares His Torah, written on a Torah scroll, with the Torah written on the hearts and minds of the sage.

TORAH AND COVENANT ARE ONE IDEA

And so, when God agreed to share the Torah with us, He required commitment on our part. He demanded a covenant.[16] The Ark in which the Torah is kept is called the "Ark of the Covenant."[17] In the morning blessings of the Torah, we say, "Who chose us amongst the nations (the covenantal commitment) and gave us His Torah." Covenant and Torah are one blessing; one doesn't make sense without the other.

Through this covenant, God let us know that until the Torah actually changes us—puts us in harmony with God's vision for man—we are merely tourists of the Torah. And that was never the idea.

MOSES ACHIEVES DAAT

And so we have:

- *chochmah*—the wisdom of the intellect
- *binah*—the wisdom of the heart
- *daat*—the wisdom of action

---

15 Talmud, Tractate *Makkot* 22b.

16 In fact, the Torah describes many such covenants with God. See, for example, Exodus 34:10, 27; Leviticus 26:25, 45; Numbers 4:23; Deuteronomy 5:2.

17 Numbers 10:33, 14:44; see Chapter 20.

We see the relationship to these different kinds of wisdom in the growth of Moses:

- While tending to his father-in-law's sheep, Moses saw a burning bush.[18] The bush was aflame but it was not being consumed.[19] Moses was curious. He began to ask questions, approached the bush, and tried to understand.[20] This was the search for *chochmah*, the flash of insight.
- Moses then deepened his understanding. He understood that the source of this fire was holy—that the presence of God must be in this place. And, so, he responded; he internalized what he saw. Moses "hid his face, for he was afraid to look at God."[21] He reached a level of *binah*.
- But he wasn't done. He entered into a prophetic state.[22]

However, even then, Moses was being reactive—an act of submission. God wanted more from him—to liberate the suffering Jewish People: "Come...and you shall free My people, the Israelites, from Egypt."[23] God wanted from him the knowledge of action—the wisdom of *daat*, where his actions flowed naturally from what he knew.

This is the commandment of Jewish engagement. Moses could not escape this responsibility. To do so would be to be false to his God and false to himself.[24] And so, after his initial resistance, he no longer questioned.[25] He spent the rest of his life acting on what he knew to be true. His wisdom of *daat* was complete.

DAAT TORAH

There is one more level above the level of *daat*. After the Exodus, Moses began to sense and anticipate what God wanted of him. His natural

---

18 Exodus 3:2.

19 Ibid.

20 Ibid., v. 3.

21 Ibid., v. 6

22 See, however, *Ramban* ibid., v. 5.

23 Exodus 3:10.

24 Based on Rabbi J.B. Soleveitchik.

25 Exodus 4:18.

thinking was in harmony with God's will.[26] This is a special level of *daat* called *daat Torah*.

The Talmud tells us of three occasions when Moses actually initiated laws:[27]

- Moses added a day to the Jewish nation's preparations for receiving the Torah, turning six days at the foot of Mount Sinai into seven.
- Secondly, Moses divorced his wife.[28] This was because Moses needed to be pure and ready for prophecy at any time of the day or night. Miriam, in fact, criticized her younger brother for doing this, which led to her getting *tazaraat*—a kind of skin disease,[29] thereby delaying the whole nation while she recovered.[30]
- Finally, and most astonishingly, Moses broke the first set of Tablets that contained the Ten Commandments after finding out that the Jewish People had built the Golden Calf.[31]

In each case, God confirmed Moses' decision.[32] Moses had reached the level where he was pure *daat Torah*—a living Torah scroll. Moses could, on rare occasions, anticipate the thoughts of God not yet revealed to man. He could reveal what God was destined to reveal.

Only Moses could think with such Torah-harmony that his thoughts were included in the Torah itself. But we don't have to be Moses to have some level of *daat Torah*. When the great sages of every generation think about life, challenges, or the type of advice they give to people, their thinking is also *daat Torah*, for it is also forged on the anvil of a lifetime of being immersed in Torah.

Our job is to become so naturally attuned to the Torah's methodology of thought—to its values and sensitivities—that we too can develop

---

26 This is in contrast to the prophecy that Moses was to receive from God.

27 P. 87a.

28 Targum Onkelos to Numbers 12:1-2

29 *Tzaraat* is often incorrectly translated as leprosy.

30 Numbers 12:1–15.

31 Exodus 32:19; Deuteronomy 9:17.

32 Talmud, Tractate *Shabbat* 87a.

increasing levels of our own *daat Torah* to think about ourselves and the world around us as a Jew. This exalted state is no romantic dream. It is available to us all.

32
THE WISDOM OF QUESTIONS

My mother made me a scientist without ever intending to. Every other Jewish mother in Brooklyn would ask her child after school, "So? Did you learn anything today?" But not my mother. "Izzy," she would say, "did you ask a good question today?" That difference—asking good questions—made me become a scientist.

Isidor Rabi, Jewish Nobel physicist, A Jew Asks Why

THE BEGINNING OF WISDOM IS THE QUESTION

The fifth wisdom is the wisdom of questions. There comes a point where we have reached the highest form of wisdom that is within our grasp. But there are always things that are beyond our understanding. These are called "*mi yode'a*—who knows?"[1] The recognition that something goes beyond our own understanding is a wisdom in and of itself. The search itself is the first step to a deeper understanding.

The question of a wise man is half the answer.

The beginning of wisdom is a question. A wise question will, in and of itself, show a deeper understanding.

1 As in the song at the end of the Passover Seder, *Echad Mi Yode'a*—"Who Knows One?"

"The question of a wise man is half the answer," say the Sages.[2] It already points and guides us to the solution.

NEVER WALK AWAY FROM A QUESTION

As we saw, when Moses saw that the burning bush was not getting burned up, his curiosity was aroused, and he approached closer to try and understand.[3]

Moses could also have kept his distance from the bush and tried to figure out what was going on from afar. After all, the bush was burning; it was hot, and the strangeness that it didn't burn must have made Moses uncomfortable. Had he done so, perhaps Jewish history would have been very different. However, Moses embraced the discomfort, and what an opportunity that turned out to be! Moshe's curiosity wasn't just intellectual; it also emerged from his heart. He didn't just approach the bush for more information. He approached it open to the possibility that pursuing this mystery may change his life forever.

There is a straight line from Moses' curiosity, which led to the Exodus, and a part of the Haggadah that we read on the Seder night of Passover, for we seem to celebrate our national birth by asking questions.

Early in the Haggadah, we ask, "Why is this night different from all other nights?" Soon after, we read about the four sons who ask four different questions. Actually, only the wise son, the evil son, and the simple son ask.

The fourth son does not know how to ask. The Haggadah teaches that it is our responsibility to teach him how to ask questions.[4] We cannot rest when there is a Jew who does not know how to ask questions! He

---

2 *Ramban, Milchamot*, Tractate *Bava Batra*; *Migdal Oz*, Maimonides, Laws of Repentance, chap. 5.

3 Exodus 3:2–3.

4 The language of the Haggadah is "You should open for him…" In the *Shulchan Aruch* (*Orach Chaim* 473:7) this is codified as "if the child is not yet wise, the father should teach him how to ask."
Some commentators understand that the next lines of the Haggadah are a part of the father's response to this child: "Could it be that we need to say from the first of the month? etc." is a part of the answer of the father to this child.

will not engage, his curiosity will not be aroused, and he will stay where he is from a spiritual standpoint.

In fact, on the night of the Passover Seder, we do unusual things just to arouse the questions of young children sitting around the table. At one stage, we wash our hands as if to eat bread, but then dip *karpas* (a vegetable) in salt water and eat it instead. This, too, is to arouse questions.[5] Even a learned person, and even one conducting the Pesach Seder on his own, should do so in the form of questions and answers.[6]

Isn't it fascinating? The very night that we became a nation we celebrate by asking questions! This is a very Jewish way of grasping the most profound of events. The Torah instructs us, "And you should tell your child..."[7] We have to tailor-make the Exodus story to the understanding of each child.[8] But how do we know what each child needs? We look at his questions.

WE ARE ALL THE FOUR SONS OF THE PASSOVER SEDER

In truth, we all have elements of each one of the four sons within ourselves.[9] As people, we cannot be categorized and labeled. Sometimes negative emotions—e.g., anger, fear, or shame—interfere with our grasp of an issue. Sometimes, we feel so overwhelmed by an area that we simply don't know where to start, or we're too nervous to do so. We are the son who doesn't know how to ask.

Sometimes we may use our entire intellectual prowess to resist embracing areas of our growth that we are too fearful, angry, or ashamed to face up to. This is really what the Haggadah means by the evil son, for a child is not held accountable for evil behavior. This child also has a place around the Seder table.

And sometimes, we find ourselves apathetic and disengaged. We are the simple son requiring stimulation from the outside.

---

5 *Rashi / Rashbam, Pesachim* 114a. This is the reason brought by the *Mishnah Berurah* 473:21.

6 Tractate *Pesachim* 116a.

7 Exodus 13:8.

8 Rabbi Yitzchak Bordiansky, the Mashgiach of Kol Torah.

9 *Sefat Emet*.

We have different relationships with different aspects of our Judaism and we relate to God in different ways at different times. We are all four sons in one.

This is the lesson of the Seder. We declare that everyone's questions are important. No question is illegitimate, and there is no person on this earth who does not deserve the dignity of an answer to a genuine question. The *Mah Nishtanah* song ("Why is this night different from all other nights?") is traditionally said by the youngest child at the table. Even his questions are worthy of the entire table's attention.[10]

SOMETIMES, ALL WE ARE LEFT WITH IS THE QUESTION

"The purpose of knowledge is to know that we don't know," said the Chassidic master known as the "*Yid Hakodesh*—the Holy Jew."[11] The *Yid Hakodesh* was echoing what the Sages tell us, "Teach your mouth to say 'I don't know.'"[12] It takes confidence to say "I don't know," but our love for truth, of wanting to do the right thing, has to be stronger than the urge to say something, especially when asked.[13]

We may never find an answer to our question, but we grow immensely from asking.

We see this from the story of Mordechai and Esther read in the Scroll of Esther on Purim. When Mordechai was telling Esther that she needs to go in front of the king, he ends by saying, "Who knows whether it was just for such a time that you reached the position of royalty?"[14]

This seems strange. Mordechai had already told her that she has to go in to save the Jews. He just finished saying that if she hesitates to take the plunge, the Jews will be saved another way.[15] He should have ended with a powerful declaration that empowered Esther to complete her mission. Yet, he ends as if uncertain of her mission—"Who knows?"

10 *Chayei Adam* 130.

11 His real name was Rabbi Yaakov Yitzchak Rabinowitz.

12 Talmud, Tractate *Berachot* 4a.

13 Rabbi Chaim of Volozhin, *Ruach Chaim*, ibid.

14 Book of Esther 4:14.

15 Ibid.

The commentators explain that Esther had a question, "Why me? How did I get into this mess? Why was my successful and fulfilling life suddenly turned on its head?" Mordechai answers her, "Who knows?" There are some parts of our life we cannot explain. We are left with questions. We cannot always understand our journey. Sometimes, we see ourselves or others taking unexpected turns. We won't always have an explanation. We can only turn in awe to our omniscient God and declare that we will embrace and respect the mission that is the trajectory of our life.[16]

JOB AND THE REFUSAL OF INAUTHENTIC ANSWERS

God tests Job with terrible suffering. Job's friends come to comfort him and also to explain to him why God is doing this. Job rejects their explanations. Seemingly, their faith is greater than his. Yet, in the very last chapter, God surprisingly praises Job and condemns his friends.[17] This is because the explanations of Job's friends of God's behavior were drawn from pat answers. They had been told why there was suffering in the world, and they repeated them. However, they didn't really believe their own answers. Job, on the other hand, wouldn't accept answers that didn't seem authentic.[18] It wasn't for lack of faith in God that he questioned, but rather the very opposite. He was struggling to reconcile his belief in a just and all-powerful God with the issue of suffering.[19] Better to be left with an authentic question than to reconcile with a superficial answer.

Job's questions were a part of his faith. Through his own tribulations, he was coming to deepen his understanding of how God operates in this world. The search itself enhanced his depth of understanding. The courage to keep on asking questions was a delight in the eyes of God.

Job's courage to keep on asking questions was a delight in the eyes of God.

---

16 Rabbi Y.Y. Jacobson.

17 Job 42:7.

18 *Malbim*, Job, ibid.

19 Job 42:2–3.

No area of Judaism is too sacred to question.[20] It is for this reason that Maimonides, the searching thinker who looks to understand the reasons behind the mitzvot, stands on a higher plane than the simple believer.[21] (By this, he meant the observable effect of mitzvot, not their source or ultimate reason on God's side.) This does not mean that we are being asked to live in a state of constant existential angst.

As the Alter of Kelm put it:

> *Once you have accepted this reasonable tradition, you should intellectually analyze it and study proofs as if you have never heard the concepts before. You should analyze it until you come to a point where your intellect is independently convinced of the foundations of Judaism...In the end, you are rooted in tradition but led by your reason and intellect.*[22]

Without real questions, we would not grow in our understanding. We might acquire more information, but we won't acquire more wisdom. We might stretch the mono-dimensional plane on which we are operating, but we won't break through to a new dimension. We won't get deeper and more profound, and that is not the kind of faith that our God is asking of us.

---

20 It is true that asking questions about God's essence are generally unanswerable. But the limitation there would be epistemological—having to do with the limits of what is knowable and not because of the illegitimacy of asking.

21 *Guide to the Perplexed* 351. This is also the view of *Duties of the Heart*, intro. and 1:3, in contrast to *Kuzari* 2:26, 5:1.

22 Alter of Kelm, *Chochmah U'Mussar*, vol. 2, p. 76. See also Rabbeinu Bachya, Deuteronomy 13:7.

33

THE WISDOM OF SILENCE AND PROTEST

Learn to be silent, so that you will know how to speak.

Rabbi Mendel of Vorke

Silence takes many forms. There is the silence in the face of tragedy, such as, "and Aaron was silent."[1] There is the silence in the face of personal attacks, such as, "and to those who curse me, let my soul be silent."[2] There is also the silence that allows us to appreciate that the voice with which we speak always has layers and layers of depth that will be left below the surface. "Not every thought should be said," claimed the Kotzke Rebbe.[3]

The late Rabbi Moshe Shapiro was told of a new recording device that would turn off every time the speaker paused and turn back on when he resumed speaking. Rabbi Shapiro responded by saying, "In other words, this is a machine that leaves out the main thing that needs to be heard."

---

1 Leviticus 10:3. This was after the death of his two sons, Nadav and Avihu, for bringing a strange fire in front of God.

2 Said at the end of the *Shemoneh Esreh*, the silent prayer.

3 Based on *Kochav Hashachar*, by Simcha Raz, as quoted by Menachem Posner, Chabad.org.

Imagine, said Rabbi Yitzchak Hutner, that there is a brilliant and wise rabbi lecturing to his students. When that rabbi is pausing, he is thinking about what his students are ready to hear. He is figuring out how to translate the unfathomable depth of Judaism into that which they can conceive. Imagine, he said, that a student could read the silences of the rabbi. He would then have full access to his wisdom, and not just what the rabbi chose to communicate.[4] Perhaps this is what the Kotzke Rebbe meant when he stated that silence is the most beautiful of all sounds.[5]

Imagine that we could hear the silences of the Torah itself. This is what the Kabbalists try and do; they try to understand the level of the Torah that is called *sod* (secret)—that which starts out hidden from the eye.[6]

Perhaps the most important silence is the ability to be by yourself. Until you can be by yourself, you cannot be with anyone else either. Today, more than ever, we are in need of quiet, not only to hear the voices of others silenced by all the noise but to hear the voice within ourselves. When we do this, we will also hear others—the tones and nuances with which people tell us things, not just their electronic one-liners. And we will learn how to speak.

We are in need of quiet so that first we can hear the voice within ourselves.

TEACH YOUR MOUTH TO SAY "I DON'T KNOW"

Ethics of Our Fathers tells us:

> *A wise man does not speak before one who is greater than him in wisdom or age. He does not interrupt his fellow man's words. He does not hasten to answer. His questions are on the subject and his answers to the point. He responds to first things first and to latter things later. Concerning what he did not hear, he says, "I did not hear."' He concedes to the truth.*[7]

---

4 Rabbi Yitzchak Hutner, *Pachad Yitzchak*.

5 Based on *Kochav Hashachar*, by Simcha Raz, as quoted by Menachem Posner, Chabad.org.

6 We will discuss the wisdom of the Kabbalah in Chapter 36.

7 *Ethics of Our Fathers* 5:7.

The wise man will not butt in with his own ideas while his teacher or friend is speaking, thereby missing the teaching moment by the other. He will really listen. The wise man may give speeches, but he knows that "not every speech should be written down."[8] He will write profound things, but he will know that "not all writings are fit for print." He will know that, in fact, erasing is more important than writing.[9] And he will know, as Ludwig Wittgenstein put it, "Whereof one cannot speak, thereof one must remain silent."[10]

WHEN OUR VOICES NEED TO BE HEARD

It would be wrong to think that Judaism holds up silence as some meta-principle. Many situations require our voices to be heard. "Love that does not contain the element of criticism is not love," say the Sages.[11] However, this mitzvah to reprove our neighbor[12] requires exceptional wisdom and great sophistication.[13] First and foremost, we must do this by example, as Reish Lakish said: "Correct yourself first, and then correct others."[14]

The idea of this is rooted in a profound understanding that, in Judaism, I cannot say something is someone else's problem. Everything is my problem. It is *my* problem because my fellow's soul shares with me its source in the collective Jewish soul which was formed at Sinai.[15] There is ultimately a very deep, even mystical sense of unity among us that leads to us all being responsible for each other.[16] We all share each other's spiritual reality.[17] We all have some element of our neighbor inside of us.

---

8 Kotzker Rebbe, based on *Kochav Hashachar*, by Simcha Raz, quoted by Menachem Posner, Chabad.org.

9 Ibid.

10 End of *Tractatus Logico-philosophicus*.

11 *Midrash Rabbah,* Genesis 54:3.

12 Leviticus 19:7.

13 *Maharal, Netiv Hatochachah*, chap. 1.

14 Talmud, Tractate *Bava Metzia* 107b.

15 *Rashi*, Exodus 19:2.

16 Rabbi Moshe Cordevero, *Tomer Devorah* 1:4.

17 *Ritva*, Talmud, Tractate *Rosh Hashanah* 29a, explaining, "For all of the Jewish nation is responsible for the other."

It is *my* problem because I need my fellow as he needs me to repair the world.[18] It is *my* problem because my moral sensitivity demands that I not be a passive bystander when wrong is being perpetrated.[19] And it is *my* problem because of my deep concern and love for my fellow Jew's spiritual wellbeing.[20] Judaism is not about simply caring for yourself and letting the rest be damned.

If we failed to prevent an outrage that we could have prevented, we will pay the price as if we committed the outrage ourselves.[21] Noah, a holy man, never reached his true greatness because he never reached out to correct his generation.[22]

Jews have been and must continue to be the voice of protest at injustice in the world.

The Hebrew word for reproof—*tochachah*—comes from the word *hochachah*, which means "to prove"; in the recipient's mind and heart, that matter is proven as a value he now wants for himself. Rebuke is probably the last thing—especially in our day—that will achieve this. Rather, we have to hug these people close and inspire their Torah commitments through authentic and unconditional love.[23]

PROTEST

Even when we know that our efforts at constructive reproof will be fruitless, often-times we must still protest.[24] Protest is not to effect change as much as it is the moral voice that keeps the issue—and our souls—alive. We get used to injustice and all sorts of evil. Protest tells us that even though we feel helpless right now, we refuse to lose our sensitivity; we refuse to accept that this is norm.

We learn of Abraham risking his life by protesting against the idolatry of his time. From that time on, Jews have been the quintessential

18 *Ramchal, Daat Tevunot*, p. 189; see Chapter 3.

19 See Chapter 9.

20 *Chatam Sofer*, introduction to responsa on *Yoreh Deah*.

21 Talmud, Tractate *Sanhedrin* 27b; *Shavuot* 39a; *Rashi*, Deuteronomy 29:28.

22 *Kedushat Levi*, Genesis 6:9.

23 *Chazon Ish*, *Yoreh Deah* 2:22.

24 *Shaar Hatziun* 508:3.

conscience of the world, protesting injustice wherever we have seen it, taking moral stands when others have been too frightened to do so. This is our holy chutzpah.[25]

In the story of Esther, Mordechai refuses to bow to Haman, willing to risk all for the sake of what he believes in.[26] Edmund Burke is reputed to have said, "the only thing necessary for the *triumph* of *evil* is for good men to do nothing."

But protest is a tricky business. Personal feelings, animosity, and a sense of heroism can so easily cloud one's judgment. Judaism has rules as to when and when not to take such action. When should protest reach the level of active rebellion, as in the case of the Maccabees against the Greeks in the Chanukah story? And when should our protest be silent but continue to act unintimidated, even if it leads to our own death, as in the case of Rabbi Akiva?[27]

We cannot rely on our moral compass for these decisions; there are too many heated emotions and feelings of self-righteousness that distort our thinking. Moreover, once unleashed, we cannot know where the process will lead to and what hatred and violence will follow. It is so easy to become our own god and believe in our cause more than we believe in the God-given principles that were given to us. Our own take of what Hashem wants, even if it is coming from "deep inside of us," may be gloriously wrong, which is why we look to Torah authorities for guidance before embarking on a journey that involves carving out your own path.

"Aggressiveness is an important trait that is needed for the world. But it is like fire: In limited and directed amounts, it is good for cooking, etc. But when it surges forth unbridled, it can destroy everything."[28]

Moreover, it is so easy to hate "the enemy" and justify everything in the name of fighting evil. "An act of protest, which causes damage to

---

25 Every person is obligated to say, "When will my deeds reach the deeds of my forefathers Abraham, Isaac, and Jacob?"; *Tanna d'Bei Eliyahu*, chap. 25.

26 Book of Esther 3:2.

27 Talmud, Tractate *Berachot* 61b.

28 Rabbi Moshe Yechiel Weiss Tzuriel, *Beit Yechezkel* 5:6 (p. 181).

another, must be pure in its intent. It may not contain even a trace of personal benefit."[29]

THE STILL SMALL VOICE

In that awe-inspiring tune, *Unetaneh Tokef*, which we say on Rosh Hashanah and Yom Kippur, the words read, "And He will blow on the great shofar; and a thin, still sound will be heard."[30] Sometimes we hear God speaking to us through a great noise—a mighty upheaval in our lives. But sometimes we must listen carefully—deep inside ourselves—for the "still quiet voice."

---

29 Rabbi Yaakov Naiman, author of *Darkei Mussar*, as quoted in *MiShulchan Gavoha*, Numbers 25:13.

30 Based on Kings I 19:12.

34

THE WISDOM OF THE ORAL LAW

Learning the Torah is a spiritual workout.

Shimon Peres, former President of Israel

THE WRITTEN TORAH REQUIRED AN ORAL ONE

Anyone who studies the Torah will realize that, for all its majestic messages, there must be an accompanying explanation to the written text. Just two of many examples:

- The Torah tells us to slaughter animals "as God commanded you."[1] However, nowhere in the Torah does it explicitly state how to slaughter an animal. God must be referring here to the explanation He gave us in the Oral Law.[2]
- The Torah tells us to wear things it calls "tefillin" between our eyes.[3] Yet, nowhere in the written text do we understand what tefillin are and where between the eyes they need to be. Should they be round or square? Blue, pink, or black? Should they be pointed or flat? What substance should be used in making them? Should anything be written inside of them, and if so, what?

1 Deuteronomy 12:21.

2 *Rashi*, ibid.

3 Deuteronomy 6:8.

In short, if God gave us the Torah as a way of revealing His will to man and then failed to reveal all these details, He has played a nasty trick on us.[4] The message begins, but it is unintelligible to the recipients.

Imagine getting a call from God Himself, but when you pick up, all you get is static. You know God is telling you something, but you cannot make out the message. That is how the Torah would be without the Oral Law.

Let's take another example: the Shabbat. The Torah tells us not to do any *melachah*—creative work—on the Shabbat.[5] Yet, it does not define what *melachah* is,[6] even though the Shabbat is central to our identity as Jews.[7] It is only through the Oral Law that we know that there are thirty-nine categories of forbidden work and that these are taken from the categories that went into building the Tabernacle, as we explained above.[8] The connection between the Shabbat and the Tabernacle is a deep one,[9] but we are only alerted to that through the Oral Law. Had there not been an Oral Law, the form of the Shabbat itself would have been unfathomable!

There are hundreds of such examples in the Written Law. Even the vowels and punctuation in the Written Law are part of the Oral Law.[10] Someone who tries to understand what Judaism is all about from the Written Law alone will be left dumbfounded and confused. In fact, without the accompaniment of the Oral Law, it can be stated that one is not studying the Torah at all.[11] Without the Oral Law, there would not be a single mitzvah that we could understand fully.[12]

---

4 This is especially true since God makes it clear that there are consequences to our observance and non-observance.

5 Exodus 31:14.

6 *Smag*, introduction. The Written Torah only mentions two prohibited acts, carrying (Exodus 16:29; Numbers 15:32) and lighting a fire (Exodus 38:3), each for a distinctive reason; see Tractate *Shabbat* 95a, *Tosafot* ad loc., and *Shabbat* 70a.

7 Exodus 31:16.

8 Talmud, Tractate *Shabbat* 49a–b, as per *Tosafot* there.

9 See Chapter 23.

10 *Smag*, introduction.

11 Rabbi Joseph B. Soleveitchik, *Kinus Teshuvah* lecture, 1979, as reported by Arnold Lustiger in *Jewish Action*, Fall 1993. See also *Maharal*, *Gur Aryeh*, Exodus 15:25.

12 *Maharal*, *Beer Hagolah* 4, p. 50.

Both the Written Law (the Five Books of Moses) and the Oral Law comprise the spiritual grandeur of the word of God given at Sinai.[13] Moses received the entire Oral Law,[14] although in a highly condensed fashion.[15]

ORAL LAW COULD NOT HAVE BEEN GIVEN IN A WRITTEN FORM

As we have shown, it is obvious from looking at the Written Law that there is an Oral Law accompanying it.

The original text of the Torah is in reality no more than a shorthand text that is so brilliantly composed that it makes sense even in its shorthand face, while its longhand meaning is discernible only by making use of the Oral Law's keys. It is only in this longhand form that we can understand the specific instructions for day-to-day living and for all the changing circumstances of mankind.

The Written Torah is in the form of principles and generalities, while the Oral Law represents the applications of the Torah to new situations.

But why did God see the need to separate the Torah into two parts—a written and an oral?

One reason is that God wanted the Chumash text to be comprehensible at its basic level to even to a five-year old.[16] Then, anyone ready for the next level can climb upwards by using the Oral Law, while those who are not ready can still have a relationship with the Torah.[17]

But there is another, equally profound reason. As life unfolds, there is no end to new situations that arise. Each generation faces unique circumstances, technology advances, and no two people live the same lives. Since each individual is constantly being exposed to different situations, conceivably without end, we will always have to know how given

---

13 Maimonides, introduction to the last chapter of Tractate *Sanhedrin*, the Eighth Principle of the Thirteen Principles of Faith.

14 Talmud, Tractate *Berachot* 5a and several other places; *Sifri*, beg. *Parashat Behar*.

15 *Ohr Hachaim*, Leviticus 13:37; *Midrash Tanchuma*, *Parashat Ki Tisa* 16; This is the eighth of the Thirteen Principles of Faith.

16 *Ethics of Our Fathers* 5:21: "At five, a child should learn Chumash."

17 *Maharal*, *Tiferet Yisrael*, chap. 69.

principles apply to these new situations. A Written Law that would attempt to contain all possible eventualities would have been endless.[18] Therefore, the solution was to give a Written Torah in the form of principles and generalities, together with an Oral Law in the form of particulars,[19] but which is never complete in its new applications.[20] A major consequence of this is that it allows the human impulse to innovate without compromising the integrity of the law.[21]

Any attempt to incorporate all of the Oral Law into the written text would have been still-born. It would have simply been too long, requiring huge libraries and then huge libraries more.[22] Had all of Oral Law been written out, the text could never have contained all the tools of interpretation,[23] nor could it have contained all the possible applications to new situations.[24]

Had the Torah been a written text only, other major problems would have arisen. A Written Law alone could not avoid all ambiguities, for there is always more than one way to understand a written text.[25] The Oral Law resolves possible contradictions between different verses,[26] and it tells us what the intention of the verse really is.[27]

During the time of the Romans, when the Jews were being persecuted mercilessly and Torah study was outlawed, the main principles of the Oral Law were written at first in the form of the Mishnah and then expanded by recording later discussions between the sages on

---

18 Ecclesiastes 12:12: "There is no end to the making of many books."

19 *Midrash Tanchuma, Parashat Noach* 3.

20 *Maharal, Beer Hagolah* 1.

21 *Chazon Ish*, as brought in *Peer Hador*, vol. 3, p. 79; see also Rabbi Tzadok HaKohen, *Machashavot Charutz*, p. 113.

22 Talmud, Tractate *Eruvin* 21a, based on Ecclesiastes 12:2.

23 Talmud, Tractate *Shabbat* 31a.

24 *Midrash Tanchuma, Ki Tisa* 16; *Midrash Rabbah* Exodus 41:16. One has only to look at a major Torah library to begin to understand the extent of the Oral Law. The writing down of the Oral Torah has resulted in so many volumes and so many libraries; a digitalized program of such books, *Otzar HaChochmah* has over 90,000 books.

25 Rabbi Joseph Albo, *Sefer Ha'ikkarim* 3:23.

26 *Smag*, introduction.

27 *Ramchal, Maamar Ha'ikkarim*, chap. 10.

the Mishnah. This is known as the Gemara. The Mishnah and Gemara combined comprise the Talmud.

The extreme oppression of the Romans was making it near impossible to ensure a perfect transmission from one generation to the next.[28] But even then, the law remained essentially oral. This is because the Mishnah, and even the expanded Gemara, is written in such a way that it still requires a teacher for it to be fully accessible.[29]

THE HUMAN MIND—THE REPOSITORY OF THE ORAL LAW

The holiness of the Written Law is contained in its letters. They are the vessels that hold its holiness.[30] This means that the Written Torah has an independent reality from us; it is written with letters on parchment. We can study it and integrate it, but its essential holiness still remains in the Torah scrolls. Hence, there is always a distinction between our reality and the reality of the Written Torah. We are here, and the Torah scroll is there.

The true place of the Oral Law remains in our minds and not in any text.

Still, the holiness of the Oral Law cannot be contained by the written word. The true place of the Oral Law remains in our minds and not in any text.[31] This creates a type of bonding with the Torah that otherwise would not be possible. In fact, had there not been an Oral Law, we would never have been able to become totally one with the Torah. This is the seminal characteristic of the Oral Law.

---

28 The first writing of the Mishnah was written by Rabbi Yehudah HaNasi who took advantage of his close relationship with the Roman ruler Antoninus to produce this great work. An additional reason necessitated the writing down of the Oral Law. The Jewish people had begun to spread throughout the Diaspora and their connection to a purely Oral Law would be more tenuous.

29 Therefore, the Talmud is full of statements such as: "There is no order to the Mishnah"; "This statement is written abbreviated," i.e., with gaps in the sentence; "The words of the Talmud are poor in this place [i.e., the idea is not expressed with all its details] and rich in another place."

30 Rabbi Tzadok HaKohen, *Resisei Laylah*, p. 156.

31 *Maharal, Tiferet Yisrael*, chap. 68.

Since the Oral Law resides in us, we can become living Torah scrolls, affecting a total fusion of the Torah with man.[32] Each person, at the level of his understanding, can become a repository of the Oral Law.[33] Hence, the Rizhiner Rebbe, when asked why he didn't write books, answered, "I write my books on the hearts and minds of my students."

THE JEWISH MELODY OF THE ORAL LAW

It is interesting that although other religions tried to co-opt the Written Law,[34] there was never an attempt to co-opt the Oral Law. As one non-Jewish translator of the Mishnah (the kernel of the Talmud) put it, "The Oral Law speaks with a melody that only a Jewish ear can hear." The Oral Law cannot be co-opted because no text can fully contain it. Existing as it does in the hearts and minds of the Jewish People, it is an unsteal-able commodity.[35]

---

32 Ibid. See also Rabbi Chaim son of Betzalel (the brother of the *Maharal*), *Sefer Hazechuyot*, and Rabbi Tzadok HaKohen, *Machashavot Charutz*, p. 113.

33 See Chapter 27.

34 Notably the Christians, who call it the Old Testament. However, already prior to this, the Greeks had ordered a translation of the Torah into Greek known as the Septuagint. See Rabbeinu Bachya, Exodus 34:27, and *Yalkut Shimoni*, *Parashat Ki Tisa*, end.

35 *Maharal*, *Beer Hagolah* 4; *Chiddushei Aggadata* (vol. 2), Tractate *Gittin*, p. 123.

35
THE WISDOM OF PROPHECY

The pyramids fell, great empires came and went, but in the eternal words of our Torah, there has been no change.

Shimon Peres, former President of Israel

THE ACCURACY OF PROPHECY

If God has a purpose for this world, He must have a way of revealing that purpose. That message was contained in the Torah. Bringing the Torah to earth had to involve a process that was accurate and clear.[1] The logic of the Sage could not reliably reveal God's wisdom. Subject to human limitation, wisdom can always be wrong.[2] Do we not see a long history of great philosophers all arguing with each other, each using his best logic? Only prophecy could ensure the integrity and clarity of the process.[3]

Hence, belief in prophecy is one of the Thirteen Principles of Faith.[4] Prophecy is highly accurate in two ways: First, the prophet knows for

1 *Ramchal, Derech Hashem* 3:3:4.

2 *Rashba*, responsa 8:9.

3 Ibid.; Rabbi Tzadok HaKohen, *Machashavot Charutz*, no. 17, p. 142.

4 Maimonides, *Mishneh Torah*, Laws of the Foundations of Torah 7:1.

sure that he is having a prophetic vision.[5] Second, every prophet is clear about the interpretation of any parable or other aspect of his vision.[6]

MOSES' PROPHECY—REVELATION OF GOD'S WILL

Although there were many different levels of prophecy,[7] Moses' prophecy towered above all the rest. He was but the human instrument that God used to communicate, with no subjectivity of his own.[8] This was because he was tasked with revealing God's Torah to mankind.[9] At Sinai, not only did Moses speak to God face-to-face, but so did the entire Jewish People.[10] In this way, the Jewish People were able to authenticate Moses' prophecy.[11] Moses sustained his level of prophecy for the rest of his life.[12] Other prophets only had individual moments when they had their prophecies, and they only prophesized in visions or dreams.[13]

Moses was but the human instrument that God used to communicate, with no subjectivity of his own.

PROPHETS AFTER MOSES

After the Torah was revealed, the role of subsequent prophets was primarily to reprove the nation.[14] In this role, they were fearless, lonely men of faith. Jeremiah nearly lost his life when he entered the Temple and dramatically announced that if the people do not repent, the

---

5 *Ramchal, Daat Tevunot* 180, p. 202.

6 *Derech Hashem* 3:3:4.

7 *Mishneh Torah*, Laws of Foundations of Torah 7:2–3.

8 *Sifri, Parashat Matot*: God spoke through the throat of Moses. Numbers 12:8. This is known as prophecy through a clear lense; Maimonides, *Shemoneh Perakim*, introduction to *Ethics of Our Fathers*.

9 Numbers 12:6–8; *Derech Hashem* 3:5:2.

10 *Siftei Chachamim*, Numbers 30:2; Maimonides, *Shemoneh Perakim*, introduction to *Ethics of Our Fathers*.

11 *Mishneh Torah*, Laws of Foundations of Torah 8:2.

12 Numbers 12:8.

13 *Derech Hashem* 3:5:2.

14 *Mishneh Torah*, Laws of Foundations of Torah 9:2; see also ibid., Laws of Repentance 4:2; Rabbi Joseph Albo, *Sefer Ha'ikkarim* 3:8. A secondary task was to clarify certain Torah laws. See, for example, Isaiah 58:13–14; see also how the Talmud, Tractate *Bava Kama* 2b, understands from Kings I 22:11.

Temple would be destroyed.[15] He was accused of making up bad news, of being a heretic, and of being worthy of execution. Not even this made a dent in his courage, and he continued with his mission:

> *Amend your ways and your wrongdoings, and I [God] will let you go on living...in the land that I gave to your ancestors forever...[But] You steal, you kill, you commit adultery, you swear falsely...and then you come and appear before Me in this house that bears my name [the Temple] and you say: "We'll be safe."...Do you believe that this house that bears My name is a refuge of thieves?*[16]

The prophets had no armies and no backup. They had only their own voice as the messenger of God, unsparing in articulating the foibles and failings of the age. And yet, remarkably, their message has retained relevance and potency—often in unmatched prose—through the ages.

> *Thus said God, the Lord...Who gave breath to the people upon it and life to those who walk thereon: I, the Lord...have summoned you, and I have grasped you by the hand. I...appointed you a covenant people, a light of the nations—opening eyes deprived of light, rescuing prisoners from confinement, from the dungeon those who sit in darkness.*[17]

RUACH HAKODESH

In the Bible, we have two sets of books that are revealed prophecy. The first is the Five Books of Moses, which comprise the Torah. The second is the set of books called the Prophets—the *Neviim*. There were many prophets, but only those with a message for future generations were included in Prophets.[18] These include forty-eight men and seven women.[19]

---

15 Jeremiah 26:1–6.

16 Ibid. 7:3–11.

17 Isaiah 42:5–7.

18 Talmud, Tractate *Megillah* 14a.

19 Ibid., 14a–14b. The females were Sarah, Miriam (the sister of Moses), Deborah, Chanah, Abigail (to whom King David was married), Chuldah, and Esther (of the Purim story).

A third group of books, called the Writings (*Ketuvim*), were revealed at a level lower than prophecy (even if some of its authors were prophets) called *ruach hakodesh*—Divine inspiration. This, too, is a level of great clarity.[20] The amazing thing is that, in every generation, there have always been great people who have experienced *ruach hakodesh*.[21] In fact, even today, every parent who names a child does so with *ruach hakodesh*, so that the name matches the essence of the newborn.[22]

HOW ONE BECAME A PROPHET

Someone could not simply decide to become a prophet. Prophecy was a gift from God.[23] Still, a person could prepare himself so that he was spiritually at the right level. For a start, the potential prophet was one who had perfected his character.[24]

There were many different levels of prophecy, but all of these (other than the prophecy of Moses) worked in the same way.[25] When a prophetic vision would come over a prophet, it would take over his entire body.[26] He would no longer be in control of his emotions and senses, but rather would fall into a deep trance.[27]

This is because it was impossible to perceive the glory of God directly as Moses did.[28] Hence, he could only do so through his power of imagination, and from there it would work up to the intellect. Once it reached the intellect, the prophetic message would be engraved in his mind. Hence, it was a bestowal of Godly influence that went not directly through the mind, but indirectly through the power of imagination in

20 *Derech Hashem* 3:3:1–2; *Sefer Ha'ikkarim* 3:10.

21 Rabbi Shlomo Wolbe, *Alei Shur*, vol. 1; *Ramban*, Tractate *Bava Batra* 12a. The *Tumim*, *Kitzur Takfo Kohen*, says that the *Shulchan Aruch* was written with *ruach hakodesh*.

22 *Shaar Hagilgulim*, Introduction, 23.

23 *Ramchal*, *Mesilat Yesharim*, chap. 26. He is referring to *ruach hakodesh*, but this also applies to prophecy.

24 *Mishneh Torah*, Laws of Foundations of Torah 1:1.

25 Ibid. 7:2.

26 *Derech Hashem* 3:3:6.

27 Ibid. 3:5:3.

28 *Daat Tevunot* 180, p. 202.

the heart. Once the prophecy reached the mind, it did not require further processing, but rather was perceived as a readily-understood message.[29]

The whole process filtered the experience of God that would otherwise be too intense, and hence God appeared to the person as if seen through multiple lenses.[30] Such a person was lifted up to a different spiritual plane by the experience.[31]

THE PROPHET AND THE SAGE

Once the Torah was revealed in the world, no prophet could contradict what was written in the Torah. Neither he nor any other Jew could add or subtract from it.[32] It was now in the hands of the sages of each generation. Of course, since Torah wisdom was one of the prerequisites of prophecy, a prophet also had the status of a sage,[33] but he had no extra status in determining the law than a sage who was not a prophet. In the words of Maimonides, "Even if a thousand prophets said the law was one way and a thousand and one sages said that the law was the other way, the law would be like the thousand and one sages."[34] Anticipating that there would be disputes amongst the sages, God determined that the law should be like the majority.[35]

The prophet received a message from God. It was a top-down system. The sages, on the other hand, work with a bottom-up approach. They start by the given Written and Oral Laws and work their way upwards, as high as they can go, without limitation.[36]

Each one had an advantage and a disadvantage. The prophet had the advantage of absolute clarity.[37] The sage might err in his logic by

---

29 Ibid.

30 *Derech Hashem* 3:5:4.

31 *Mishneh Torah*, Laws of Foundations of Torah 7:1.

32 Ibid. 9:1, based on Deuteronomy 4:2. This is the principle of "It is not in the heavens"; see Tractate *Temurah* 16, amongst many other places.

33 *Mishneh Torah*, Laws of Foundations of Torah 7:1.

34 Maimonides, introduction to the Mishnah.

35 Exodus 23:2.

36 Rabbi Tzadok HaKohen, *Machashavot Charutz* 17, p. 142.

37 Ibid.

perhaps comparing two variables that should not have been compared, or in some other way.

Even if a thousand prophets said the law was one way and a thousand and one sages said that the law was the other way, the law would be like the thousand and one sages.

On the other hand, the prophet was limited by his overall spiritual stature to the type and level of prophecy he could have. Some did not see words (a higher level) but only pictures and parables.[38] A sage, by contrast can stretch his mind beyond his bodily limits. Hence, the Talmud says that, in this sense, a sage is preferable to a prophet.[39]

The Kabbalistic wisdom states: "The Divine spirit continuously rests upon a wise man, [but] upon a prophet, [only] at times."[40] A person who spends his nights and days immersed in Torah wisdom eventually becomes imbued with an almost intuitive grasp of what God wants and, in a fashion, gets far deeper than the prophet could achieve.[41]

AFTER PROPHECY STOPPED

Prophecy stopped for various reasons. For one, a prophet needed the extra boost of the holiness of the land—perhaps of the Ark of the Covenant—to gain his initial prophecy.[42] No new prophets appeared after the destruction of the First Temple, though seven of them survived into the beginning of the era of the Second Temple.[43]

The end of prophecy coincided with the greatest flowering of the Oral Law that history has known. In fact, the great desire of the nation to delve deeper and deeper into the Oral Law—levels of depth not available to prophecy—was a contributing cause to the demise of prophecy.[44]

---

38 *Sefer Ha'ikkarim* 3:9.

39 Talmud, Tractate *Bava Batra* 12a.

40 *Zohar*, Exodus 6:2.

41 *Machashavot Charutz* 17, p. 142.

42 *Sefer Ha'ikkarim* 3:11. For another reason, see Rabbi Tzadok HaKohen, *Resisei Laylah*.

43 Talmud, Tractate *Sanhedrin* 11a.

44 *Machashavot Charutz*, p. 141–42.

This was the time of the discussions recorded in the Babylonian and the Jerusalem Talmuds, as well as other great works. The gap left by the loss of prophecy was filled by this golden era of oral erudition to such a degree that the rabbis of that time are known simply as "the Sages."

36
THE WISDOM OF KABBALAH

The Zohar is written in code. Someone who does not have the keys to the code will not be able to understand it.

The Ari[1]

KABBALAH NEEDS A TEACHER

When Moses was given the Tablets by God, there was a moment of transition when God's grip (so to speak) held onto the one side of the Tablets while Moses gripped them on the far end, leaving a space in the middle.[2]

The part that God gripped reflects those parts of the unrevealed Torah—the unfathomable, indefinable universe preceding all mass right at the beginning of creation.

The part held onto by Moses became the revealed Torah, accessible to all Jews. The part in the middle consisted of the inner Torah, the mysteries meant to be revealed only to those of special merit.[3] This is Jewish mysticism—the secrets of the Torah (*Sitrei Torah*) called "Kabbalah."

---

1 As quoted in Rabbi Chaim Friedlander's introduction to the *Daat Tevunot*. See also the *Ramchal, maamar* on the Aggadot, concerning midrashim in general.

2 *Midrash Rabbah*, Exodus 47:6.

3 Rabbi Shimon Schwab in the name of the Telzer Rav, quoted in *The Dynamics of Dispute*, p. 4.

The word *Kabbalah* literally means "received"—the received wisdom—for it has remained essentially oral. Even those who wrote about it did so in such a way that their books could not be understood unless one had been taught Kabbalah orally by someone already expert in this wisdom.[4] The written works of the Kabbalists reveal little and hide much.[5] The great Kabbalist, the holy Ari, wrote all his works in the form of a parable.[6] Even the fact of the parable was disguised.[7] Similarly, the *Zohar*, the primary Kabbalistic work, was written in parables and riddles.

Therefore, if one has not had a teacher in this area of wisdom, one cannot fully understand it.[8]

THE FOUR LAYERS OF THE TORAH

Since everything that is in the Oral Law is hinted at in the Written Torah, there is a layer of understanding the Torah that is purely Kabbalistic. This is known as *sod*—secret. It is the fourth and deepest level of interpretation of the Five Books of Moses.

The four levels of interpretation are *pshat*, *remez*, *derush*, and *sod*.[9] The first letters of each form the acronym *Pardes*, which literally means a field. Journeying through the layers of Torah is like journeying through a field of wisdom that includes the greatest Kabbalistic secrets.[10]

Journeying through the layers of Torah is like journeying through a field of wisdom that includes the greatest Kabbalistic secrets.

Pshat is the simplest meaning of the text. *Remez* is that which is hinted at in the text, sometimes through their numerology or because of a specific choice of the wording or because

---

4 *Ramban*, introduction to the Torah.

5 *Raavad*, introduction to his commentary on *Sefer Hayetzirah*.

6 Rabbi Chaim of Volozhin in the name of the Vilna Gaon, as heard from him by Rabbi Avraham Simchah, his nephew. See Rabbi Chaim Friedlander, introduction to the *Ramchal's* "138 Openings of Wisdom," pp. 10–11.

7 Ibid. However, the Arizal did use an anthropomorphic model that does allow for us to understand much of what he wrote at our level.

8 *Ramban*, introduction to the Torah; *Ramchal*, *maamar* on the Aggadot.

9 Rabbi Eliyahu Dessler, *Michtav Me'Eliyahu* 4:216.

10 See below, where these four levels are also compared to a tree.

of the thematic flow of the text. They allow for the individualization and personalization of the Torah. Through *remez*, every person can understand how the Torah comes to nurture his unique qualities. Hence, everyone's names, i.e., their inner essence, are hidden in the Torah.[11]

Derush is what God wants us to understand after looking closely at the exact word-usage, grammar, and others aspects of the text. *Derush* translates into the action plan, the halachic (legal) parameters that the text speaks to us. To achieve this level, we also have to use a certain methodology of logic, like the thirteen hermeneutic tools,[12] as well as the Oral Law.[13] The Torah is like a tree, with the *pshat* as the roots and the *derush* as the branches. The *derush*, then, extends out of the *pshat*.[14] It is deep *pshat*. The higher levels also come from the same root, and all four levels are ultimately one unit.[15]

KABBALAH—THE FOURTH LAYER OF THE TORAH

Sod is the deepest level of any verse—its Kabbalistic interpretation. For those who have reached the right level, engaging all four levels of Torah interpretation will simply reflect the soul's natural thirst to know and perceive the full depths of wisdom that God put in the world.[16] Kabbalah is called "the Wisdom of Truth" because it allows us to

---

11 *Michtav Me'Eliyahu* 5:216.

12 The thirteen hermeneutic tools are tools of logic which are used to derive Oral Laws from the Written Torah. These were given by God to Moses as a part of the Oral Law. (Maimonides, Introduction to the Mishnah.) In fact, most laws that comprise the Oral Torah were derived from these. (Maimonides, *Sefer Hamitzvot, Shoresh Sheni.*) Laws and details involving common everyday occurrences were transmitted directly by Moses to the people, but laws involving infrequently occurring cases were given in such a way as to be derivable from scripture by hermeneutic rules. (Maimonides, ibid.) This prevented these laws from being forgotten. It is clear that laws derived by hermeneutic rules have the same status as laws written in the Torah and are counted as Torah commandments. (*Ramban* to *Sefer Hamitzvot, Shoresh Sheni.*) Examples of the thirteen principles are *kal va'chomer* (a fortiori argument); *gezeirah shavah,* where two exact words in different laws are linked such that we apply some of the conditions of the first law to the second law; and *hekesh* (analogy), once again linking two laws.

13 *Michtav Me'Eliyahu*, ibid.

14 *Maharal*, *Beer Hagolah* 3 (toward the end). See also *Michtav Me'Eliyahu*, *Maamar al haTorah*.

15 *Maharal*, ibid.

16 Rabbi Shlomo Zalman of Liadi, *Shulchan Aruch Harav*, Laws of Learning Torah 1:7.

understand, in the most profound way, how God operates in the world, how everything came from Him, and how it all unfolds to produce the ultimate completion of the world in the End of Days.[17] This allows us not just to believe in God, but at a certain level, to know Him.[18]

Because all of these levels come from the same root, they are ultimately one unit.[19] Hence, even if we draw the deepest most profound Kabbalistic secrets from any verse, "the verse never departs from its simple meaning."[20] God's text can hold the interpretation of the five-year old just as it can hold the most profound interpretation of the greatest of Sages.[21] All of these levels are true and implied in the text.[22] This is why the Torah was not given with vowels, so that the same verse or word could be interpreted in multiple ways and levels and not be restricted to a particular interpretation.[23]

At the same time, when it comes to translating the Torah into the world, since each level of *Pardes* exists at a different plane of reality, an event can take place at a level of *derush* but not at a level of *pshat*, and so on.[24] Hence, Jacob can be described as not dying even though the Torah reports his death.

USING KABBALAH TO FIGHT EVIL AND CONNECT TO GOD

Kabbalistic wisdom deals with the deeper aspects of God's Will.[25] Hence, its study can improve our ability to relate and connect to God.[26] Moreover, by allowing us to become aware of the cosmic dimensions of each commandment, we realize the tremendous impact of all that we

---

17 *Ramchal, Kelach Pitchei Chochmah*, beg.

18 *Ramchal, Maamar Havikuach*.

19 *Maharal*, ibid.

20 Talmud, Tractate *Shabbat* 63a.

21 Vilna Gaon, Proverbs 1:21.

22 Rabbi Yitzchak Hutner, *Pachad Yitzchak*, Pesach 52; Vilna Gaon, Proverbs 5:18.

23 *Ramban, Maamar al Penimius HaTorah*.

24 *Pachad Yitzchak*, ibid.

25 *Tikkunei Zohar* 1:4.

26 Rabbi Chaim Friedlander, introduction to the "Gates of the *Ramchal*," printed at the beginning of the *Ramchal*'s "138 Openings of Wisdom," p. 23. By learning more about the nature of God, we understand better how to serve Him.

do, and we become more committed to doing the right thing.[27] Hence, knowledge of Kabbalah has practical implications.[28]

But there is more. The study of Kabbalah gives us a deeper understanding of the nature of evil and how it comes about. This allows us to more easily recognize evil and to fight and destroy it.[29]

The same ladder that brought the forces of evil down can now be used in reverse, as a ladder to climb up on, toward great holiness.

This does not mean war, but rather a method of revealing God's light. God hid His light in order to create our physical world which, in turn, could accommodate evil. Kabbalah shows us how to reveal this light, which drives away the evil and allows the world to progress toward its final state.[30]

THE DANGERS OF KABBALAH

The study of Kabbalah is not always a good thing. Since Kabbalah is dealing with the spiritual cosmos, a mistake in this area can lead to mistaken ideas about God Himself. The failure to understand Kabbalah properly has been a source of some great tragedies in Jewish history.[31]

Mystical union is fraught with great danger, as seen in the story of the four Sages who ascended to the *Pardes*—the highest and most exalted spiritual levels capable of man.[32] These four great men wanted to learn how to discern the various frequencies of spiritual light and to interpret

---

27 "The Gates of *Ramchal*," p. 81 §120 (Friedlander ed.).

28 Examples of practical halachah having its source in Kabbalistic wisdom is the cutting of the "female" challah on Friday night, the "male" challah on Shabbat morning, and holding them together for the third meal; the way and timing of the shaking of the Four Species on Sukkot; the meaning of each of the days of the counting of the *Omer*. There are dozens of these laws.

29 Rabbi Chaim Friedlander, introduction to the "Gates of the *Ramchal*."

30 Arizal, *Shaarei Hahakdamot* 4.

31 The most famous of these was the episode of Shabbatai Tzvi, who falsely proclaimed himself as the Messiah, and after leading many thousands astray, finally converted to Islam. Shabbtai Tzvi utilized the Kabbalah to make everyone believe he was the Messiah. There were a whole string of false messiahs following Shabbtai Tzvi with the net result that restrictions were placed thereafter on the study of Kabbalah by someone not qualified to do so.

32 Talmud, Tractate *Chagigah* 14a. For an explanation of *Pardes*, see above in this chapter.

them correctly.[33] However, not all of them had fully mastered the complicated techniques necessary to enter such a deep spiritual domain.

In his desire to experience the Divine, Ben Azai "peeked" beyond his spiritual level into the high spiritual realms. His soul leaped out of his body to cleave with great love to those realms he saw, and hence he died. Ben Zoma peeked but did not have enough spiritual greatness and lost his mind. Acheir[34] "cut off the branches," i.e., he separated the world from God.

Only Rabbi Akiva was able to define the exact boundaries to which he was allowed to go, and he therefore emerged whole.[35]

If this is what happened with these great men, the rest of us are in even greater danger. Hence, while the revealed part of the Oral Law is accessible to all, the full depths of the Kabbalah should only be revealed to people who reach a certain stature in their spirituality and Torah wisdom.[36]

There is another danger. Kabbalistic wisdom can be so satisfying that the novice might be tempted to jump into it and come to rely on it for his spiritual highs at the expense of more basic Torah study, the bread and butter of his daily Judaism.[37] Although there are Jewish meditations based on Kabbalah,[38] the idea of Kabbalah as a quick spiritual fix is the very opposite of what this is all about.

---

33 Ibid., as explained by the *Maharsha*.

34 Acheir's real name was Elisha ben Avuya. He was a leading sage of the generarion. After this and other incidences he became a heretic and was from then on referred to as Acheir, which means the "Other One."

35 *Maharsha*, ibid.

36 In Proverbs 25, King Solomon wrote: "The glory of God is a hidden thing." *Rashi* tells us that the Glory of God here is referring to certain parts of the Kabbalistic wisdom that reveal God's glory in the heavens; Talmud, Tractate *Chagigah* 13a. Rabbi Chaim Vital gave a clear order to one's study of Torah: first Tanach, then Mishnah, then Gemara, and only then the secrets of Kabbalistic wisdom.

37 *Rama*, *Torat HaOlah*.

38 See, for example, Rabbi Aryeh Kaplan, *Meditation and the Kabbalah*.

THE OPENING UP OF KABBALAH IN OUR GENERATION

Over the generations, a significant change has taken place.[39] In earlier generations, Kabbalistic wisdom was only revealed to select individuals. Over time, there has been a spiritual decline, with fewer "true" Kabbalists. Therefore, God gave us the ability to understand aspects of the inner secrets of the Torah through the more external workings of the mind to achieve at least a fragment of the mystical wisdom.[40]

Our generation has a greater need to grasp the profundity of the mystical Torah, for we are more challenged to connect with spirituality in general.

Moreover, our generation has a greater need to grasp the profundity of the mystical Torah, for we are more challenged to connect with spirituality in general. It is also a time of the pre-Messianic Era, when these secrets were destined to emerge in preparation for their full revelation during the Messianic Era. Because of this, both the Chassidic and Mussar masters, amongst others, translated many Kabbalistic ideas into a vocabulary and frame of reference that we are able to grasp. This allows us to taste a little of the profundity of Kabbalistic wisdom—a taste that will give us some sense of the awesome depths that await the one who manages to reach the true levels this area demands.

39 Rabbi Chaim Friedlander, intro. to *Ramchal, Maamar Havikuach*, and intro. to "Gates of *Ramchal*," pp. 21–24.

40 Ibid.: "They had mercy on us from heaven, and gave us the opportunity to access, using the tools of our mind, which [operate on a level of the] external [reality] to achieve a drop of internal [i.e., Kabbalistic] perception."

37

THE WISDOM OF JEWISH LAW (HALACHAH)

For the halachic Jew, there is no tension between the law and ethics; between the legal determinant of how he should act and what his conscience tells him.

THE PRECISION OF THE SPIRITUAL WORLD

In Rabbi Yehudah HaLevi's book, the *Kuzari*, a king—probably the King of the Khazars—is described as having a recurring dream where he receives a message, "Your intentions are worthy; but your actions are not."[1] This dream ignites his spiritual quest.[2]

Aligning moral and spiritual intentions with actions is no simple thing. The world around us stresses that we should accept ourselves as we are in order to become ourselves. The world of halachah—Jewish law—pushes us to become our ideal self within the practical realities of day-to-day living and within the exceptional circumstances we sometimes face.

---

1 Rabbi Yehudah HaLevi, *Kuzari*, chap. 1.

2 The king was the king of the Khazars. Legend has it that he and his entire nation converted to Judaism.

The reason for this is the halachah's precision. Many people are bothered by why halachah is so detailed, but the spiritual world is just like the physical world in its need to be exacting with details.

We don't expect anything to work in the physical world—be it a microchip, a genetic splice, or something even as clunky as a motor car—if the slightest thing is not in place. Similarly, we should not expect anything in the spiritual world to work either unless it is to exact specifications.

Aligning moral and spiritual intentions with actions is no simple thing.

As Rabbi Steve Burg puts it: "In sports, the biggest arguments are, 'Was his foot a millimeter out or in?'" We simply need to be as passionate about Judaism as we are about football.

It matters a great deal whether we are eating the right amount of matzah on the first night of Passover. One little letter missing on a Torah scroll makes it forbidden to use. The Shabbat begins and ends according to exact calculations. These are acts of great precision.

If we want to strive for greatness, we will want to get the details right. We don't want an approximate computer, and we don't want an approximate spirituality. Neither do we want something that is abstract and subjective, or something that only seems to work in solitary contemplation on a mountain top.

The system that describes this precision is Jewish law—the system of halachah. Halachah makes sure that we are always first-rate and never second-rate Jews. It does so by giving clear-cut actions. It allows us to resolve the endless shades of gray in the world around us into something specific and concrete.

> *The halachah, which was given to us from Sinai, is the objectification of religion in clear and determined forms, in precise and authoritative laws, and in definite principles. It translates subjectivity into objectivity, the amorphous flow of religious experience into a fixed pattern of lawfulness.*[3]

---

3 Rabbi Joseph B. Soloveitchik, *Halakhic Man*, p. 59.

THE JEWISH SECRET THAT EVERYONE KNOWS

Left to our own devices, even the greatest of us are liable to err sooner or later, however lofty and noble our intentions.[4] Judaism teaches that we are expected to *do* the right thing. The halachah translates the Torah into a practical and reliable actualization of our commitments.

Jewish law is at the core of our mystery for survival. The Dalai Lama, the leader of the Tibetan people who suffered the loss of their country to China, once stated, "Among Tibetan refugees, we are always saying to ourselves that we must learn the Jewish secret to keep up our traditions, in some cases under hostile circumstances."

Moreover, Jewish law has massively contributed to Western legal systems. All Western legal systems are built on Roman law, which is enormously sophisticated. Yet the Romans, despite oppressing the Jews, continued to invest enormous time and energy in understanding Jewish law. The Talmud records many conversations between the Sages and the Romans debating various points of Jewish law,[5] and later, many of these concepts showed up in Roman law. It is fair to speculate that many such concepts were first learned from the Jews.[6]

THE GREAT CODIFICATION

In the 15th century, Rabbi Joseph Karo wrote a great work, the *Shulchan Aruch* (literally, "the Ready Table")—the Code of Jewish Law, which summarized all the laws of Judaism and codified them by topic. To this day, the *Shulchan Aruch* remains the preeminent guide to Jewish law. This work is so precise and well thought out—inspired as it was

---

4 Talmud, Tractate *Derech Eretz* 8.

5 The Talmud has many such examples. See, for example, Tractate *Bava Kama* 38a: "The rulers of Rome sent two representatives to the wise men of the Jews and demanded: 'Teach us your Torah.' They learned the entire Torah three times." It is apparent there that this referred to the extensive Oral Law teachings.

6 These include many concepts in damages, the Roman law concept of the reasonable man, and others.

by *ruach hakodesh*,[7] that it is the reference point for all later halachic (Jewish Law) decisors.

The *Shulchan Aruch* is divided into four major sections:

1. *Orach Chaim* deals with laws of our daily and annual cycle—prayers and blessings, the Shabbat and the festivals.
2. *Yoreh Deah* deals with all remaining issues. These include kosher laws, laws of mourning, honoring one's parents, Torah study, conversion to Judaism, and many others.
3. *Even Ha'ezer* deals with laws relating to marriage and divorce.
4. *Choshen Mishpat* deals with commercial law, laws of lending, of theft and damages, property law, and laws of court procedure.

CONTEMPORARY RESPONSA

No work, not even the *Shulchan Aruch*, can end the codification process, for every generation has its own issues. Technology advances, new medical procedures, genetics, surrogacy, and sexual identity become the new issues of the day. We live in a turbulent world where the culture and values of society are in constant flux. All of these create new questions for Jewish law. The living sages at any time must make these calls.[8]

To make a decision, the contemporary sage applies the age-old principles of the Oral Law to the new situation. He must draw on his intimate knowledge of the Talmud and its commentaries, of the earlier and later legal codifications, as well as the voluminous responsa that have been produced over the generations. He must then apply this to the unique situation at hand.

The living Sage at any time must apply Jewish law to the unique set of variables in front of him.

There is more that needs to be taken into account. The venerable scholar of the 20th century, Rabbi Moshe Feinstein wrote: "And...even when [the competent rabbi] knows the local conditions of the place, and he is fit to decide on this matter given his greatness in Torah and his

7 Rabbi Tzadok HaKohen, *Machashavot Charutz*, p. 114. For more on *ruach hakodesh*, see Chapter 35.

8 *Ramban*, Deuteronomy 17:10.

greatness in pure awe of God, still he should take into consideration the impact that his decision will have on all other places."[9]

The contemporary authority must ask: Is this a situation of life and death? What will the spiritual impact on the person be? What is his or her current commitment to Judaism? What are the long-term social and other implications of a decision this way or that? What legal precedents are there that relate to this issue directly or indirectly? What are other contemporary sages saying about this matter?

The halachic decisor is expected to consider all of this in his final decision. Only then can he come to a conclusion. His decision will be there for all the great scholars of the age to discuss and dissect. Moreover, the ruling of the sage creates a new spiritual reality.[10] And since God set up the world to work that way, God rejoices, so to speak, at the ruling of the sage.[11]

BUILDING ON THE SHOULDERS OF GIANTS

The Talmud brings a story which relates that when Moses went up the mountain to receive the Torah, he was shown an image of Rabbi Akiva, who lived over a thousand years later, asserting the opinions and understandings of Judaism in his contemporary situation. Moses at first did not recognize this as the same Torah that he had received. Then one of the students asked Rabbi Akiva from where he was drawing his opinion. Rabbi Akiva answered that this is a law from Sinai.[12]

Rabbi Akiva lived in a troubled era. There were many new issues he had to relate to. Rabbi Akiva, a master of Torah wisdom, applied Moses' Sinaitic principles as articulated by the cumulative genius of the ages. There had been no change in the God-given Torah. Rabbi Akiva was merely applying the principles of timeless law to new situations.[13]

In this way, all the cumulative wisdom of the Torah revealed by the previous generations serves as the substructure on which contemporary

---

9 Rabbi Moshe Feinstein, *Igrot Moshe, Yoreh Deah*, vol. 3, no. 81.

10 *Derashot HaRan* 1.

11 Talmud, Tractate *Bava Metzia* 59a–b, the dispute of Rabbi Eliezer and the Sages.

12 Talmud, Tractate *Menachot* 29a.

13 See Maimonides, *Sefer Hamitzvot*, the beginning of the second root.

Sages can build.[14] This creates an effect of continuous revelation, where the insights of the Torah not only inform new situations, but the situations themselves arouse insights into the Torah that escaped us before.[15]

Even if later generations will be of reduced stature than the earlier ones, the continuous revelation of Torah means that these later generations are like dwarves sitting on the shoulders of giants, building on all the Torah already revealed.[16] "Yiftach in his generation is like Samuel in his generation," say the Sages.[17] Yiftach was not as great as Samuel, but he was the greatest sage in his generation. Hence, he had just as much authority as the venerable Samuel had during his own lifetime.

The tenacity of Jews throughout the ages to keep halachah is testimony to their deepest commitment. The Jews have been to hell and back many times, but, as a community, they never let go of the details. They kept what they could through thick and thin. They never allowed history to determine their future. And, therefore, they were able to determine history.

---

14 Rabbi Tzadok HaKohen, *Tzidkat Hatzaddik* 238.

15 Rabbi Tzadok HaKohen, *Resisei Laylah*, p. 157.

16 Ibid.

17 Talmud, Tractate *Rosh Hashanah* 25b.

38

THE WISDOM OF IMAGINATION

For there are two chambers in the mind:
one is the power of wisdom and the other is the power of imagination; and when one rises one falls.

Rabbi Tzadok HaKohen[1]

THE POWER TO LEAP BEYOND OURSELVES

We saw in Section 1 that the name for man—*adam*—comes from *adameh*—"I will be like."[2] The reference is to being God-like: "I will be like the Above."[3] *Adameh* in turn comes from the word *dimyon*—imagination. It is the power of imagination that allows us to take a leap—not only in conceiving God but in imitating Him. Without imagination, we would be forever stuck in our earthly limitations, allowing ourselves to interpret only that which we can physically see.[4]

Without imagination, we would be forever stuck in our earthly limitations, allowing ourselves to interpret only that which we can physically see.

1 Rabbi Tzadok HaKohen, *Machashavot Charutz* 3.

2 Chapter 6.

3 Rabbi Tzadok HaKohen, ibid. *Adameh LeElyon*—I will be like the above, the exalted.

4 *Machashavot Charutz* 2.

With imagination, we can have a vision of ourselves breaking through to new horizons, and explore new ways of resolving our personal issues. It was this that prompted C. S. Lewis to say, "Reason is the natural order of truth; but imagination is the organ of meaning."

This possibility of man leaping beyond himself to a horizon in the distance is uniquely human. As Michio Kaku puts it in *The Future of the Mind*: "Humans are alone in the animal kingdom in understanding the concept of tomorrow."

Kaku continues, "The ability to imagine objects as episodes that do not exist in the realm of the real [and to project them into the future]. As one philosopher noted, the human brain is an 'anticipation machine,' and 'making the future' is the most important thing it does...We constantly analyze and evaluate information from many feedback loops. We do this by running [different] simulations [in which we peer]...into the future."[5]

JOSEPH—THE DREAMER AND THE VISIONARY

One of the most powerful expressions of imagination is dreams. In fact, the Sages tell us that a dream is one-sixtieth of prophecy.[6] When one sleeps, higher levels of one's soul—the *chayah* and *yechidah*—loosen their relationship with the body so that they can more freely perceive things in the upper worlds. Most prophecy also took place during sleep, because sleep further aids the detachment of the soul, allowing it to soar to those higher worlds and "see" God's attributes close to their source.[7]

Prophecy, in turn, required imagination—"In the hands of the prophets shall I imagine"[8]—as the delivery mechanism through which God imprints his message on the minds of man.[9]

---

5 Michio Kaku, *The Future of the Mind*, pp. 46–47, 54, 57.

6 Tractate *Berachot* 57a; *Ramchal, Daat Tevunot* 180.

7 Numbers 12:6.

8 Hosea 12:11.

9 See Chapter 35. There, we explained that a prophet (other than Moses) could not receive the glory of God directly, and hence could do so through his imagination and from there up to his intellect. Once it reached the intellect, the prophetic message would be engraved in his mind.

To see the potential of tomorrow, one must be able to dream—to imagine. "I am enough of an artist to draw freely upon my imagination," Einstein said. "Imagination is more important than knowledge. Knowledge is limited. Imagination encircles the world."

It is Joseph who teaches us how to dream. Joseph is involved in six dreams: two of his own,[10] one of Pharaoh's butler and baker each,[11] and two of Pharaoh's.[12]

Joseph believes that his own dreams are a kind of prophecy,[13] and he pursues those dreams doggedly—to seeming success. It all seems to happen according to his vision. He does come to rule,[14] his brothers and father do bow down to him, and his approach to serving God does seem to come about just as he had dreamed.[15]

Joseph's brothers insult him by calling him a dreamer, but the Sages consistently call him "Yosef HaTzaddik—Joseph the Righteous One."[16]

The *tzaddik* is defined by his ability to consistently do the right thing. This requires tremendous self-control and awareness, the type that allowed Joseph to resist the seductions of the wife of Potiphar.[17] However, this definition surely contradicts our stereotype of what a dreamer is. We think of dreamers as being chilled, open-ended people, sometimes even spacey—certainly not abundant in discipline and boundaries. But those are the wrong kinds of dreamers.[18]

To see the potential of tomorrow one must be able to dream; to imagine. It is Joseph who teaches us how to dream.

The right kind of dreamer is one who has synergy between his intellectual side and the imaginative, curious, creative side of his brain.[19]

---

10 Genesis 37:5–11.

11 Ibid. 40:5–11.

12 Ibid. 41:1–7.

13 *Ramban*, Genesis 42:9.

14 Genesis, 41:37–39.

15 *Machashavot Charutz* 4:2, p. 14.

16 See for example, Talmud, Tractate *Yoma* 35b; *Avot D'Rabi Natan* 16:2.

17 Rabbi Tzadok HaKohen, *Takanat Hashavim* 6.

18 *Machashavot Charutz* 4:1.

19 Ibid., end of par. 3.

The intellectual side sets the values, the goals toward which we hope to work. When these goals are dominant, our power of imagination will work to achieve the ends.[20] The will "pulls the power of imagination with it. Then, all the passing and superficial thoughts that a person unwittingly has are also harnessed to serve God."[21]

This was exactly the formula that Joseph used. Joseph's pursuit of dreams was just the stuff that is needed for Joseph to make his spiritual climb. Through his dreams, Joseph was able to vividly depict the spiritual achievements he wished to make. To that he added his enormous strength of character to actualize that vision—a powerful combination indeed.[22]

"Imagination allows us to escape the predictable," said Bill Bradley.[23] "It enables us to reply to the common wisdom that we cannot, by saying, 'Just watch!'" And there was no one who showed this more than Joseph.

Joseph is the dreamer and the doer all in one. Prior to the coming of the Messiah, there will be a "Mashiach ben Yosef"[24]—a precursor to the actual Messiah who will come from the lineage of Joseph. This Messiah is the *doer*; he reflects man's efforts to achieve redemption, rather than simply waiting for God to do so for us.[25] In fact, we all have a part of Mashiach ben Yosef inside of us. We all have to make our contribution to this effort.[26]

There is no vision bolder and more astonishing than the pursuit of the Messianic dream. Joseph, the dreamer, is the leader of this vision, and also the one who takes the practical steps to get it done.

IMAGINATION GONE WRONG

Dreams and visions are tools. They can drive us to heights of spirituality, but they can also invite us into an abyss of self-deception. The

---

20 Ibid., 1, 3.

21 Ibid., 3.

22 Ibid. 4:1–2.

23 Bill Bradley, *Values of the Game*.

24 Lit., "the Messiah, son of Joseph."

25 Rabbi Hillel of Shklov, *Kol Hator*, in the name of the Vilna Gaon.

26 Ibid.

first, tragic victims of the power of imagination were none other than the first man and woman.[27] The snake seduced Eve with the words, "And you will be like God."[28] The root of all emptiness, falsehood, and illusions are rooted in the desire of man to be something more than he can ever be. Reaching up is a great thing, but when arrogance replaces humility, man overreaches and he becomes a danger to himself and others.[29] It was because Adam and Eve were so holy that they were capable of such an egregious sin.[30]

What is clear from the Joseph story is that it is only if our dreams are aligned with God's vision for us and the world that they are worth something. Joseph looks for signs of this. On the orders of Pharaoh, he is rushed out of the most hopeless imprisonment, going from darkness to light in a flash, as it says, "and they rushed him from the dungeon."[31] In one conversation with Pharaoh, Joseph, the freed slave-prisoner, is appointed ruler over all of Egypt. Similarly, the redemption of the Jewish People from Egypt happened so fast that our bread did not have time to bake.[32] The *tzaddik*, who relies so much on his own efforts to achieve greatness, is clearly shown how everything is in God's hands.[33]

The first, tragic victims of the power of imagination were none other than the first man and woman.

As a visionary, Joseph never loses sight of this. If his vision will align with God's, then it will come about. And if not, it will ultimately fail. He begins and ends his conversation with Pharaoh by pointing out that it is God alone who can provide the solution to his dream.[34] Joseph delivers God's message to Pharaoh: "You hid from Me that you dreamed that you are standing, as a god, by the river. But I am now telling you that

27 *Machashavot Charutz* 1.

28 Ibid.

29 Ibid.

30 Ibid.

31 Genesis 41:14.

32 Rabbeinu Bachya, Genesis 41:14.

33 Joseph's recognition of this is repeated again and again.

34 Genesis 41:16; see Rabbeinu Bachya ad loc.

I control all your food—your ability to even stay alive." Later, Pharaoh experienced his first plague through this same river, and his final demise was also through water—by the Red Sea.[35] Joseph dreams and Pharaoh dreams. Both sets of dreams are true. But Joseph knew what Pharaoh did not: For while Joseph was pursuing his dreams, God was churning the big wheels of history.[36] God sent Joseph to Egypt to pave the way for the exile of his family to that land.

35 Ibid.

36 *Ohr Hachaim*, Genesis 41:16.

39

THE WISDOM OF PRAYER

Prayer is the primary food for the upper worlds
and the soul of man himself.

Rabbi Chaim of Volozhin[1]

PRAYER AS RELATIONSHIP

It may seem strange to talk of prayer as a wisdom. Really, prayer is an art—an art of the soul—and like all great arts, it requires practice, focus, and discipline. It *is* a wisdom.

Prayer is a way of approaching and connecting with the Divine. In the culminating act of prayer—the *Shemoneh Esreh*—we approach God by taking three steps forward and stand before God.[2] The three steps remind us of the three instances when the word *va'yigash*—"and he approached"—was used by three different people.[3] Each one involved an appeal. In the first, Abraham appeals to God to save the people of Sodom.[4] In the second, Judah appeals to Joseph, then the viceroy of

---

1 *Nefesh Hachaim* 2:9.

2 Talmud, Tractate *Yoma* 53a; *Shulchan Aruch, Orach Chaim* 123:1. The dominant custom is to begin by taking three steps backwards and then three forwards. However, the former is only to facilitate the latter.

3 *Rama*, glosses on the *Shulchan Aruch, Orach Chaim* 95, in the name of the *Rokeach*.

4 Genesis 15:23.

Egypt, not to take Benjamin into captivity.[5] In the third case, Elijah stood off the false prophets of the Baal, turned to God and said, "Answer me, O God, answer me."[6]

Each one of these added a dimension to our understanding of prayer. Abraham taught us to pray even for evil people, e.g., the people of Sodom. We are all capable of repentance. Judah taught us how to include in our prayers the principle of "all of Israel is responsible one for the other," therefore he risked his life for Benjamin.[7] Elijah taught us that we have to pray that there will be a sanctification of God's name (*kiddush Hashem)* in all of our actions. And so, we take all three steps at the beginning of the *Shemoneh Esreh* to incorporate all three levels of understanding.

After our three steps, we then stand angel-like with our feet together,[8] just as later, with the leader's repetition of the *Shemoneh Esreh*, we imitate the angels by saying "*Kadosh, Kadosh, Kadosh*—Holy, Holy, Holy..."[9]

And now, facing God, we are ready to speak to Him—directly, in the second person, "You"—for an entire nineteen blessings. It is this awareness—that we can stand opposite our God, so to speak, and have a conversation with Him—that is the very essence of the Jewish definition of prayer.[10] Even if our requests are not answered, just by talking to God we achieve the main object of prayer, i.e., the relationship itself.[11]

When you miss someone you are close to, he or she is in your thoughts. You long to have contact. We should strive for that same type of relationship with God. The soul needs to be fed like the body, and just as we get physically hungry if we have not eaten for a while, and we get

---

5 Genesis 44:18.

6 Kings I 18:37.

7 Talmud, Tractate *Sanhedrin* 27b; Tractate *Shavuot* 39a.

8 Talmud, Tractate *Berachot* 10b, quoted in *Shulchan Aruch, Orach Chaim* 95. We know this about the angels from Ezekiel 1.

9 *Ben Yehodaya*, Tractate *Berachot* 10b.

10 *Chiddushei Rabbeinu Chaim HaLevi, Tefillah.*

11 *Malbim*, Psalms 41:17. In the words of the siddur *Avodat HaLev*: "Since the definition of prayer is the focusing of our thoughts toward God, it is readily understood that praising Him or making requests of Him are secondary...The core of prayer is the intention (focus) of our hearts."

emotionally hungry to see a person we love, so too, our souls get spiritually hungry when we have not prayed for a while.[12] The desire to pray is the desire to connect. The prayer is the actualization of the desire.[13]

Hence, prayer is the only commandment that begins before the commandment itself. From the moment we begin to take three steps forward to start the silent prayer, we have already begun the mitzvah.[14] Approaching God is a part of the relationship.

It is this awareness—that we can stand opposite our God, so to speak, and have a conversation with Him—that is the very essence of the Jewish definition of prayer.

THE LABOR OF THE HEART

What's hard about prayer is "getting the experience." All relationships require work, and a relationship with God is no different: it requires time, energy, and commitment.[15] No authentic relationship can simply be an intellectual process; the relationship must move me. I must have feelings. God wants our heart.[16] And hence the Torah calls prayer "service of the heart," as it says, "and you should serve Him with all your heart."[17] Like all relationships, our prayer relationship with God will require work, and it will be a learning curve.

Our relationship with significant others is multi-faceted. We talk, we share, we argue. We sometimes feel close, and we sometimes feel distant. We trust, we honor, and we love. So too, when it comes to God, we cannot be mono-dimensional. We cannot reduce our feelings toward God to one word, be it faith, love, awe, or trust. We will feel

---

12 *Kuzari* 3:7.

13 Rabbi Tzadok HaKohen, *Tzidkat Hatzaddik* 42; *Duties of the Heart*, tenth consideration.

14 Rabbi Yitzchak Hutner, *Pachad Yitzchak*, based on the *Ritva*, who says that if you decide to go and pray in the further of two synagogues, you get rewarded for the extra distance. This is because the moment you left your home to go and pray, you began the relationship.

15 Based on Dena Heller, *Moreshet* (2000).

16 Talmud, Tractate *Sanhedrin* 106b. The Sages prove this with a verse: "And God will look to the heart" (Samuel I 16:7).

17 Deuteronomy 11:13; *Rashi*, ibid. Hence, prayer is referred to as *avodah she'balev*—work of the heart; Maimonides, *Sefer Hamitzvot*, positive mitzvah 5.

different things at different times, and we must find different ways of expressing this.

We might turn to God with questions to which we may never find an answer. "Why?" We may feel frustrated and upset and direct those feelings toward God. These too reflect a relationship. They too show connection.

No authentic relationship can simply be an intellectual process; the relationship must move me. I must have feelings. God wants our heart.

Asking for our needs is yet another way of connecting to God. We are in constant need, and we recognize that He is the source of fulfilling that need. We use our needs to propel us to a profoundly spiritual experience.[18]

Many of us who pray are so focused on the words that we forget the big picture. It is an awesome moment when we finally feel that we are communicating with the Divine! It's a direct connection to the Almighty.

DIFFERENT CONVERSATIONS

As we've learned, depending on the time of day or week or year, and the emotional and spiritual mood we are in, our prayer relationship with God will look different at different times.[19] The common denominator is that through all these different conversations, we are trying to lose ourselves in prayer—to be totally caught up in the moment of connection. The more intimate the dialogues, the more authentic the relationship, the more focused our prayer-mediation will be. Chanah (Hannah) is described as pouring out her soul to God,[20] and indeed we often see a similar language used for prayer.[21]

We don't always easily hear the dialogue in prayer. God doesn't boom out an answer in the form of prophecy. Nevertheless, by praying, we get to know God better. We get to know that God loves us. We become alert to God's way of communicating with us: His constant guiding and

---

18 *Maharal, Netiv HaAvodah*, chap. 1.

19 Rabbi Shlomo Wolbe, *Alei Shur*, vol. 1, p. 114.

20 Samuel I 1:15.

21 Rabbi Chaim of Volozhin, *Nefesh Hachaim* 2:14.

vigil, His provision of the opportunities of life, and His preventing us from all the pitfalls we might fall into. In the first blessing of the silent prayer, we say that God is "[our] Helper, [our] Savior, and [our] Shield."[22] Sometimes we are on track and just need a bit of help ("our Helper"); we need God to make it happen for us. Sometimes we are headed in the wrong direction and need to be saved and redirected ("our Savior"), and sometimes we are so vulnerable that we need to be protected from ourselves and others ("our Shield"). In these later cases, God says "no" for our own good. "I have lived to thank God that all my prayers have not been answered," said the English poet, Jean Ingelow. And that thanks is yet another conversation with God.

TURNING THE DAY INTO A PRAYER

Prayer cannot end with our formal prayers. We must continue to talk to God from deep inside our hearts, using our own words and feelings throughout the day. To be aware of God is one thing. To have a relationship with Him throughout the day is entirely another.

The early righteous ones would meditate on their prayer until they would reach a level where their souls no longer felt clothed and constrained by their bodies. They were able to focus their minds to such a degree that they reached a level close to prophecy.[23] This didn't just happen, however. They didn't just walk up to God and begin a conversation. They prepared an hour before they even began their prayers.[24]

Today, many of us struggle with the art of prayer because we struggle with deep relationships in general. But God says, "Show up anyhow. Any conversation that we have is good." That conversation can take place in any language. But the Hebrew version, when someone can manage it, is particularly

Today, many of us struggle with the art of prayer because we struggle with deep relationships in general. But God says, "Show up anyhow. Any conversation that we have is good."

22 The Hebrew words are *ozer, moshia, u'magen*.

23 *Shulchan Aruch*, *Orach Chaim* 98:1.

24 Ibid., based on the Mishnah, *Berachot* 30b.

powerful. So much thought and wisdom went into the formulation of the Hebrew prayers so that they contain an entire spectrum of everything that needs to be corrected in this world.[25]

Praying is a uniquely human trait. The Sages identify us as "praying beings."[26] Prayer is one of the richest experiences any human can have.

---

25 Rabbi Chaim of Volozhin, *Nefesh HaChaim* 2:12.

26 Talmud, Tractate *Bava Kama* 3b.

SECTION 4

PATTERNS OF GROWTH

40

NURTURING YOUR UNIQUE YOU

It is not for you to finish the work, but neither are you free to exempt yourself from it.

Ethics of Our Fathers[1]

BE YOURSELF

Goethe said, "If you treat an individual as he is, he will remain how he is. But if you *treat him* as if *he* were what *he* ought to be and could be, *he will* become what he ought to be and could be."

The same applies (even more so) to ourselves: Treat yourself as you are and you will remain as you are; treat yourself as you can and should be, and you will become as you can and should be.

Becoming ourselves—all that we should and can be—is what Judaism is all about. God is neither interested in any one of us becoming a spiritual robot, nor becoming a clone of anyone else. God wants you to be you, and me to be me, and this authentically and quintessentially unique you and me are of enormous significance. Each life is so precious in Judaism because it is truly never replaceable. "Whomever sustains one soul it is as if he sustains the entire world."[2] In fact, one may break the Shabbat

---

1 *Ethics of Our Fathers* 2:17.

2 Talmud, Tractate *Sanhedrin* 4a.

in order to extend someone's life, even if we assess that they will die a few seconds later,[3] for every second of every life is of infinite value.[4] And yet, after all that concern for the other, Judaism tells us, "Your life comes first."[5] The first person whose infinite worth as a human being you have to understand is yourself.

Failure to recognize your own potential is to live a lie. It is to lie to oneself and that, said the Kotzker Rebbe, is the worst kind of lie. The Kotzker Rebbe did not mean this in a literal sense, for Judaism certainly would consider false evidence, a false oath, and other kinds of lies as worse. What he might have meant was in the vein of Rabbi Simchah Bunim of Peshischa's remark that the only sinners he could not reform were liars, and among the liars he included those who lied to themselves. "'Thou shalt not steal,'" he said, "always meant that you should not steal from yourself, just as you must not steal from anyone else."[6]

To lie to oneself is the worst kind of lie.

BELIEVING IN YOURSELF

We are commanded to believe in God, and this leads us to believe in ourselves. For if we believe in God, we must believe that He created us, is involved with us, and is thrilled when we do become the best "us" that we can be. This is what it means when it says at the crossing of the Red Sea that "they believed in God, and Moses His servant."[7] In fact, they believed in God and each and every one of His servants.[8] So, too, the verse says of the Jewish People, "God placed him alone, and no foreign nation is with him."[9] He guided "him," in the singular, for each Jew is important in and of himself.[10]

---

3 *Shulchan Aruch, Orach Chaim* 329:4.

4 *Biur Halachah*, ibid.

5 Talmud, Tractate *Bava Metzia* 62a.

6 See also Chapter 4.

7 Exodus 14:31.

8 Rabbi Tzadok HaKohen, *Tzidkat Hatzaddik* 154.

9 Deuteronomy 32:12.

10 *Shelah*, ibid.

Erroneously, some people believe that a person has to "acquire" good behaviors, qualities, feelings, and thoughts. In truth, there is no need to *acquire* anything! We need only to *uncover* the good that is already within us, the pure *neshamah* that Hashem has planted in each and every one of us.[11]

Although you can certainly apologize for your behavior when it is not good, you should never apologize to yourself or anyone else for being you. You can never live properly until you access your real self and like what you see.

The starting point for this is to know with absolute certainty that God believes in you, for otherwise He would not have created you. The Sages interpret the words "He is a God of faith"[12] as meaning that God had faith in all that he created.[13]

No matter what the external factors in life may bring, we can always retreat to this core identity and feel secure.[14] No matter how besieged you feel, you can always connect with that identity and find your own voice. This is what the Sages mean by their statement: "Do not be wicked in your own eyes."[15]

This whole idea was perfectly summarized by Hillel when he stated, "If I am not for myself, who is for me? And when I am for myself, what am I? And if not now, then when?"[16]

"If I am not for myself, who is for me?" I have to take charge of my life. No one but me can arouse the force that lies within me.[17] Only I can choose to fulfill the potential within me.[18]

Rabbi Weissmandl, famous for his efforts to save the Jews of Europe from the Holocaust, put it like this:

---

11 "Know Yourself" (by the author of *Bilvavi*), pp. 44–45.

12 Deuteronomy 32:4.

13 *Sifri*, ibid.

14 Ibid.

15 *Ethics of Our Fathers* 2:14.

16 Ibid. 1:14.

17 Maimonides, commentary to *Ethics of Our Fathers*, ibid.

18 Bartenura, commentary to *Ethics of Our Fathers*, ibid.

> *Ladies and gentlemen, I want to tell you who I am. And even though it is not accepted protocol [that a person should bestow on himself titles], I have no other way. I am one of the unlimited tens of thousands of people that God created in his world, by virtue of believing in His world and hence deciding to create it, and by virtue of the fact that He believed that through this person [i.e., myself,] there would be a certain benefit in increasing His glory in the world.*
>
> *This is neither arrogance, nor pride, nor lording it over others. [For] every man is created because God first believed in him and only then created him. Every person is obligated to say, "For me the world was created." I am the person that God has been waiting for and expecting.*[19]

Hillel continued: "And if I am for myself, who am I?" For all that I have achieved, I still have an infinite amount of potential.[20] That recognition is meant to be an enabling and a motivating force. We had better get up and get moving. Hillel's statement can then be interpreted as: "And if I am only for what I have already become, and I have stopped growing, then I am biologically alive but not spiritually alive. Who am I then?"

"And if not now, when?" Don't wait for that moment of inspiration. It may be long in coming. Don't wait for something to happen that will allow you to begin living. There will always be a reason to wait, but these reasons never match up to the opportunity of now. The growth-day is today.

"And don't say when I will be free, I will study. Perhaps you will not ever be free."[21] Our days will always be full with urgent business matters, relationships, study, work, medical issues, or something we need to order or buy. For every day brings a new "busy-ness"—and you will go through life always waiting for "tomorrow" to clear your plate and

---

19 Rabbi Weissmandl, *Ish Chamudot*, pp. 855–61.

20 Bartenura, commentary to *Ethics of Our Fathers*, ibid.

21 *Ethics of Our Fathers* 2:4.

start growing.[22] We are never fully in control of our lives, and this will apply to our future as much as our present.[23]

Every day that passes means that change will be harder. Our character traits become more set, we learn to be more comfortable with whom we are, and our negative reactions to things become entrenched.[24] The easiest time in our lives to change and grow is most likely to be today.

We have to develop a certain sense of urgency about our growth. "The day is short, and the work is great,"[25] and the spirituality we are engaging is endlessly deep.[26] Imagine that a king told a servant, "All the gold you can gather from my treasury until tomorrow is yours." Would such a person go to sleep, knowing that every minute he was sleeping he was losing vast amounts of wealth?[27]

The only way we will take charge is if fulfilling our values mission becomes the absolute priority of our lives.[28]

If we do that, the physical, material, and other impediments may not go away, but we will be so much more equipped to face them. "I wish I could tell you that it gets better," comedian Joan Rivers once quipped. "But it doesn't get better. YOU get better."

GROWTH FROM WHERE YOU ARE

Maimonides regarded someone who overcame his instincts as greater than one who was naturally righteous.[29] The former reflects human achievement; the latter reflects a handout from God. The primary goal is the process itself—the act of growing, the act of successive approximations to getting it right.[30]

---

22 Rabbeinu Bachya, commentary to *Ethics*, ibid.

23 *Maharal*, commentary to *Ethics*, ibid.

24 Maimonides, ibid.

25 *Ethics of Our Fathers* 2:15.

26 Bartenura, commentary to *Ethics*, ibid.

27 Rabbeinu Yonah, commentary to *Ethics*, ibid.

28 Maimonides and other major commentators.

29 Maimonides, *Shemoneh Perakim* (introduction to *Ethics*).

30 Rabbeinu Yonah, *Ethics* 2:17; in some editions, §16.

God has His own definition of greatness. It is someone who takes a step forward from wherever he is.[31] It doesn't matter how observant we are right now. The idea is to grow. Every little action counts. Every step forward is exactly what you are supposed to be doing right now. It is the amount of growth we achieve from our starting point that interests God, and that is what should interest us as well.[32]

A great person who is no longer growing, who is just holding onto his spiritual level, is not as great in God's eyes as someone just starting out on his journey but who keeps on taking tiny steps every day.[33] It doesn't matter how great or distinguished we are, or how simple and lowly we are in the eyes of our fellow man. God has a different measure!

King Solomon stated, "A man of kindness deals kindly with himself."[34] He nurtures a positive self-image, he stays engaged, and he gives himself access to all the opportunities of the day. Not to do is to be cruel to oneself, and that is actually a form of wickedness.[35] To sustain growth and maintain emotional and spiritual health, we have to be kind to ourselves, but not too kind.[36] We should be living on the very edge of our comfort zone. To do less is to lose a part of ourselves.

---

31 Rabbeinu Yonah, ibid.

32 Rabbi Eliyahu Dessler, *Michtav Me'Eliyahu*, vol. 1, *Kuntres Habechirah*.

33 Rabbi Yitzchak Hutner, *Pachad Yitzchak*.

34 Proverbs 11:17.

35 Based on *Sefer Hachinuch,* mitzvah 75. See Rabbi Gantz, *Parashat Mishpatim*—the Psychodynamic of Wrongdoing. See also Rabbi Shlomo Wolbe, *Maamar Yemei Ratzon, Maamarei Elul, Maamar Rishon, Hitchadshut.*

36 Rabbeinu Yonah, Proverbs 11:17.

41

PRINCIPLES OF GROWTH

We must appreciate our world, our mission, our greatness to fuel our commitment when we encounter roadblocks along the way.

Rabbi Daniel of Kelm[1]

CHANGE AND FAITH

Judaism is a system of change. This system cannot be separated from its faith anchor. It cannot be secularized. We trust the process because we trust its source.[2] We trust that we are getting exactly what we need, and that others impact on our lives for reasons that are ultimately good. Without this, we can never have the equilibrium and peace of mind to engage ourselves in lasting change.[3]

In addition, God-awareness tells us that doing God's will is a serious matter. When an issue is serious, we take action whether or not we know we will succeed. For example, when someone's life is in danger, we do whatever we can to save it without considering the odds of success. Belief in God tells us that it is worth taking risks to grow.[4]

---

1 *Brisk*, p. 23.

2 Vilna Gaon, *Even Sheleimah* 3:1.

3 Ibid. 3:2.

4 Rabbi Yisrael Salanter, *Ohr Yisrael*, letter 5, as described by Rabbi Levi Lebovits, *Panu Derech*.

Furthermore, our belief informs our values. It is no good becoming a more competent or better put together Mafioso. Such a person will simply become better at doing the wrong thing.

Finally, faith tells us that God is rooting for us because He made us in His image,[5] and His whole reason for making us was to set us up to do good.[6] We were set up for success, not failure!

At any stage of our lives, we may be very down on ourselves. The solution is not to learn to become comfortable with this "me," warts and all. The idea of a positive self-image—an essential human ingredient—is to enable us to identify a starting point that will allow us to grow from there.[7] The Jewish message is, "Like yourself, but never accept yourself as the final you that you must become."

WHEN WE BECOME OUR HABITS

Why is change so hard? Because long-term negative behavior becomes a habit, and habits become automated. The Talmud states: "When a person commits a sin and repeats it, it becomes as if permitted."[8] When someone does an act for the first time with the knowledge that he shouldn't be doing it, he is very distressed; the second time he does it, he is less upset; and the third time, it already feels normal.[9]

Thankfully, that same habituation process can be used for good character as well. Habits give us structure—a way to safely negotiate our day.

INSPIRATION AND PASSION

All change begins with a moment of inspiration when we feel the passion and excitement to reach beyond our habituated self. It is this that was meant when the Sages say, "A *mazal* in the heavens hits him and orders him, 'Grow.'"[10]

---

5 *Ethics of Our Fathers* 3:14.

6 See Chapter 3.

7 Rabbi Nachman of Breslov, *Likutei Moharan* 141:282.

8 *Yoma* 86b.

9 "Know Yourself," by the author of *Bilvavi*, p. 45.

10 *Midrash Rabbah*, Genesis 10:6; *Zohar*. This is often quoted with the word "angel" substituting for the word *mazal*.

However, inspiration doesn't last. Hence, we pray to God, "Don't throw me away in my old age."[11] This means that when things in spirituality are old and stale, when they have lost their freshness and energy, we pray that God should still stay with us. And this is what is meant in our daily prayers: "He who renews the act of creation every day," i.e., that He keeps us fresh and inspired.[12]

If this passion could translate into our new habits, we could become the new "us." But inspiration does not last long enough to cover the slow process toward habituation. We might try to bridge this gap by resorting to sheer will and determination. However, this means pushing against ourselves, day by day, hour by hour. Fatigue inevitably sets in. This is why, for most of us, our New Year's resolutions don't last.

All change begins with a moment of inspiration when we feel the passion and excitement to reach beyond our habituated self.

To cover the gap between inspiration and habituation, we need freshness and passion, and here Judaism provides a unique system: A Jew gets up in the morning. He says the morning blessing, "Blessed are You, O God, who gives sight to the blind." I open my eyes; I can see! I can hear and touch and taste and smell. Remarkable. I feel so blessed. The blessings focus on the fact that I can sit and stand and walk. They relate to the fact that I have clothes and shoelaces. They sensitize me to the amazing fresh opportunity I have on this day. My gratefulness to God for what He has given me allows me to energize myself for the day ahead, to recommit to the plan, and to move it forward. Voltaire said it well when he stated, "God gave us the gift of life; it is up to us to give ourselves the gift of living well." Gratefulness for our gifts leaves us fresh and optimistic. It allows us to make our day count.

BRIBING THE SELF

Are we ever totally honest with ourselves? The Talmud tells us that the Kohen Gadol (High Priest) was not allowed to sit on the panel that

---

11 Psalms 71:9.

12 *Degel Machaneh Ephraim*, beg. *Parashat Eikev*.

would declare a leap year.[13] This is because adding a month would place Yom Kippur further toward the winter. The High Priest had to do his service barefoot on the floors of the Temple. The later the month, the colder the floors were likely to be. This great and holy man was suspected of falsely calculating the leap years because of the comfort of his feet on the holiest of days! Nobody thought that the High Priest would deliberately subvert the calculation. Despite this, his inner biases were strong enough that he might subconsciously make the wrong calculation.[14]

Similarly, the Talmud says that a judge may not hear one side of a dispute without the other side present, even if he comes later to present his arguments.[15] Should the judge see some redeeming argument presented by the first litigant, he will have already bought into that idea, and he will have a certain resistance to change.[16]

This is sobering. If we are not aware of our biases that tell us not to change, how are we going to counter them? Fortunately, we can train ourselves in critical awareness. Without self-awareness, nothing is going to happen. As Dr. Mark Griffiths put it, "Living without self-awareness is like driving your car at night with the headlights off—technically, you can still drive, but you will eventually have a collision."

To achieve self-awareness, we Jews dedicate a significant chunk of time thinking about both the big picture and the details of whom we are and where we want to go. Many observant Jews do a *cheshbon ha'nefesh*—an accounting of the soul—before going to bed every night. "What did I do right and what did I do wrong? How could I have improved on each aspect of the day?"

Once a year, we spend a whole month (Elul) preparing for Rosh Hashanah, the Jewish new year. We then begin the Ten Days of *Teshuvah* (repentance), ending with Yom Kippur. On Yom Kippur, we fast for a whole day and go through the details of our sins for that year.

---

13 Tractate *Sanhedrin* 18b.

14 See Daniel Kahneman, *Thinking Fast and Slow* (or for an easier read, Michael Lewis, *The Undoing Project*) to see how extensive these thinking biases are.

15 Talmud, Tractate *Sanhedrin* 7b.

16 *Rashi*, ibid.

We verbally articulate these sins (*vidui*), for thoughts alone allow us to keep things fuzzy.[17] Four days later, before the inspiration can wear off, we begin a process of consolidation by celebrating Sukkot.

All of this is a lot more serious than a New Year's resolution. What we are trying to launch is a momentum for sustainable change.

THINK SMALL, THINK SLOW

Tomas Chamorro-Premuzic points out the big difference between wanting change and wanting *to* change. Most people don't really want *to* change—i.e., a whole process; they want *to have changed*. They long for the results that come from change, but they are not committed to doing the work that such change requires.[18] Change is hard.

One of the reasons for this is that to change, we must think small and not big. The great principle of growth is, "Do not leap to the heavens."[19] It is not the grand leaps of spirituality that will be sustained, but the extra little push to do another kindness or be patient for a minute longer.[20]

It is with the ground firmly under our feet that we inch forward.[21] You can decide in a moment of inspiration to become righteous and holy, but you can't do it all at once. Engaging in spiritual growth is a process, and someone who takes it all on in one shot will drop it just as fast. This is one perspective of Rabbi Tarfon's maxim: "You are not required to complete the task, but you are not free to exempt yourself from it."[22] Don't think of perfection now—of completing the task. Think of moving forward.

It is not the grand leaps of spirituality that will be sustained, but the extra little push.

Growth is a slow business.

---

17 *Sefer Hachinuch.*

18 Tomas Chamorro-Premuzic.

19 Rabbi Shlomo Wolbe, *Alei Shur*, vol. 2, p. 26, in the name of Rav Yeruchum Leibovitz.

20 Ibid.

21 Ibid., p. 27.

22 *Ethics of Our Fathers* 2:21.

GREATNESS LIES IN THE DETAILS

William Blake once commented, "He who would do good to another must do it in Minute Particulars: general Good is the plea of the scoundrel, hypocrite, and flatterer."

When he died, the great Rabbi Chaim Friedlander left his diaries with their daily entries. People were so surprised to see what he had written: "Once a week, think about the mitzvah of loving my neighbor." "Twice a week, pray for my fellow man." On one occasion, he entered a commitment to refrain from giving his own opinions on what was happening in the world for just five days.[23]

Rabbi Friedlander broke down his growth into mini-steps. He never said to himself, "Start being kind," or "stop getting angry." He took a step, and if it stuck, then he came back to that step a little later and took another one.

But this is not just a methodology. Small actions are, in and of themselves, the true value of our spirituality.

In the Torah, the culminating act of Abraham's kindness was his hospitality to the three angels whom he thought were people.[24] The Torah describes this incident in unusual detail. It was not the kindness of the mega-philanthropist endowing a building, or even the heroic kindness of going to Africa and inoculating people against cholera. It was the kindness of a man in his home to three utter strangers.

The Torah goes into the minute nuances of the event: what Abraham said, what Sarah prepared, Abraham's running to and fro, three slaughtered animals so that Abraham could serve the delicacy of one tongue for each guest,[25] served with butter and milk, and all served by him personally.[26] Clearly, just taking care of hunger was not the goal.[27]

The greatness of Abraham's kindness lay in the details and not in grand ideas. Beware the man who talks love but he pushes to get ahead

---

23 *Siftei Chaim*, intro. to festivals, vol. 1.

24 Genesis 18:1–8.

25 This is not obvious from the text but is proven by the *Midrash Tanchuma*, *Vayeira*, chap. 4.

26 Genesis 18:8, as explained by *Rashi*, v. 7.

27 *Ramban*, Genesis 18:6.

in line; of the one who talks big but does little.[28] Greatness lies in Abraham's running for his guests sake,[29] in the fact that Abraham so badly wanted to give but was still able to say the equivalent of, "and if all you want to do is have a drink, I won't keep you."[30]

BE IMPERFECT

Judaism is a system that provides a vision of excellence; we can never reconcile ourselves to mediocrity. But our steps along the way will perforce be imperfect.

It is growing that is our measure of success, not perfection.

When we act, however imperfectly, we are building self-trust. We start believing in our capacity for change.

When we do act, however imperfectly, we are building self-trust. We start believing in our capacity for change. By accepting imperfection, we are more likely to achieve success, and it is those successes that build our self-trust.

If we can sustain mini-steps our whole lives, at some point we will achieve greatness. The trick is to stay with each little action until it becomes habit and before we suffer from fatigue. Fatigue sets in when one feels that one is banging one's head against a wall and not growing. It happens when each time you resolve anew to do something, you last a couple of weeks and then slip back again. People don't suffer from fatigue as a result of micro-step because they create a spiritual momentum. They don't measure growth one week or one month at a time. They just make sure that they are pointed in the right direction.

Imperfect actions also exercise our character muscles. Every time we act, it will be easier to do that act again. Even if we fall, the next round will be easier. An athlete who had an injury and now has to get fit again will do so much faster than someone who never exercised to begin with. Once in shape, we find it easier to use our character "muscles." We get used to the system of growth.

---

28 *Midrash Tanchuma* ad loc.

29 Genesis 18:6–7.

30 Ibid., v. 4.

42

THE NEGATIVE INCLINATION—REVISITED

There are three inns that a person visits during his earthly journey: the inn of Jealousy, the inn of Desire, and the inn of Honor. I managed to leave the first two fairly quickly and have never returned. But the third, the inn of Glory, I struggled mightily to leave until I felt that my very veins were snapping.

Kotzker Rebbe[1]

THE NEGATIVE INCLINATION

In Chapter 8, we introduced the idea that everyone has a *yetzer hara*—a negative inclination, as well as a *yetzer hatov*—a positive inclination. Our negative inclination is that which tells us to lust after the sensual, be arrogant, and engage in the forbidden. It begins with the materialistic desires of the body and ends with real negativity. The insidiousness of the *yetzer hara* is not that it seduces us with the full knowledge that we are doing something wrong. That happens, but it is relatively easy to control, if we so desire. It is when the *yetzer hara* sneaks

1 As quoted by Menachem Posner, Chabad.org, based on *Kochav Hashachar*, by Simcha Raz.

into our persona and takes over our identity that the real problems begin. Hence, the prophet Joel called the *yetzer hara* "the hidden one."[2]

The choice to do good over evil is the stuff of righteousness, but there is a more fundamental choice to be made than choosing good over evil. It is to choose that the *yetzer hara* does not speak with our voice. If we can view our negativity as an "other," we can then separate our core identities from our negativity. We are not our *yetzer haras*. Our essence is good and pure. Any bad that I find within me exists only due to the garment—the body that covers the soul.[3] Hence, we can shed that persona that tells us that we must reconcile ourselves with our bad habits. We can know with certainty that it is inconsistent, not just with our life's purpose, but with the very essence of our being.

It is when the yetzer hara sneaks into our persona and takes over our identity that the real problems begin.

The *yetzer hara* has no life of its own.[4] It can only be sustained by us adopting it and nurturing it.[5] When we say, "*I* don't want to get out of bed, but I *should*," the side of me that doesn't want to get up becomes the "I," whereas the voice of goodness becomes the "should"—the voice outside of myself. By doing this, we give life to the *yetzer hara*. We become the host of a spiritual virus. But we do more than that. We give our identity over to this outside force.

To allow this, we simply have to be passive, for the *yetzer hara* never sleeps. It is always energized. *Ethics of Our Fathers* tells us: "You should run to do an easy mitzvah, and flee from a sin."[6] We have to actively run to do a mitzvah and flee from sin.[7] We cannot be good by just being; we have to choose goodness.

---

2 Talmud, Tractate *Sukkah* 52b.

3 "Know Yourself," p. 44, by the author of *Bilvavi*.

4 It was created by God only as a potential.

5 Talmud, Tractate *Shabbat* 105b observes that the verse says: "'You should not have *within you* a foreign god.' (Psalms 81:10). What kind of foreign god exists within the body of man? This is the *yetzer hara*."

6 *Ethics of Our Fathers* 4:2.

7 Rabbi Chaim of Volozhin, *Ruach Chaim* ad loc.

Since our souls are pure, this is nothing but self-deception, and the last person we want to fool is ourselves. We have to dig deep until we meet the real "I." We have to turn our "should" back into our "I"—to do good so often that we naturally identify with this as whom we are. "Righteous people are governed by their *yetzer tov*."[8]

THE THREE BIG YETZER HARAS

In *Ethics of Our Fathers*, we read, "Jealousy, sensuality, and honor take a person out of this world."[9]

Jealousy is wanting something that is not yours. It is the desire to be someone that you are not—to be someone else. Jealousy is so powerful that even though Cain and Abel each had half the world, it was not enough.[10]

Sensuality is the opposite of giving. Giving is taking from within yourself and giving beyond yourself to another person. Sensuality is the desire to give to yourself—to take in rather than give out. It is giving directed in the wrong direction.[11]

The three big sensuality drives are the sex drive, the food drive (which includes addictions), and the drive for materialism and money. Money is a double-whammy. It is also rooted in a drive for power. Through money, even the incorruptible can become corrupted.[12] (See more below in Chapter 53.)

Arrogance is the inability to try and be great with reference to one's own potential. The arrogant person must be better than others. He must lord it over others. In extreme cases, the arrogant person finds it hard to accept any higher authority, including God. "And your heart will be raised up [in arrogance], and you will forget the Lord your God."[13]

Arrogance, *gaavah*, is the opposite of *gevurah*—the expression of self-control and the setting of boundaries. Whereas *gevurah* is expressed

---

8 Talmud, Tractate *Berachot* 61b.

9 *Ethics of Our Fathers* 4:28.

10 *Chidushei Harim*, *Kitvei Chassidim*.

11 Rabbi Eliyahu Dessler, *Michtav Me'Eliyahu*, vol. 2, "The Traits of the Forefathers."

12 Kotzker Rebbe, as brought by Menachem Posner, Chabad.org.

13 Deuteronomy 8:14, 11. See below, Chapter 52.

inwards—control of self—*gaavah* is expressed outwards in the desire to control others.[14] (We will deal with this in Chapter 52.) In extreme cases, this can lead to aggression. "The rewarding aspect of aggression, including feelings of superiority and dominance, underlies the hedonistic component of bullying."[15]

There is an additional problem with arrogance. Because he believes he is already great, an arrogant person stops growing. "Even the greatest person—who has never sinned—must pray to God that he not come to believe in himself, for self-aggrandizement is worse than the worst sin," said the Kotzker Rebbe.[16]

ANGER—THE ONLY NEGATIVE TRAIT

It emerges that sensuality is kindness turned in the wrong direction, just as arrogance is strength of character gone wrong. The trait is essentially a good one gone wrong.

Sensuality is kindness turned in the wrong direction.

So, too, with every trait; none of them are intrinsically negative. Each can be used for good and for bad. There is only one trait, the trait of anger, which does not have any redeeming features.[17] Whereas sensuality is the "good of bads" (because it can be so easily re-channeled), anger is the "bad of bads."[18] That is because anger is a loss of control,[19] and this is the reason why the Sages compare anger to serving idolatry.[20] For he who loses his temper doesn't really believe that God is looking after him and giving him exactly what he needs.[21] The Talmud tells us that we generally follow the laws of Beit Hillel over

---

14 *Michtav Me'Eliyahu*, ibid.

15 R. Douglas Fields, "The Roots of Human Aggression," *Scientific American*, May 2019.

16 As quoted by Menachem Posner, Chabad.org.

17 *Orchot Tzaddikim*, introduction.

18 *Shelah Hakodesh*, letter 200.

19 Talmud, Tractate *Shabbat* 105a; Maimonides, *Mishneh Torah*, Laws of Attributes 2:3.

20 *Tanya*, *Iggeret Hakodesh*, chap. 25.

21 Hence, Rabbah son of Rav Huna said: He who loses his temper, even the Divine Presence is unimportant in his eyes; Talmud, Tractate *Nedarim* 22b.

Beit Shammai because the former were always pleasant and never got insulted.[22]

CHANNELING THE YETZER HARA FOR GOOD

We saw in Chapter 8 how our impulses for sex, ownership, and wealth can be channeled for good.[23] Not only that, but if we go to the source of our sensual drive, we will see that it is really inverted giving. Someone steeped in sensuality can really become a very giving and caring person![24]

So too, the drive for power (pride) and honor has its place, such as the need for a Torah sage to accept enough honor to legitimate the effective transmission of his Torah.[25] Jealousy, too, has its place: One *ought* to be jealous for the sake of one's spouse or for God, as we see many times in the Torah and prophets.[26] We even see this trait attributed to God Himself.[27]

All of these examples show how we actually can use our *yetzer hara* for good. But we need to know that even when what is being asked of us is to simply control our urges, it is the *yetzer hara* that gave us the choice to begin with—the choice to become the master of our own good.[28] Whichever way you look at it, this pesky *yetzer hara* is actually a force for good in disguise.[29]

---

22 Talmud, Tractate *Eruvin* 13b. The Talmud adds a third reason, that Beit Hillel always declared the words of Beit Shammai before they announce their own opinions.

23 *Yefeh Toar*, ibid.

24 *Degel Machaneh Ephraim*, beg. *Parashat Vayigash*.

25 Proverbs 3:35. The Talmud in Tractate *Sotah* 5a says, "Any wise man who does not have an eighth of an eighth (i.e., the smallest amount; *Meiri*) of pride, is not a wise man."

26 Numbers 25:11; Kings I 19:10.

27 Exodus 34:14.

28 See Chapter 3.

29 *Ramchal, Derech Hashem* 1:2:1.

43

CHALLENGES AND TESTS

I've never wanted to serve a God Whose ways would be understandable to mere mortals.

Kotzker Rebbe[1]

FINDING THE HIDDEN POTENTIAL

The word for "test" in Hebrew is *nisayon*. According to some, the root of this word is *nes*,which means "miracle."[2] A test is that which brings out the miracle of self—the part of us that we had no idea was inside of ourselves.[3] It is the capacity to rise above one's nature—to be supernatural within one's own self.[4]

In Psalms, we read, "Our entire soul must praise God."[5] We have to find new resources within ourselves to develop all the missing aspects of our "I."[6]

1 As quoted by Menachem Posner, Chabad.org, based on *Kochav Hashachar*, by Simcha Raz.

2 Rabbi Mordechai Miller of Gateshead, England.

3 *Nes* can also mean a banner, i.e., the glories of untapped human potential that then act as an inspiration for the whole world.

4 *Mimaamakim*, Exodus, p. 53.

5 The common translation of this is "Let every soul praise God." However, the literal translation is as in the text.

6 *Shiurei Daat*, Rav Elya Meir Bloch, *Yesurim shel Ahavah*.

Were we not forced to push against the existing reality of our own personality, we would never bring out the hidden miracle of the self. "Treat a person as he is and he will remain as he is," said Ralph Waldo Emerson. "Treat him as he could be, and he will become what he should be."[7]

One who has really internalized this idea—that the test is really his friend and is there to elevate him—will face most difficulties in a matter-of-fact manner, as this is exactly the reality he anticipates in this world. He doesn't think, "This is so unfair," and "why me?" He simply focuses on facing the challenge itself. He sees suffering for what it is—as a means, not as an end. He understands that this world (in its entirety) is a means, and that the ultimate state of man in the World to Come is to be in a state of spiritual happiness without any pain or suffering.[8]

A test is that which brings out the miracle of self—the part of ourselves that we had no idea was inside of ourselves.

He wastes no emotional energy on what he deserves or on comparing with others; he simply engages the issue itself.

Without challenges, we would naturally grow where we are strongest. It would leave us with vast gaps in our personality.[9] Resolving that gap—that incompatibility between our existing state and our potential—is what a test is all about.[10] The test is a gift of growth to allow us to transition from being people with a good heart and some good actions to actualizing *all* of our potential.[11]

FACING THE IMPOSSIBLE

By its very nature, a test puts us in a situation whose resolution we do not know how to achieve.[12] A test tells us to leap into the darkness

---

7 See Chapter 41 above.

8 *Ramchal, Derech Hashem, Daat Tevunot.*

9 *Maharal, Netzach Yisrael*, chap 7.

10 Rabbi Elya Meir Bloch, *Shiurei Daat*, suffering.

11 *Maharal, Netzach Yisrael*, chap. 32; *Netiv Hayesurin*, chap. 3.

12 Rabbi Moshe Shapiro.

where seemingly we have no control. Despite that, we are being asked to take responsibility.

But how can God ask us to take responsibility for something beyond our control? Our first instincts are to conclude that, indeed, we are not responsible. "Am I my brother's keeper?" says Cain of Abel.[13] Someone else, certainly not me, must be at fault: "The wife You gave me, gave me to eat,"[14] says Adam, and she, not me, must take responsibility. Or our instincts are simply to flee, as Jonah did.[15] Or they are to refuse to understand that God would do such a thing, as was the case of Job.[16] Surely, God's world is an orderly one, where everything makes sense.

We can only resolve this with a leap of faith that God believes in me and my potential. But this faith is built on solid foundations and a sound rational basis. It is nothing like an initial leap into religious fervor. It is, rather, extending what we know just a little further than we can know—to stretch our horizons of what we know about God, i.e., that He *does* care for us and believe in us in general, into the arena of faith, i.e., that then He surely does; so too in this case.

If God believes in me, then I am being asked also to believe in myself and to stay the distance.[17]

My faith tells me that not only does God not give me a test that I cannot handle,[18] but also that the test is absolutely in my best interest. For what the test does is strip us of our superficiality, leaving our essential self. It asks the essential me to take myself into the unknown, based on my trust that this process is good for me.[19]

PROCESS RATHER THAN RESULTS

The Jews entered Egypt as a small family-tribe of seventy people, were then enslaved, and somehow emerged as a new nation. No human

---

13 Genesis 4:9.

14 Ibid. 3:12.

15 Jonah 1:3.

16 This is the theme of the entire book of Job.

17 See, for example, Tractate *Bava Batra* 15b, concerning Job.

18 *Ramban*, Genesis 22:1.

19 *Maharal*, *Netiv Hayesurin*, chap. 1.

could have predicted such an unlikely result. The irony of it was that the process itself helped to produce the result. The suffering of the slavery purified the Jews like an iron furnace purifies metal—to the point where they were ready for redemption. The darkness served to elevate and raise them.[20] The Jews were not only asked to believe in the result but also in the process. This was their test.

Seen this way, it is not the resolution of the issue that is central. It is the way we approach the issue. In fact, a particular challenge may be so essential to our purpose in life that we will never resolve it.[21]

We may have to live with this difficulty our entire lives. Our job will be to turn it into an instrument of both growth and happiness.

We all dream that somehow, if things were different, life would be so much better. So many of us say, "I am fine. But it wouldn't hurt if God let me make a little more money." The saintly Chafetz Chaim overhead someone utter those words and responded: "And how can you be so sure that it wouldn't hurt you? Since this is your lot, it would seem that you are definitely best off as you are."

WHO AND WHAT IS BEING TESTED

Ethics of Our Fathers tell us that Abraham underwent ten tests.[22] In all of these, Abraham was asked to go against his basic nature of kindness that he had spent a life-time perfecting.

In the most dramatic of these, Abraham was ordered to take his son, Isaac, and to sacrifice him on an altar.[23] Abraham was being asked to kill a beloved son, the only son who seemed eligible to continue his life-task.

---

20 *Sefat Emet*, *Va'era* 5638; *Ohr Gedalyahu*, Exodus, p. 12, note 4 there; p. 7.

21 We may have to live with this difficulty our entire lives. Rav Eliyahu Dessler, *Michtav Me'Eliyahu*, vol. 4, p. 22. Rav Dessler makes passing reference to this idea in numerous places: In vol. 3, p. 30, he refers to this poetically (in Hebrew): This is your life, and its entirety is challenges. In vol. 3, p. 197, he says that when a person refuses to use the attributes and personality as well as material objects (*keilim*) he's been given correctly, his challenge may increase. In fact, a person is granted certain attributes already before birth. (Vol 2, p. 156.)

22 *Ethics of Our Fathers* 5:3.

23 Genesis 22:2.

The Torah calls this Abraham's test—his test alone, and not Isaac's. "And it happened after these things that God tested Abraham."[24] Yet Isaac, despite only getting to know about the plan on site, also rises to the challenge. He is ready to die for God.[25] So why wasn't it his test as well?

For Isaac, whose attribute was *gevurah*—total control and boundaries, sacrificing his life to God was no test. He saw his whole life as nothing else. But for Abraham, it was different. Abraham had built his whole life as a giver. His connection to God was through seeing God as the ultimate giver and his desire to imitate Him. In addition, the way he connected others to God was by teaching them about this kindness.[26]

Abraham was now being asked to go against everything that he had stood for—to go against his life's work. Abraham was asked to be cruel for the sake of God, whom he believed was totally kind and giving.[27]

Why did God ask such a thing?

Abraham was being asked to go against everything that he had stood for—to go against his life's work.

God was testing whether Abraham was kind because he was naturally a nice person, or whether he had developed his attribute because he saw this as the way to serve God.[28]

Put differently, did Abraham believe in God only so long as he could understand His every move? The way to test this would be to see whether Abraham could go against his character if this is what God wanted of him now.[29]

For three days, Abraham and Isaac walked together.[30] The Torah tells us nothing about Abraham's thoughts and feelings during this

24 Ibid. 22:1.

25 Ibid. 22:6–9.

26 Talmud, Tractate *Sotah* 10b.

27 Rabbi Eliyahu Dessler, *Michtav Me'Eliyahu*, p. 162.

28 *Michtav Me'Eliyahu*, ibid.

29 Tractate *Sanhedrin* 89a; Vilna Gaon, Tractate *Berachot* 33b.

30 Genesis 22:6.

time. The overwhelming emotions that Abraham felt were too deep and profound to be described in words.[31]

Eventually, Abraham resolves these feelings. He is ready to overcome a lifetime of compassion and to lift the knife that will kill his son.[32] At that moment of resolution, the angel of God calls on him, "Abraham, Abraham." Abraham answers, *Hineni.* "Here I am, I am ready."[33]

The story then takes a dramatic turn. Instead of being told to sacrifice his son, he is told to change course and hold off. God shows him a ram which he sacrifices instead.

Abraham is ready for this too. *Hineni*. This was the same word that Abraham used when God first approached him about the sacrifice.[34] Now his *hineni*, his commitment, was resolved at a much higher level. It was the culmination of the three days of struggle—the painful journey to the mountain.[35]

Every Rosh Hashanah, we blow the shofar in memory of the binding of Isaac when a ram with its shofar (horns) was sacrificed instead.[36] This is because Abraham's test, his two *hineni*'s, reflect the journey we must all take. We start with simple faith. Then we become more thoughtful, and we have questions. We then resolve them at a higher level.

The fact that Abraham overcame these challenges showed that his kindness was not just a natural trait which he happened to enjoy expressing.

All of Abraham's ten tests required him to go against his character. For example, Abraham was asked to circumcise himself at the age of ninety-nine.[37] By circumcising himself, Abraham would be entering into a special relationship with God, thereby creating a division between him and all of those people with

31 *Seridei Aish*, with commentary of the *Gachalei Aish*, Rabbi Avraham Aba Weingart.

32 Genesis 22:10.

33 Ibid., v. 11.

34 Ibid., v. 1.

35 *Seridei Aish*, with commentary of the *Gachalei Aish*.

36 Tractate *Rosh Hashanah* 16a.

37 Genesis 17:1–2.

whom he was trying to connect.[38] All his instincts told him that this was the wrong thing to do.[39] Yet, God commanded and he obeyed.

He thereby showed that where the will of God required something else, he was capable of that too.

UNDERSTANDING WHAT IT WAS ALL ABOUT

God only gives us tests that we are capable of withstanding.[40] The greater our soul, the more need God has to challenge us to fulfill our potential. That does not mean that we always understand the purpose of our test at the time. When Moses asked God for an insight into this, God's answer to Moses' request was: "My face may not be seen" as the events are unfolding.[41] A human being may not stare at that level of God that will provide a full answer, a place above time and all human reality.[42] Nevertheless, "You will see My back,"[43] meaning we may gain some understanding of why this or that challenge was in our best interests in retrospect. There will come a time, during the Messianic Era, when we will understand the whole picture of this world and hence how everything was necessary to bring the world to completion.[44]

38 *Michtav Me'Eliyahu*, vol. 2, *middot ha'Avot*.

39 Vilna Gaon, *Kol Eliyahu*, beg. *Parashat Vayeira*.

40 *Ramban*, Genesis 22:1. See also Proverbs 3:11; Psalms 94:12; Talmud, Tractate *Arachin* 16b.

41 Exodus 33:18–20. See Tractate *Berachot* 7a.

42 See *Ethics of Our Fathers* 4:19; *Maharal*, *Netzach Yisrael*, chap. 18.

43 Exodus 33:22–23.

44 *Ramchal*, *Daat Tevunot* 54.

44

THE INNER SPIRIT OF JUDAISM

The totality of serving God is dependent on fixing one's character flaws.

Vilna Gaon[1]

A TORAH CREATES THE TUNE—MAN SINGS THE SONG

To fulfill the trust that God has in us, we have to understand the inner spirit of Judaism. The Torah cannot give us an exhaustive list dictating all our neighborly relations, how to conduct every financial transaction, all the laws of the environment or taxation, or of bodily health.[2] God wanted to leave these things to our own spiritual creativity. What God did was give us examples of the type of behavior that He wants from us so that we could understand the principle involved: "Do not spread gossip";[3] "Do not take revenge or bear a grudge";[4] "Don't stand idly by while your fellow man's blood is spilled";[5] "Don't curse the deaf";[6] "Rise before the old and the wise."[7]

---

1 *Even Sheleimah* 1:1.
2 *Ramban*, Deuteronomy 6:18.
3 Leviticus 19:16.
4 Ibid., v. 18.
5 Ibid., v. 16.
6 Ibid., v. 14.
7 Ibid., v. 32.

God then says to man, "And you should do the righteous and the good."[8] It is as if He is saying, "OK, you get the idea. Now go do the rest yourself. Don't just stick to the letter of the law. Soar above that into the inner spirit of what I am trying to tell you."[9]

Take the example of kindness. The Torah could never detail the endless opportunities to give—a smile in the right place, standing for someone on the subway, or simply passing the salt to the other end of the table. Marriage in particular has so many giving moments every single day: The little bits of housework, the constant sensitivity to one's spouse's needs and moods, child-rearing, and the financial burden are just a short-list of the never-ending giving possibilities.

For this reason, the Torah did not legislate the nature of our kindnesses to our fellow man, but left it up to our own creative spirituality. There is only one way that this kind of kindness can be sustained; it must come from within. Our character trait of giving must push us to give.

The sum total of all the mitzvot creates a harmony—the blending of different *kedushot* that make up the melody of life. We need to tune into that spiritual melody, the inner harmony that will allow us to become a Torah personality. "We must find God where we find ourselves," said Rabbi Shimshon Raphael Hirsch.[10] By that, he meant that we must create within ourselves that inner synergy that naturally connects with the Divine.

This is a seminal point. It is about capturing the essence of what Judaism is all about, which is so easy to miss from the outside. It is about how ordinary people become extraordinary. It is what allows all the details to combine in producing all the essential elements of being human.

---

8 Deuteronomy 6:18.

9 *Ramban* ad loc.

10 As quoted in Dayan Grunfeld's introduction to *Horeb*, p. cxvii.

The Sages filled in some details,[11] but, in the end, enormous areas of activity were left up to our own discretion.[12] Each person must apply his unique character and personality in each situation such that his thoughts and actions are in harmony with the Torah.[13] It is not good enough to just "do" the commandments. After all, these occupy but a small part of most people's day. The Torah personality intuits the internal logic of the Torah—its methodology of thought—and acts accordingly.

The sum total of all the mitzvot creates a harmony—the blending of different kedushot that make up the melody of life.

THE TORAH PERSONALITY BUILT THROUGH TORAH EXAMPLES

How do we develop a Torah personality? Each one of the mitzvot stimulates a different part of our character.

Let's take cruelty to animals. The Torah gives us a few examples:

- Feed your animal before you feed yourself.[14]
- Don't muzzle an ox when he is on the threshing floor.[15]
- Don't slaughter a mother and its child on the same day.[16]
- Don't harness an ox and a donkey (who don't feel comfortable next to each other) to the same plow.[17]
- Help your neighbor unload his animal.[18]

This is not, and cannot be, an exhaustive list. We need to use these examples to develop our sense of mercy toward animals in general. By

---

11 Talmud, Tractate *Bava Metzia* 108a, applies this verse—"And you should do the righteous and the good"—to someone who wants to sell his land, saying that he must offer it first to the owner of the adjacent land. Tractate *Yoma* 71a says that from this we learn that we should always speak gently. Tractate *Taanit* 16b states that the implications of the verse are that we must not only be honest but we must act beyond suspicion of acquiring anything by dishonest means.

12 *Maggid Mishnah*, *Mishneh Torah* Laws of Neighbors 14:5.

13 Ibid.

14 Deuteronomy 11:15.

15 Ibid. 25:4.

16 Exodus 22:28.

17 Deuteronomy 22:10.

18 Exodus 23:5.

starting with this list, we train ourselves to be the kind of righteous person that naturally extends the sensitivity to animals in new areas.[19]

There once was a cow being led to slaughter. It ran into the arms of the great Rabbi Yehudah HaNasi and cried. Rabbi Yehudah said to it, "Go, since for this you were created!" Of course, the rabbi was right, but since he did not show compassion for the cow, difficult travails fell upon him.[20] The Torah cannot legislate compassion of this sort, but for someone of Rabbi Yehudah HaNasi's stature, the lack of it was tantamount to a sin.

Or take hunting. The Torah does not prohibit hunting for pleasure, but this is an obvious extension of the list.[21] It doesn't tell us not to stomp on an ant without any cause, or not to chase a frightened cat under a car, even though these acts do not benefit us in any way (however, see note[22]). The Torah personality doesn't need to be told this. Rabbi Chaim Pinchas Scheinberg lived on the fourth floor. He once saw an ant walk over his couch. He asked a departing guest whether he would mind taking the ant out to the garden downstairs.

What we are being asked to do is to tune in to the inner spirit of Judaism. For this reason, there is no mitzvah in the Torah commanding us to work on our character in general. For character development is

---

19 *Ramban*, Deuteronomy 6:18.

20 Talmud, Tractate *Bava Metzia* 85a.

21 *Noda B'Yehudah II*, *Yoreh Deah* 10. See Leviticus 17:13, where hunting is allowed for purposes of food. However, the two famous hunters in the Torah, Nimrod (Genesis 10:8–10) and Esau (Genesis 25:27) are both considered evil.

22 This does not mean that we may not kill or scare away animals where there is a reason. "It is a Torah prohibition to cause pain to any animal. On the contrary, one is obligated to save every animal from pain, even those that are ownerless and including those that belong to non-Jews. However, if they are causing pain to people, or if a person needs them for healing purposes or for any other productive purpose, it is permissible even to kill them, and we are not concerned that, in the process, we are causing them pain, for the Torah allowed us to slaughter animals [for the purpose of eating meat]"; Rabbi Shlomo Gantzfried, *Kitzur Shulchan Aruch* 191:1. The *Kitzur Shulchan Aruch* continues (191:2–6) with other laws relating to this, including the obligation to help an animal up a hill lest his owner will whack it to get it do so. It is also prohibited to castrate it.

implicit in every mitzvah we do, each one nurturing a different aspect of self.[23]

Once that character is developed, the Torah personality will not just find his life punctuated with mitzvot but will be permeated with a spirit of Torah that will be reflected in his every action: in the way he speaks, in the way he acts, in his sensitivity and in his overall character. Such a person has cracked the code that allows him to now live on the inside of his Judaism.

There is no mitzvah in the Torah commanding us to work on our character in general. Character development is implicit in every mitzvah we do.

JUDAISM REQUIRES THE STAMP OF MY INDIVIDUAL PERSONALITY

There is another reason why the Torah could not mandate every detail. We are all unique, and we all have different personalities and character profiles:[24]

- Some of us are naturally laid back, while some of us are intense.
- Some of us stay calm through thick and thin, while some of us are easily upset.
- Some of us are brimming with confidence, while some of us have poor self-images.
- Some of us have food cravings all day, while others seem more ascetic.[25]

To be authentic, the spiritual "I" of the Torah personality perforce must have the stamp of individual personality.

Embracing Judaism in this way puts us in tune with our inner selves so that, ultimately, there is no contradiction between our outer and our inner selves. It allows us to be authentic at every level. Maimonides tells us that every Jew has to be a doctor of his own soul. We have to learn

---

23 Rabbi Chaim Vital, as brought by Rabbi Shlomo Wolbe, *Alei Shur*, vol. 1.
24 Miamonides, *Hil. Deot*, 1:1.
25 Ibid.

about our whole body—the big picture of ourselves. We must know what our healthy parts and unhealthy parts are.[26]

BE BALANCED!

If we will follow the whole Torah system, some of the commandments will direct us toward giving, and some of them will direct us toward self-restraint; some toward the right, and some toward the left.[27] We ought not to be angry people, but we should not become totally unresponsive either.[28] We ought to live simply, but not so simply that we neglect our necessities.[29] We ought to be humble, but not to the point where people walk all over us. We ought to be charitable, but our needs must come first. The overall effect is to avoid the unhealthy extremes[30] and to become well-rounded and holy Torah personalities. Maimonides calls this the *middle trait*,[31] popularized as the "golden mean."[32]

There is a difference between being balanced and being normal. Normal means being in the middle of the bell curve, an average. It is a term of comparison. Jews are anything but normal. We are here to tell the tale because we are the most abnormal nation on earth, the people who never feared breaking norms in order to set a new standard. "A nation that dwells alone."[33]

If the definition of normality is the average of all people—a bell curve—then there is no idea to be normal in Judaism. There *is*, however, a strong idea to be balanced.[34] Such balance will emerge from

---

26 Maimonides, *Shemoneh Perakim*, chap. 1.

27 Ibid., chap. 4.

28 Maimonides, *Mishneh Torah*, Laws of Attributes 1:4.

29 Ibid.

30 Ibid. §3.

31 Ibid. §4.

32 Maimonides does not use this word. It appears to have been taken from a non-Jewish source, probably Aristotle.

33 Numbers 23:9.

34 The distinction between normal and balanced is an important one. Often the two are confused. A two-year-old who doesn't make it to the bathroom on time or a four-year-old who throws a tantrum—these behaviors would be highly abnormal in someone much older. These examples relate to natural maturation—with growing up—rather than with conscious development of one's character, which is my focus here.

passionate pursuit of spirituality. Be passionately balanced! According to Maimonides, there is a commandment in the Torah that instructs us on this idea. It is the mitzvah of "walking in His ways."[35]

This "way of God" is exactly why God chose Abraham and his descendants: "For I have known him that he would command his children and his household after him that they would keep the way of God."[36]

Walking in God's ways, then, is not one-size-fits-all. To be a Jew is to know yourself. It is to own your Torah in a way that allows you to create your own balance—your own personal walk with God.[37]

---

35 *Mishneh Torah*, Laws of Attributes 1:5, 7; *Shemoneh Perakim*, chap. 4. In Chapter 8, we referred to this verse in a different context, as the source of one of the two commandments to be kind to our fellow man.

36 Genesis 18:19.

37 See Rabbi Aaron Soloveitchik, *Perach Mateh Aaron*; *Mishneh Torah*, Laws of Attributes, chap. 1.

45

LOVE, MARRIAGE, AND RELATIONSHIPS

What has God been busy with since the Six Days of Creation until now? He has been putting couples together.

Midrash Rabbah, Genesis

LOVE IS A RESULT, NOT A STATE OF BEING

One of the greatest errors we can make is to imagine that love is something that "happens" to us—that we fall in love. However, "To fall in love is to create a religion that has a fallible god," as Jorge Luis Borges put it. It is to create an illusion that makes us very unwise in our relationships, and this is why, in the end, it spawns disillusion.[1] Such love is truly blind in the sense that it does not allow us to see the other person with the remotest accuracy.

If we want to get love right, we have to stop using love as a state of being, as in using "I love you" to mean "I am in love." Love is a process that emerges over time. Singer Joan Baez stated, "The easiest kind of

---

1 Based on Francis Bacon's phrase: "It is impossible to love and to be wise," and Miguel De Unamuno, who stated: "Love is the child of illusion and the parent of disillusion" (*The Tragic Sense of Life*).

relationship for me is with ten thousand people. The hardest is with one." This is true because our relationship with the ten thousand doesn't seem to require anything of us. Hence, they amount to ten thousand non-relationships.

LOVE COMES FROM GIVING

The Torah explicitly tells us to love God,[2] our fellow man,[3] the stranger, and the convert.[4]

If love is a feeling, then indeed it cannot be commanded. God cannot order us to feel something that we don't. But if love is a process, then we can be directed to that process. This is indeed the case.

The Hebrew word for love, *ahavah*, comes from the root *hav*, which means to give.[5] Judaism sees the source of love as giving. When one gives to another person, he comes to love him. The more that someone invests in his fellow, the more love will flow from one to the other.

Parents tend to love their children much more than children love their parents because, in typical situations, parents give more to children than the other way around. The giving of the parent is that which *generates* their love, and not the commonly believed idea that we give to someone *because* we love them.[6]

The ultimate giving opportunity is in marriage, and that is why it leads to the deepest expressions of love. "Isaac married Rebecca; she became his wife; he loved her."[7] First he married her, then he loved her. Of course, to want to give to a potential spouse for the rest of your life, certain things have to be in place: chemistry, attraction, shared values, and emotional enthusiasm. But true love comes later.

God cannot order us to feel love, but He can direct us on a process.

2 Deuteronomy 6:5.

3 Leviticus 19:18.

4 Ibid., v. 34; Deuteronomy 10:19.

5 Rabbi Shimshon Raphael Hirsch, Genesis 22:2.

6 Rabbi Eliyahu Dessler, *Michtav Me'Eliyahu*, vol. 1, *kuntrus ha'chessed*, part 1.

7 Genesis 24:67.

Neither can this giving be turned into a partnership—a quid-pro-quo of giving. Marriage requires each spouse to give unilaterally without any expectations of receiving anything in return, again and again. Giving triggers a giving-love-giving cycle. "Through giving, we draw closer to someone. When we are closer to him, we get to know him better, recognizing more and more of his inner virtues. And then we want to give to him even more and deepen our love further."[8] Where do we learn this from? From God Himself, Who takes care of people's needs all day and expects nothing in return.[9]

GIVING IN OTHER RELATIONSHIPS

As humans, we have a deep need to be givers. In one study, two different signs were put up at hand-washing stations in a hospital. One reminded doctors and nurses, "Hand hygiene prevents you from catching diseases." Another read, "Hand hygiene prevents patients from catching diseases." The study measured the amount of soap used at each station. Doctors and nurses at the station where the sign referred to their patients used 45% more soap or hand sanitizer.[10] The idea that their action was helping someone else was a great motivator.

RELATIONSHIPS REQUIRE MORE THAN LOVE

People will stay in abusive relationships because "I love him," and they will break up because "everything is there, but the spark is missing."

The problem with this is not that we are using a false measure but that we are using an exclusive one. Love is only one of the ingredients in a successful marriage.[11]

Mature love is an act of responsibility, of saying, "let's commit to living our life together." That life may involve difficult moments in the

---

8 Rabbi Yirmiyahu and Rebbetzin Tehilah Abramov, *Two Halves of a Whole*, p. 107.

9 *Kuntrus ha'chessed* ad loc.

10 https://www.beckershospitalreview.com/quality/20-hospitals-with-great-hand-hygiene-programs.html. There are certainly many other factors that improve medical handwashing in hospitals. See Peter D. Le Roux, Joshua Levine, W. Andrew Kofke, et al., *Monitoring in Neurocritical Care* (e-book).

11 Sarah Chana Radcliffe, *Ezer Kenegdo*.

realms of health, finances, or disagreements. They may involve the opposite—the mundane of running a home. It involves dealing with a range of emotions, including anger and frustration, as much as it does enjoying and appreciating day-to-day life. It involves learning how to communicate and share, as well as bringing up children together. Most important of all, it involves sharing meaningful long-term goals, values, and perspectives. When choosing a spouse, shared values is the single most important indicator of how successful the marriage is likely to be.

LOVE WITH ONE REQUIRES SENSITIVITY TO ALL

The most basic relationship element of all is mutual respect.

In Hebrew, the word respect—*kavod*, is the same as honor. *Kavod* (כבוד) comes from the word "heavy"—*kaveid* (כבד). Honor is the weight or value you give to someone (or something).[12] When I respect someone, I value them.

The Sages say, "Let the honor of your friend be as precious to you as your own."[13] They also say, "A man should love his wife as he loves his own body, but he should honor her more than he honors himself."[14] All of this is the honor that precedes love. Failure to honor your spouse is so basic that it may be grounds for divorce.[15]

Respect is that which gives boundaries to the relationship. It says, "I cannot use the 'love word' to justify behavior that is insensitive or not caring." It also says, "Even when I am angry and upset and not feeling any warm vibes toward my spouse, I am still bound to respect his/her dignity and needs." Respect is the minimum scaffolding of the relationship that allows the relationship to continue to function until passion can be restored. When I hear the words, "I don't respect him/her anymore," I know the relationship is going to be hard to save. A frequent reason that wives divorce their husbands when they catch them viewing pornography is not necessarily the pornography per se, but because

12 Rabbi Moshe Shapiro, based on Rabbi Shimshon Raphael Hirsch.

13 *Ethics of Our Fathers* 2:5.

14 Talmud, *Bava Metzia* 58b.

15 *Beit Yoseph, Even Ha'ezer* 154.

they lose respect for their spouse and sense the spiral of emotional distancing that it engenders.[16] Love without respect quickly collapses.

TRUST

The next rung on the relationship ladder is trust.[17] Trust is built on respect. The corollary of trust is trustworthiness. I trust my partner, meaning that I consider him or her trustworthy. And I ask for trust in return because I claim to be trustworthy. This is not just the (big) issue of whether spouses remain faithful to each other. It has to do with the secure feeling that your spouse wants the best for you and is willing to sacrifice for this.

Let the honor of your friend be as precious to you as your own.

Trust creates the lens through which we interpret the actions of the other. Your husband comes home late for dinner without telling you because he bumped into an old friend. If there is trust, you see him as just insensitive. If there is no trust, you might think it is because he does not love you.[18]

Trust is that which allows us to be vulnerable and feel safe. It is the platform on which we rest when we feel challenged by our life. It is the certain knowledge that our spouse believes in us and will do so even when we fail.

If there is no respect, there will never be trust. And if there is trust, then—and only then—will there be love. Respect, trust, and love must come in that order.

---

16 The role of pornography in divorce cases has been well documented. In 2005, Dr. Jill Manning, a specialist in this area, claimed before the US Senate that 56% of divorce cases involve one party having an obsessive interest in pornographic websites. Dr. Manning's specialty is described as "betrayal trauma," which reads to the point we are making here. An article by Lauren Vinopal on Fatherly.com brings research showing that it is specifically when the spouse was not aware of the habit that led to a greater likelihood of divorce.

17 Sarah Chanah Radcliffe, *Ezer Kenegdo*.

18 Rabbi Shlomo Wolbe, *Kuntres Le'chatanim*.

LOVE AS CLEAVING

God created the first person as a male-female being. There was initially just one human, an androgynous being with the male face looking one way and the female the other.[19] The face of man represents the first point of contact we have with a person's inner spirituality.

This meant that the full force of man's spirituality, i.e., his face, turned to the world in every direction. Adam had no back, meaning he had no weakness. Since man was complete, he had no needs, and therefore the two faces looked away from each other, rather than turning toward each other, for they had nothing to give to one another.

Then God said, "It is not good for man to be alone."[20] This situation was "not good," i.e., not according to its intended state. God therefore split Adam into a half male-Adam and a half female-Adam (who became Eve).[21] Each one now had a face, but they also both had a back—a place of lack and deficiency. Now they could turn to each other to give themselves over to the other, which is exactly what each one lacked.[22] They then became one again as they had once been at the outset of creation.[23] Since then, marriage has been about giving ourselves to our partners and thereby completing ourselves with literally our other half.[24]

Each of us has a back—a place of lack and deficiency. What we lack is the other.

This idea is revealed by God's instructions to man: "Therefore, a man should leave his mother and his father, and he should *cleave* to his wife,

---

19 *Rashi*, Genesis 1:27.

20 Genesis 2:18.

21 Ibid., 21–22. The normal translation, that "God took man's rib," is a valid but minority opinion (see for example *Targum Yonatan*). The Hebrew word is that God took one *tzela* of man. *Rashi* (v. 21) shows that this word means "side," and not rib. *Rashi* then quotes the Talmud (Tractate *Eruvin* 18), which says that the original being was two-faced—male and female. This is reinforced by Genesis 1:27, where the verse states: "And God created man in His image; in the image of God He created *him*, male and female He created *them*." Apparently, man was both a singular (*him*) and a plural (*them*) simultaneously.

22 *Tur*, beginning of *Even Ha'ezer*.

23 Genesis 2:23.

24 *Kuntrus ha'chessed* 1:6.

and they should become as one flesh."[25] Note that it does not say that a man should *love* his wife, but rather that he should *cleave* to her. And what does that do? The verse continues, "And they should become one flesh." The goal of marriage is to feel a sense of unity. There is no deeper satisfaction in a relationship than where the spouses feel that they are inseparable. Not that they live two lives together, or that they have a partnership, but rather that they are just one unity. One flesh.

Here is a new definition of marital love: Love is becoming one.

LOVE AS HOLINESS

The Jewish recipe for successful marriage requires an attitude that the couple's home is a mini-Sanctuary, and the couple themselves are the bearers of God's name within that sanctuary. The Hebrew name for a woman is *isha* (אשה); for a man, it is *ish* (איש). Each one of these names is a combination of the word *eish* (אש)—fire—plus one other letter—a *yud* (י) for a man, and a *hei* (ה) for a woman. Those two letters spell one of God's names—*y-ah* (י"ה). Remove God's name, and the couple are like two fires that will consume each other. Insert God's name and the relationship is nurtured toward holy unity.[26]

---

25 Genesis 2:24.

26 Talmud, Tractate *Sotah* 17a.

46

KINDNESS—THE QUINTESSENTIAL JEWISH TRAIT

Rabbi Moshe Leib of Sasov would say he learned about loving others from watching two peasants drinking in a saloon.

One turned to the other and said, "Ivan, do you love me?"

His friend responded, "Of course I do!"

"Then Ivan, tell me what hurts me!"

Ivan responded, "I don't know."

"How can you say you love me if you don't know what hurts me?!"

The Sages tell us, "There are three signs indicating Jewishness: [Jews] are shameful, merciful, and bestowers of kindness."[1]

In the last chapter, we saw how marriage in particular and relationships in general are a function of giving. If you want to have warm feelings toward someone, give to them.[2]

1 Tractate *Yevamot* 79a: "This nation has three signs: the bashful, the merciful, and the kind."

2 *Derech Eretz Zuta*, chap. 2.

Giving leads to love because when you give to someone, you put something of yourself into that person.[3]

Abraham had a big question: How does one start the Jewish People? What would be the right quality to be the foundation for all generations to come—humility, simplicity, wisdom, tenacity, honesty? Abraham had strong elements of all of these. However, in the end, he concluded that he had to focus on kindness.

How so? Because by being kind we are imitating God's kindness, which underlies everything He does in this world.[4]

And so, kindness creates an unshakable bond between mankind and his Creator. Abraham declared that this is what Jews will always stand for: A nation of kindness and philanthropy, sensitivity and caring.

Abraham the Monotheist was a gift to the whole world, while Abraham the Giver defined the very nature of the Jewish People.[5] His kindness elevated Abraham to the degree that his very name "Avraham" means "*Av Ram*," the elevated father of the Jewish People.[6]

How does one start the Jewish People? Abraham concluded that he had to focus on kindness.

Hence, when a potential convert asked Hillel to teach him all of Judaism on one foot, he stated, "What is hateful to you, don't do to your neighbor. This is the entire Torah. The rest is a commentary. Go and study."[7]

LOVE YOUR NEIGHBOR LIKE YOURSELF

The commandment of "love your neighbor like yourself"[8] isn't commanding a feeling. Rather, it means that you should actively work toward the same goodness for your neighbor as you have for yourself.[9]

---

3 *Michtav Me'Eliyahu*, vol. 1, *kuntrus ha'chessed*.

4 *Maharal, Netiv Hachessed*, chap. 1; see Chapter 11.

5 *Sefat Emet* 5640, sect. beg. "and He appeared to him."

6 *Maharal, Netiv Gemilut Chassadim*, chap 1. "*Av Ram*" (אב רם) literally means, "the father of elevation." (See *Rashi*, Genesis 17:5, who offers a different interpretation on Abraham's name as Av Ram.)

7 Talmud, Tractate *Shabbat* 31a.

8 Leviticus 19:18.

9 *Ramban*, Leviticus 19:18. The *Seforno* (ibid.) and the Vilna Gaon say the same thing.

Love is an action. We don't have to feel love; we have to *do* love. The verse in fact says, "You should love *for* your neighbor like yourself."[10] The implication of loving *for* is to act. We *do* love.

For Maimonides, feelings are also involved, but he is quick to stress that without actions, those feelings are meaningless.[11] We should be actively concerned, says Maimonides, with the protection of the body, money, and honor of our fellow humans.[12] We should speak the praises of other people.[13] We should be concerned for their spiritual well-being.[14]

GIVING VS. MERCY

But Judaism does not advocate giving without feeling. "Loving-kindness demands more than a momentary tear and a cold coin. Loving-kindness means empathizing with one's fellow man, identifying with his hurt, and feeling responsible for his fate."[15] "One who gives a coin to a poor person is blessed with six blessings, but he who (also) soothes him with words gets eleven."[16]

Kindness is the act of giving to fulfill the need of another. Mercy is the feeling of discomfort at someone else's pain that moves us to want to do that kindness. Judaism is saying that even though mercy is a Jewish identifier, as we stated above, our kindness will be better when not borne of it. Mercy runs its course, sooner or later. "A man who sees another man on the street corner with only a stump for an arm will be so shocked the first time [that] he'll give him sixpence. But the second time, it'll only be a three-penny bit. And if he sees him a third time, he'll have him cold-bloodedly handed over to the police."[17] The Talumd explains: "Acts of kindness are greater than charity since they can be done

10 This is pointed out by many commentators. See, for example, the *Chizkuni*, ibid. In Hebrew, the word for "neighbor" in the verse is *l'rei'acha,* where the prefix "*l*" means "to /for."

11 Maimonides, *Mishneh Torah*, Laws of Attributes 6:3, *Sefer Hamitzvot*, positive mitzvah 3.

12 Ibid.

13 Ibid.

14 Rabbi Yitzchak Abuhav, *Ethics of Our Fathers* 1:12.

15 Rabbi Joseph B. Soloveitchik, *Kol Dodi Dofek*, p. 15.

16 Talmud, Tractate *Bava Batra* 9b.

17 Bertroit Brecht, *The Threepenny Opera*, translated by Desmond I. Vesey and Eric Bentley.

for both the rich and poor. Charity can only be done with one's money, while acts of loving-kindness can be performed both personally and with one's money."[18]

Mercy runs its course, but kindness is present even where mercy is not.

Why is this so? Because part of the motivation of mercy-giving is to get rid of one's own distressful feelings. Kindness as an act of mercy is not sustainable. What is needed is the development of kindness where the trait itself pushes from the inside to give. To be kindness-driven is to look for giving opportunities even when they don't stare at us in the face. To be mercy-driven is to be aroused only when our heart is being tugged by the person in front of us.[19] To be kindness-driven, as we shall see in the next chapter, involves the Jewish principle of *noseh b'ol*—sharing the load. It is a subtle difference between this—the ability to identify with and share the pain or simply the needs of our fellow—and the giving that arises through guilt and the tugging of our heartstrings.

MERCY

Mercy is a meta-principle of Judaism as well. However, Jewish mercy, as we shall see, is not simply the act of feeling sorry for someone. On Mount Sinai, God revealed to Moses His Thirteen Attributes of Mercy.[20] God told Moses that when the Jews sin, they should appeal to His thirteen attributes, and He will forgive them.[21] Therefore, we say these attributes repeatedly on Yom Kippur.

Each attribute has human application; the Godliness in us includes these attributes.[22] For example, God suffers our insulting behavior toward Him and continues to bestow kindness on us. This teaches us not only to tolerate others who have hurt us but to continue to shower kindness on them, waiting patiently for an opportunity to fix the damage. God gives us the gift of repentance, forgiving us and bestowing us

---

18 Talmud, Tractate *Sukkah* 49b.

19 *Michtav Me'Eliyahu*.

20 Exodus 34:6–7.

21 Talmud, Tractate *Rosh Hashanah* 17b.

22 Rabbi Moshe Cordovero, *Tomer Devorah*, chap. 1.

with atonement. So too, we should be gracious to those who ask our forgiveness, reaching out to them to make it as easy as possible for them to reconcile. We should embrace them with extra closeness after the fallout.[23]

God created us to begin with, whether we deserved it or not. So too, we should show kindness without justification. We should not allow the hurt that someone has caused us to override the good that he has done for us in the past. We should feel pain and pity when we think of how far they have fallen, never with gloating or condescension. If someone has acted terribly toward us and then goes through a challenging period, we must help him rather than saying that he brought his troubles on himself.[24]

SACRIFICING SPIRITUALITY FOR THE REAL DEAL

By engaging in kindness, Abraham paid a spiritual price. It is hard to meditate and reach Kabbalistic heights when you are washing off the idolatrous dust from the feet of strangers. Abraham was a great Kabbalist, but he wasn't as great in this area as some of those who preceded him—a direct result of his focus on kindness.[25] It must have been tempting for Abraham to follow the models of high and spiritual people who spent their days meditating on God and the cosmos.[26] Yet, he decided against this. "God has enough angels in heaven," he reasoned.[27] "Does he need another one on earth?"[28]

Ironically, it was only Abraham, with his hands dirtied by the dust of idolatry, who became the forefather of the Jewish People, and not the holy Shem, Hanoch, or Ever who preceded him.[29] "For I have known,"

---

23 Ibid.
24 Ibid.
25 *Chatam Sofer*, introduction to his responsa on *Yoreh Deah*.
26 Ibid.
27 Ibid.
28 Ibid.
29 Ibid.

says God, "that he will command his children and his household after him, and they will keep the way of God, doing charity and justice.[30]

It was no coincidence that those same angels that brought out Abraham's great hospitality announced to him the birth of Isaac.[31] Abraham and Sarah's dedication to kindness led to the possibility of the ultimate kindness: the giving of life to a new human being. At that point, they were truly imitators of God, His partners in producing life itself.[32]

KINDNESS—A JEWISH FUNDAMENTAL

Kindness, as we have seen, is a Jewish fundamental,[33] a key to unlocking all the rest of the Torah.[34] This attribute is what Jews have always been about. "Simple human solidarity was the *shtetl*'s source of strength," wrote Amos Elon,[35] but it has also played a central role in our connection with God. God loves those who give. And so, Abraham earns the most exalted title of all: "Abraham, My beloved one."[36] We are his descendants, and this is our legacy.

---

30 Genesis 18:19.

31 Ibid. 21:1–3.

32 Rabbi Menachem Rekanti, *Taamei Hamitzvot*, no. 1.

33 Rabbeinu Bachya, *Gates of Repentance* 3:13; see further in Chapter 11.

34 Michah 6:8: "And what does God demand of you but doing [acts of] justice and loving kindness and walking modestly with your God."

35 Amos Elon, *The Israelis*. He continues: "A ghost of the *shtetl* lingers on in the modern living institutions of Israel."

36 The *Shelah* states that the trait of kindness is none other than the trait of internal love of God.

47
CHARITY

And [my father] said to me constantly that man was not created for himself, but to help others, as far as his ability allows.

Rabbi Yitzchak of Volozhin[1]

ONE TENTH TO CHARITY

Maimonides writes:

> *While one eats and drinks himself [on a festival], it is his duty to feed the stranger, the orphan, the widow, and other poor and unfortunate people, for he who locks the doors to his courtyard and eats and drinks with his wife and family, without giving anything to eat and drink to the poor and the bitter in the soul—his meal is not a rejoicing in a Divine commandment but a rejoicing in his own stomach…Rejoicing of this kind is a disgrace to those who indulge in it.*[2]

All but the poorest Jews are required to give *maaser*—a tenth of one's income to charity.[3] However, this is a mitzvah-investment with

1 Intro. to his father's work, the *Nefesh Hachaim*.

2 Maimonides, *Mishneh Torah*, Laws of Resting on Holidays 6:18.

3 *Shulchan Aruch*, *Yoreh Deah* 149:1.

an excellent return. The Sages understand the verse that states, "You should surely tithe,"[4] as saying, "Take a tenth in order that you should become rich."[5] You look after God's creations, so to speak, and He will look after you. The late Bernard Hochstein, a significant philanthropist, would get up at fundraising dinners and assure his audience that taking a tenth would be the best business investment they could make.

The saintly Chafetz Chaim urged wealthy people to go beyond even 20% of their earnings. (He said the same to ordinary people who were living in an area where poor people are prevalent.)[6]

LEARN GIVING BY GIVING

We become givers by giving. Maimonides tells us that if we have one hundred dollars, it is better to give one dollar to a hundred people rather than twenty dollars to five people, for example, because the act of giving one hundred times will help us to become more charitable.[7] The same applies to all other areas of our giving. By practicing, we get used to opening the door for people, or being alert to whether they have somewhere to sit on the subway or the bus. Our actions—and even the clothes we wear—condition us until we do these things as a matter of course.[8] Giving takes training.

By repeated giving we condition ourselves to give as a matter of course.

THE CITY FUND

The Sages decreed that every town has to have two food distribution systems—one for the locals (the *kupah*) and one for poor visitors (the *tamchui*). All citizens were required to contribute to this. While the locals were to get their food weekly, the out-of-towners got a daily distribution.[9] This made sense; a hungry stranger would show up in

---

4 Deuteronomy 14:22.

5 Talmud, Tractate *Taanit* 8b. This is because the word "to tithe" has the same letters as the word "to get rich"; see also Malachi 3:10.

6 Chafetz Chaim, *Ahavat Chessed* 2:20.

7 Maimonides, commentary to *Ethics of Our Fathers* 3:15.

8 *Sefer Hachinuch* 99.

9 Talmud, Tractate *Bava Batra* 8b.

town and would know that he would be fed, while a local could get his supplies for the week and plan accordingly.

In my neighborhood in Jerusalem, comprising several thousand families, there is a small, weekly collection of about one dollar from every family to be distributed to the poor. This service is known as the *Kupah shel Tzedakah* ("the Tzedakah Box"), and there are neighborhood and city-wide collections across many cities in Israel. *Kupah shel Tzedakah* is the modern version of the original *kupah*. In my neighborhood, the *kupah* has a representative servicing every few buildings, and we are all visited by the representative every week.

NECESSITIES

We only have to give for necessities. Jewish law states that we do not check whether a person who requests food is an imposter or not, but rather we feed him immediately.[10] However, if he is asking for clothing, we are entitled to check out his story.[11] If he checks out, we must give.

The Torah did not define what a necessity is, for one man's luxury is another's necessity. For many Americans, the morning is unthinkable without a cup of coffee half the size of a traffic cone. (In Europe, where the cups are so small, I feel the coffee is more for smelling than for drinking.) For some, a certain quality of clothing is a necessity. Others feel that they wouldn't survive a day without a car.

Once, there was a very wealthy man who lost all of his money. The great sage Hillel hired a horse and took this man around himself. Hillel felt that being led on a horse was a necessity for this man, not a luxury.[12]

The verse states that "you should open your hand...sufficient for his lack *which he lacks*."[13] This is interpreted as "that *which he perceives* he lacks."

---

10 *Shulchan Aruch, Yoreh Deah* 251:10.

11 Ibid.

12 Talmud, Tractate *Ketuvot* 67b: Hillel the Elder obtained for a poor person of noble descent [who lost all of his money] a horse upon which to ride and a servant to run in front of him. One time he did not find a servant to run in front of him, and Hillel himself ran in front of him for three *mil*, to fulfill the dictate "which is deficient for him."

13 Deuteronomy 15:7–8.

Of course, such a man should get used to living a simpler life, but it was not Hillel's job to teach him this. We are charged with helping, not dishing out advice.

CHARITY PRIORITIZATION

Soon enough, even the multi-billionaire will realize that he does not have the means to service even a small percentage of the world's needs. As a result, we have to prioritize our giving. Family comes before others. The poor of your city comes before the poor of other cities.[14]

Many opinions say giving to institutions or people in Israel has the same status as giving to someone in your own city.[15] This is because every Jew has a stake in the land of Israel, and therefore the needy in Israel are always considered "the poor of your city."[16]

We must move in concentric circles of giving, going as far as our means allow.

Rabbi Shimon Shkop tells us how to do this. Instead of looking at our kindness being in tension with our personal needs, we need to expand our concept of self so that it automatically embraces the community as well.[17]

Despite this, one should not harden one's heart to anyone, giving at least a little to anyone who requests it.[18]

---

14 Talmud, Tractate *Bava Metzia*, based on the verse in Exodus 22:24.

15 Such charity certainly takes precedence over giving to another Diaspora country. See next footnote.

16 *Shulchan Aruch*, *Yoreh Deah* 251:3, based on the *Sifri*, Deuteronomy 15:7. The verse talks about an impoverished person "in your land."

17 Rabbi Shimon Shkop, *Shaarei Yosher*, introduction: A person ought to clarify the quality of his "I"...and someone who walks in the ways of the Torah will find that his "I" includes all of the Jewish People.

18 This is because besides the positive mitzvah of "open your hand to the poor" (Deuteronomy 15:11), there is a negative mitzvah not to harden our hearts (Deuteronomy 15:7). While the positive mitzvah only requires one to be generous according to one's prioritization scale, the negative mitzvah requires that even if you have given your allocated amount, you must nevertheless give something; *Tzafnat Paneach*, *Mishneh Torah*, Gifts to the Poor 10:5.

THE BURDEN OF EMPATHY

The great enemy of giving is indifference. Elie Wiesel almost woke up the world with these words: "Indifference, to me, is the epitome of evil. The opposite of love is not hate, it's indifference. The opposite of art is not ugliness, it's indifference. The opposite of faith is not heresy, it's indifference. And the opposite of life is not death, it's indifference."[19]

Great philanthropist Zev Wolfson explained his (staggering) giving by saying that he did not want to be the richest man in the cemetery.

In the previous chapter, we learned about giving and mercy. Here we add the third component of the triple cord—empathy. Empathy begins with caring and ends with taking responsibility.

"And Moses grew up, and he went out amongst his brethren, and he saw their suffering."[20] Still, Moses did not merely *see* the suffering of the Jewish People and then continue his daily business. Moses "put his eyes and his heart to the matter"; he would constantly envision his brethren's suffering in his mind.[21] The midrash tells us that in order to really feel their pain, Moses removed his princely garments and went out into the field to make bricks and mortar with his brethren.

Moses learned this from his great-grandfather, Levi, one of the twelve sons of Jacob. Levi foresaw the future with Ruach Hakodesh (a level just below prophecy) that the Jews would be enslaved. In Egypt, the tribe of Levi, being that they were Kohanim (priests), was excused from slavery, but Levi could not live with the idea that their lives would go on normally while their brethren were experiencing a time of trouble. Therefore, as a message for the future, he gave each of his sons a name that impressed upon them the idea that they were to share the pain of their brethren.

- *Gershom*—I was a stranger (*ger*) there (*sham*) in a foreign land.
- *Kehat*—Their teeth were blackened and knocked out.
- *Merari*—Because everyone has it so bitter (*merirut*).[22]

---

19 *US News and World Report*, Oct. 27, 1986.

20 Exodus 2:11.

21 *Rashi*, ibid.

22 Genesis 46:11; See the *Shelah*, Exodus 6:14, who points out the difference in language when talking about the tribe of Levi in contrast to the other tribes.

For the rest of their lives, even after the Jews were redeemed from Egypt, the sons of Levi would bear testimony—in their very names!—to the pain that was.

Life cannot go on as usual when the Jewish People are in trouble. One must not just notice, but feel the pain—feel that because something is happening to our fellow, something is happening to us as well.[23]

During World War I, the wife of the Chafetz Chaim (1838–1933) woke up in the middle of the night to find her husband not in his bed. She went looking for him, and found him sleeping on a bench. She asked for an explanation. He responded: "The Jewish People are in the middle of a war. There are people who have lost their houses. Whole communities have been dispersed. There are many Jews out there tonight who do not have beds. Under such circumstances, how can I sleep in my own bed?"

We need to expand our concept of self so that it automatically embraces the community as well.

The term that we use in Judaism for this is "*noseh b'ol*"—sharing the burden. This idea is empathy perfected. We ought to be feeling an emotional load when someone else is in pain; we ought to be sharing his burden.[24]

Noseh b'ol involves feeling for the person, even when he is not around, to arouse our mercy. The Chafetz Chaim bore the load of his brethren and felt their pain, even if no one in the world would know about it.

Noseh b'ol begins with caring. The Talmud states that Pharaoh consulted with three advisors whether to enslave the Jews: Balaam, Job, and Yitro (Jethro):

- Balaam advised Pharaoh to go ahead and was ultimately punished by death.
- Job remained silent and was condemned to a life of suffering as a result.

---

23 Lydia Denworth, "I Feel Your Pain," *Scientific American* (Dec. 2017), quoting Adam Smith.

24 Note the distinction between this concept and the concept of mercy discussed in the previous chapter.

- Yitro, who was bitterly against the enslavement, fled and merited that his descendants would be a part of the *Sanhedrin*.[25]

Each one of these punishments was commensurate with the advice they gave.[26] If so, how was Job's intense suffering in accordance with his stance? Job kept quiet because he felt that there was nothing he could do. But he should have screamed out, for when you feel pain, you cry out even if it does not help.[27] The fact that he remained unmoved in the face of terrible travesties indicates that some feeling must have died within him. It was to revive that something, to be able to feel pain, which was the purpose of his suffering.

Job should have cried out at the pain of others even though he felt that there was nothing he could do.

Maimonides takes this further, saying that we should not just feel empathy for others, but wonder whether we have contributed to their pain. We should engage in introspection to see what of our own spiritual deeds might be responsible for this situation.[28]

SENSITIVITY IN GIVING

Jewish giving is not all about what or how much we give. It is also very much concerned with how we give. Maimonides lays out eight levels of charity, ordered to reflect levels of sensitivity by the giver to the recipient.[29]

The lowest three levels involve being asked to give, and giving either unwillingly and tinged with resentment. The poor person has the discomfort and burden of having to ask.

The other levels involve giving before being asked. Levels five to seven involve various combinations of the giver not knowing who the recipient is and/or vice-versa. This anonymity reduces the shame of the poor person.

---

25 Talmud, Tractate *Sotah* 11a.

26 *Maharsha*, ibid.

27 Rabbi Yitzchak Zeev HaLevi Soleveitchik (known as the Brisker Rav) to Tractate *Sotah*, 11a.

28 Maimonides, *Mishneh Torah*, Laws of Fasts 1:2–3.

29 *Mishneh Torah*, Laws of Charity 10:7–14.

The eighth and highest level is to set the person up so that he can generate his own finances. One might find him a job, sponsor his professional training, or give him a loan so that he can start a business.

The moral of all these levels is that one should not only care to give but should also care how to give. It takes many years of growth to become a truly caring and giving person. Our job is to begin. And then to keep on growing.

48

HAPPINESS

To know how to live—surely that is the greatest of wisdoms.

HAPPINESS—A WHOLE-BEING EXPERIENCE

Happiness is not a state of being; it is a state of becoming. And that becoming has to move toward life, not away from it. In addition, it is a whole-being experience. A person who is anxious, depressed, or unhappy will find that even the things that ought to be sources of joy bring no pleasure. Hence, one cannot achieve happiness by a single event or achievement. Rather, being happy involves the entire way that you are living.[1] Moreover, happy living requires a consistent application of a certain way of life. We know that lottery winners are not happy for long,[2] and neither are professors who achieve their dream of gaining tenure.[3] Income, promotions, and even fame gives the person a boost before they then return to their base-line of happiness.

---

1 Daniel M. Habron, "Happiness and its Discontents," in "The Stone" (the philosophy section of *The New York Times*), April 13, 2014.

2 https://www.cnbc.com/2018/06/06/winning-the-lottery-makes-you-more-satisfied-with-life-for-10-years.html

3 https://www.chronicle.com/article/Why-Are-Associate-Professors/132071. Professors are actually happier while working toward tenure than they are once they've earned it.

The happy person is not so because of this or that particular thing. He is happy because his whole being is happy—because he feels his life is meaningful.

And that happiness is not a luxury. "The *Shechinah* (the presence of God on this earth) only rests upon one who is in a state of joy."[4] A prophet could not have prophecy if he was sad or depressed, and hence prophets would play harps and violins to up their mood.[5] "And it was," says the verse, "when the musician played, that the hand of God was upon him."[6]

Just as happiness reflects our overall state, so too with its opposite. "Unhappiness, like happiness, says something about your whole personality. Whereas back pain does not: It is just a sensation, something that happens to you...Our language also marks the difference: You merely *feel* a pain, but you *are* depressed, anxious, melancholy, or whatever. Similarly, you might have a depressive or anxious or cheerful personality. But we never talk of someone having a 'painful' or 'pleasureful' personality."[7]

The core problem is the pursuit of making the body happy, instead of following the agenda of the soul.

DOES JUDAISM STRESS HAPPINESS?

A culture can be understood by its language. For example:

- Eskimos have multiple words for snow because each type of snow is seen as distinct. For most of us, however, it is all just snow.
- Turkish have a special word for the eldest big brother. This means that he is not only the eldest of the siblings, but he is in a category of his own.[8]

---

4 Talmud, Tractate *Shabbat* 30b.

5 Maimonides, *Mishneh Torah*, Laws of Foundations of the Torah 7:4.

6 Kings II 3:15.

7 "Happiness and its Discontents."

8 In truth, Hebrew also has a special word for the eldest brother, the *bechor*. However, this word has other meanings too.

- In Hebrew, there are many words for joy and pleasure. In one of the seven blessings at a wedding, we mention no less than ten such words.[9]
- This tells us that Judaism is a culture where happiness is a central idea. In fact, Judaism's many words for happiness allow us to express the full range of joy available to mankind.

Judaism's dramatic vision is one where the entire creation joins in a symphony of joy: "Let the heavens rejoice, and let the earth be glad; let the sea roar, and all that is in it."[10] Every chapter that was particularly dear to David was commenced with the word "happy" (*ashrei*) and terminated with the word "happy", implying that the joy of serving God embraces all aspects of our lives.[11]

The reason that Judaism is a happy religion is because, as King David's Psalms repeatedly assure us, the result of righteousness is happiness: "Be glad in God, and rejoice, you righteous; and shout for joy, all you who are upright in heart."[12]

What does this mean? Judaism is neither guaranteeing a happy ending in this world to all who embrace it, nor will it be the all-cure for depression or many other challenges. We will explore, in this chapter, what it does provide by way of happiness and how it does so.

---

9 *Sasson, simchah, gilah, rinah, ditzah, chedvah, ahavah, achvah, shalom, reut*. Six of them are obviously words for joy. *Ahavah, achvah, shalom, v'reut* translate more easily as "love, oneness, peace, and friendship," respectively. (All four are used in *Shir Hashirim* [Song of Songs] to characterize the relationship between Hashem and Israel [*ahavah nafshi*; *achot lanu*; *ra'ayati*; *kemotzeit shalom*].) However, Rabbi Belsky reported that Rabbi Yitzchak Hutner explained how these two are expressions of love that are born of joy or lead to joy. Indeed, the *Kuntres Birkat Hatanim* by Rabbi Meir Mintzberg divides the ten words into five for the bride (*simchah, rinah, chedvah, achvah, reut*) and five for the groom (*sasson, gilah, ditzah, ahavah, shalom*), and he explains each one as parallel for a certain type of joy to the other.
In addition Avot D'Rabi Natan (34:10) also brings down ten languages of joy, using the obvious six above and adding *tzahalah, alizah, alitzah*, and *tiferet*. *Shir Hashirim Rabbah* (1:29) brings down yet another variation, including the words *sisah* and *pitchah*.
From all this we see that there are actually as many as sixteen words in Hebrew for joy.

10 Ibid. 96:11.

11 Talmud, Tractate *Berachot* 10a.

12 Psalms 32:11; see also 97:12.

HAPPINESS CANNOT BE THE GOAL

The first principle of happiness is that we can never make it a goal. If you aim to be happy, it will elude you. Happiness is a consequence, not a goal. "Happiness cannot be pursued; it must ensue," said Victor Frankl.[13]

It must be this way because to pursue happiness is to focus on yourself, and selfishness is the straightest road to misery.

We shouldn't get married in order to be happy. Rather, the goal of marriage is to have a meaningful relationship with our spouse—a goal that is larger than just ourselves. The result will be happiness. The Talmud reports that once Rabbi Bruna prayed especially well and was smiling the entire day.[14] Rabbi Bruna aimed for a truly spiritual experience. The result was happiness.

There is no specific mitzvah in the Torah to be happy, but happiness is the consequence of living a spiritual life—of being spiritually full.[15] The same with sadness; it is not a transgression, but it's the basis of all transgressions.[16] We became exiled "because you didn't serve God with joy."[17] We were lacking that level of passion that in turn deprived us of happiness. We did so because we didn't have the right values. The values in turn determined the messages we gave ourselves. We began to think that financial security, our own professional expertise, or our social acceptance were what mattered to us. We began to look for happiness in all the wrong places.[18]

If you want to be happier, be kinder and live a more meaningful and righteous life. "The door to happiness," said Viktor Frankl, "opens outward."[19]

The *mashgiach* (dean) of the Mir Yeshiva turned up to the funeral of a simple man, explaining that this man was always happy, and therefore

---

13 Viktor E. Frankl, *Man's Search for Meaning*, p. 140.

14 Talmud, Tractate *Berachot* 9b.

15 Rabbi Eliyahu Dessler, *Michtav Me'Eliyahu*, vol. 1, p. 3. There are many verses that correlate happiness with being spiritual, e.g., Psalms 84:5, 106:3; Isaiah 56:2, and more.

16 *Netivot Shalom*.

17 Deuteronomy 28:47.

18 See *Michtav Me'Eliyahu*, ibid., p. 7.

19 Viktor E. Frankl, *The Doctor and the Soul: An Introduction to Logotherapy*.

he must have had good character because bad character ruins one's happiness.[20]

Two Hebrew words sound exactly the same:

- *Osher* with an (אושר) א means happiness.
- *Osher* with an (עושר) ע means wealth.

This is to tell us that the only person who is truly wealthy is the one filled up with the meaning of life. The consequences of such an approach will be a deep sense of wellbeing, a sense that we are living a worthwhile life. And then we will be happy.[21]

Happiness is a consequence, not a goal.

HAPPINESS MUST COME FROM WITHIN

The second principle of happiness is that it can never come from the outside. "Who is happy? He who rejoices in his portion."[22] No amount of money, no type of acquisition, and no job can bring us happiness if we are not happy on the inside. The "outside" seeker will have no rest. He will be a restless soul, always searching where happiness can never be found.[23] We dream of money. We dream of being a celebrity. However, I have talked to numerous world-class dancers, sportsmen, and other celebrities. Though they were rightfully proud of their achievements, not one of them said that this made them happy.

HAPPINESS, FAITH, AND GRATITUDE

The third principle of happiness is faith and gratitude. Faith is such a great key to unlocking joy because the person who trusts in God is willing to let go. He has no problem being faithful to his God because he is faith-full. The man of faith believes that everything he has is from God, and that therefore he has received exactly what he ought to.[24] He knows that every investment of effort he makes in overcoming his

---

20 Told by Rabbi Dovid Povarsky, quoted in *Kol Mishalotecha*, p. 20.

21 *Orchot Tzaddikim*, gate 9, the Gate of Joy.

22 *Ethics of Our Fathers* 4:1.

23 *Reishit Chochmah*, chap. 12, the Gate of Love.

24 *Orchot Tzaddikim*, the Gate of Simchah.

challenges will be worthwhile.[25] "I will surely rejoice in God; my soul will be overjoyed with my God."[26]

But he goes further. He is grateful even for just being alive—for every breath he takes.[27] This creates a momentum of happiness. Such a person is emotionally and spiritually healthier and thus able to accomplish more. This reinforces his sense of well-being and increases his happiness, which again allows him to accomplish even more.[28]

When we thank God every morning for our sight, ability to walk, and the clothes on our back, we heighten our awareness of all the beautiful things that we have—not the things we don't have or that other people have. The Torah is constantly reminding us to be grateful: The Jewish People brought the first fruits to the Temple and declared their gratitude.[29] We say a blessing on every morsel of food we eat. We celebrate our freedom on Passover by imagining that it is we, personally, who were redeemed.[30]

The man of faith believes that everything he has is from God, and that therefore he has received exactly what he ought to.

Gratitude, combined with trust, is the means through which we interpret experiences, including challenges. Trust means we believe that God sends us a challenge because it was just what we needed. Gratitude allows us to view the challenge in the context of all the things we can truly be grateful for.[31]

An unhappy person misses so many opportunities to rejoice. He might score well on his tests, but he will see no value in getting ready for a life not worth living. He may find his partner in life, but his mental frame is to reinterpret all events through the prism of his misery.

---

25 *Reishit Chochmah*, the Gate of Love, chap. 12.

26 Isaiah 61:10.

27 *Shivtei Yisrael*. The Sages (*Yalkut Shimoni* 889 to Psalms, chap. 150) tell us that the verse from Psalms: *"Kol ha'neshamah tehalel Kah"* (Every soul will praise God) should be understood as: *Al kol neshimah u'neshimah*—on each and every breath—I should praise God. (The word for soul, *neshamah*, and the word for breath, *neshimah*, have the same letters.)

28 Gila Feder, *Letters to a Friend*, p. 64, in the name of Rabbi Weinberg.

29 Deuteronomy, chap. 26.

30 Haggadah of Passover.

31 Talmud, Tractate *Taanit* 21a, concerning Nachum Ish Gam Zu.

He convinces himself that living with such thoughts is normative. He mistakenly thinks it is impossible for life to be any different.[32] He can prove his position by ticking off his difficulties, but difficulties on their own don't increase or decrease happiness. It is our interpretation of the difficulties that determines our happiness in those situations.

HAPPINESS IS JEALOUSY-FREE

Although we can and should be happy in this world, true happiness comes only in the World to Come. That is the happiness of basking in the light of God.[33] This world is a place where we are given what we need in order to grow. There is no point comparing ourselves to others, because God gives us exactly what we need in order to fulfill our potential. This allows us to escape the great happiness killer—jealousy. At root, jealousy is the thought that somehow this other person has what I really need to make myself happy—"If only I had her looks," "If only I had his speed," If only I had her money." The message I am giving myself when I am jealous is that I am dissatisfied with my lot; that I am deprived; that life is unfair to me. Therefore, a key element of joy is trust, trust that God is looking after us, and that He is giving us our best shot at fulfilling all of our potential.[34]

---

32 Rabbi Yerucham Levovitz, *Daat Chochmah U'Mussar*, vol. 2, p. 139.

33 *Ramchal, Mesilat Yesharim*, chap. 1. His exact wording there is "to derive pleasure from God."

34 *Orchot Tzaddikim*, Gate of Joy.

49
REPENTANCE

You can learn three things from a child; he cries when he needs something, he is always happy, and when he falls he always gets up.

Rabbi Levi Yitzchak of Berditchev

GOD WORKS WITH BROKEN UTENSILS

We think that we are unfixable because of our sins. God tells us that we are wrong. He will work with us just as we are.[1] He is willing to work with broken utensils (*keilim shevurim*). But He tells us more. There is a way that we can fix ourselves, and it is neither painful nor scary. It is the mitzvah of *teshuvah*.

The Kabbalists tells us that before God created this world, He created other worlds and destroyed them.[2] He then used the remnants of those worlds to create our world.[3]

It was into this reality that God said, "Let there be light."

What was the purpose of all of this destroying and creating worlds? It was, say the Kabbalists, so that every type of moral and spiritual

1 Jerusalem Talmud, Tractate *Makkot* 2:6.

2 *Midrash Rabbah*, Genesis 3:7.

3 *Derash Ohr Hachaim* on *Rosh Hashanah* of the *Tiferet Yisrael*.

destruction that could ever take place will have already been done when God destroyed the universes. God built our universe based on the destroyed remnants of those worlds. So now, every type of destruction already has its solution built into the fabric of creation.[4] Any type of distortion or sin we might do has already been done and corrected. The force to correct our actions now exists long before we commit any sin. That force is *teshuvah*.

Teshuvah tells us that we are never stuck, no matter how bad we have been or how many times we have messed up. We can pick ourselves up, dust ourselves off, express regret for our actions of the past, and commit anew to fulfilling our potential.[5]

Every type of sin already has its solution built into the fabric of creation.

We don't have to wait for Yom Kippur or any other special opportunity to do this. We don't need a rabbi or any intermediary. God runs a twenty-four hour-a-day hotline, and we have His number.

BROKEN TABLETS

When God gave us the two Tablets of stone at Sinai through Moses, the Jewish People worshipped the Golden Calf and Moses broke the Tablets.[6] Then, on Yom Kippur, the Day of Atonement, Moses brought a second set of Tablets down,[7] which was successfully delivered. This meant that the final bringing of the Torah in this world was *after* sin. It was given on the quintessential day of repentance and forgiveness—Yom Kippur. The Torah and forgiveness are tightly bound with each other.[8]

---

4 *Ramchal*, *Daat Tevunot*, vol. 2.

5 The elements of *teshuvah* are:

1. Separate oneself from sin.
2. Regret the past.
3. Commit to the future.
4. Beg forgiveness from any person aggrieved by your action and make any restitution required.
5. Say aloud the first three steps (known as *vidui*).

6 Exodus 32:19.

7 Ibid. 34:29.

8 *Rashi*, ibid. 33:11.

When the Ark of the Covenant was built to hold the Tablets, the broken Tablets were also put into the Ark. The first Tablets tell us to do Teshuva. The second Tablets tell us that it is possible.[9]

And why did God go to all this trouble? Every human soul that has lapsed, every Jewish man or woman who has opted out of his or her mission...they are His loss! And He feels our pain at having messed up. In the words of Isaiah: "In all their troubles, He is troubled."[10]

DRAWING ON OUR OWN GREATNESS

In order to do *teshuvah*, the sinner must raise himself from any feelings of lowliness. His true place is in holiness—in greatness—and not in sin. Our worthiness stems from God creating us in the image of Himself.[11] This makes us the worthiest beings in creation. We have within us a spark of holiness that is never tainted by sin.[12] "A myrtle among thorns is still called a myrtle," is how the Sages put it.[13] When a person knows this fundamental truth, there is no place for sadness, even when we have botched our mission many times. Regret, yes; but not sadness.

THE UNIQUE STATUS OF SOMEONE WHO DOES TESHUVAH

Evil is often the mirror image of good. It is the same force going in the opposite direction.[14] Since the negative action is the opposite of a positive one, it already contains within it the possibility of redemption.[15] The sinner can take the same force that produced the impurity and transform it into the positive.

This explains a sociological mystery of our day. The Jewish world is suffering the most rampant assimilation in its history. Yet, at the same time, there is a vibrant return by Jews back to their roots—seemingly

---

9 Rabbi Moshe Shapiro. See also *Ramchal*, *Mesilat Yesharim*, chap. 2.

10 Rabbi Shimshon Raphael Hirsch, Hirsch Haggadah, quoting Isaiah 63:9.

11 See p. 91, "In the Image of God."

12 Psalms, chap. 37.

13 Talmud, Tractate *Sanhedrin* 44a.

14 Rabbi Tzadok HaKohen, *Takanat Hashavim*, no. 10; see also *Ramchal*, *Derech Hashem* 3:2:8.

15 Rabbi Tzadok HaKohen, ibid.

the very opposite of intermarriage and assimilation. But, really, inherent in the force to return is the force to assimilate. They are opposites drawing on the same energy.[16]

The sinner should not have sinned. He went where he was not supposed to go. Now, when he comes back, he brings all those areas of impurity into holiness. Hence, totally righteous people cannot stand in the place where those who return—*baalei teshuvah*—stand.[17] They provide a spiritual dimension that only they can do.[18]

In order to do teshuvah, the sinner must raise himself from feelings of lowliness.

The *baal teshuvah* is not merely coming to build on what he had before. On the contrary, *teshuvah* allows for revolutionary change. The sinner broadened his boundaries by falling off the ladder of righteousness to the right or the left. It is the nature of *teshuvah* to break boundaries and to create new merits from deliberate sins. Hence, someone who does *teshuvah* is able to multiply and broaden his good attributes and destiny way beyond its pre-determined boundaries.[19]

THE EASIEST MITZVAH

One would imagine that something as powerful as *teshuvah* would require tremendous preparation—similar to running in a marathon. Yet the Torah reassures us that this is the easiest commandment in the book:

> *For this mitzvah that I come to command you is not mysterious and inaccessible to you. It is not far from you. It is not in the heaven [forcing you to say], "Who will ascend to the heavens for us and take it from there and tell us about it so that we might do it?" Nor is it across the ocean [forcing us to say], "Who will*

---

16 *Netivot Shalom*, end of introductions to *Sefer Hamiddot*. The *Netivot Shalom* explains that this is what the Sages meant when they said, "The son of David will only come in a generation that is either completely meritorious or completely guilty." It means, he says, that each Jew will either get more engaged in his Judaism or go the other way.

17 Talmud, Tractate *Berachot* 34a.

18 Rabbi Tzadok HaKohen, ibid.

19 Ibid.

> *undertake this journey across the seas and take it from there and tell us about it so that we might do it." For the matter is very close; it is in your mouth and heart to do.*[20]

Imagine someone suffering a serious disease. The doctor is called. He announces that there is one medicine that can save the patient. The patient presumes that this medicine will be very difficult to obtain and hugely expensive, but the doctor announces that it comes from a plant growing in the patient's back garden, nor costing him anything.[21]

A person messes up. He must regret the past.[22] A person must articulate this message to God.[23] He must commit to not repeating the behavior again.[24] If he has hurt his neighbor, he must ask his forgiveness.[25]A person who says, "I will sin and I will repent" as a way to justify sin is denied the opportunity to do so,[26] but otherwise, no matter how evil one has been, *teshuvah* is still accessible.[27] No matter how alienated you feel from spirituality, an attempt to do *teshuvah* activates God's help and will cut through all resistance.[28] No matter how sad you are that you have sinned, you will heal. "There is nothing so whole as a broken heart," said the Kotzker Rebbe.

After his *teshuvah*, such a person is as beloved to God as any righteous person.[29]

Unlike other mitzvot, even if we do part of the mitzvah of *teshuvah*, it has value. It generates holiness even if it is only short-lived and we backslide again.[30]

---

20 Deuteronomy 29:11–14. This follows the *Ramban* and others who say that this is talking about *teshuvah*.

21 Rabbi Yoseph Albo, *Sefer Ha'ikkarim* 4:25.

22 Rabbeinu Yonah, *Shaarei Teshuvah* 1:4.

23 Maimonides, *Mishneh Torah*, Laws of Repentance 2:2.

24 Ibid. 2:2–3.

25 Ibid. 2:9.

26 Talmud, Tractate *Yoma* 85b.

27 *Shaarei Teshuvah* 1:1:1.

28 *Duties of the Heart*, Gate of *Teshuvah*, introduction.

29 *Mishneh Torah*, ibid. 4:4.

30 Mabit, *Beit Elokim*, chap. 12.

Hence, in the case of the spies, Caleb was able to silence the nation to make the appeal to enter the land.[31] He only captured their attention for a moment to listen to his counter-argument to enter the land. Yet, his action was deserving of being written in the Torah forever.[32]

Of all the gifts God has given us, *teshuvah* is the most mind-boggling. How it works is mysterious. But, given the facts, we would be mad not to embrace it.

---

31 Numbers 13:11.

32 Rabbi Moshe Shapiro.

50
FORGIVENESS

One who takes revenge due to his zealotry destroys his own house.

Talmud, Tractate Sanhedrin 102b

"Who is truly mighty? He who can convert an enemy into a friend."

Avot d'Rabi Natan 23

TO BE JEWISH IS TO FORGIVE

The Torah prohibits taking revenge, such as if our neighbor doesn't lend you his saw, so you refuse him your pliers.[1] It is even forbidden to lend your pliers and say, "See, I am not like you."[2] When read in context, what leaps off the page is that these two prohibitions are written in the same verse as the commandment to love one's neighbor. You cannot be a vengeful person and a loving person all in one. You cannot love your fellow man without understanding that he will err from time to time. And this understanding must extend to forgiveness.

Forgiveness is a recognition that we too share in the frailty of the one whom has wronged us. As emotionally taxing as it sometimes is,

1 Leviticus 19:18—*lo tikom*.

2 Ibid.—*lo titor*; see Maimonides, *Mishneh Torah*, Laws of Attributes 7:8.

we shouldn't see forgiveness as a super-righteous idea. Maimonides, in fact, counts it as a basic Jewish trait.[3]

If we want God to forgive us for our sins, we have to be God-like in forgiving our fellow man for emotional, physical, or other hurt.[4] (We are allowed to hold back until the person has made financial restitution, such as paying for physical damages or medical bills.) We repeat this forgiveness every Yom Kippur eve.[5] Without this, our fellow men cannot do *teshuvah* on the things they have done against us.[6]

As emotionally taxing as it sometimes is, we shouldn't see forgiveness as a super-righteous idea. Rather, it as a basic Jewish trait.

We need to make the request for forgiveness as easy as possible. When a certain chef who had sinned toward the great rabbi, Rav, failed to show up by the eve of Yom Kippur to ask Rav's forgiveness, Rav decided to go to him to appease him, even though Rav was the aggrieved party.[7]

But what about someone who has been abused by his parents, bullied at school, or beaten up by an intruder? The radical idea of the Torah is that if the person has sincerely repented, we should struggle repeatedly until we can find a way to forgive them. This may take years or a lifetime, but we must try. However, in recognition of the complexities of this situation, the Torah did not place an absolute obligation on us to forgive (see note[8]).

---

3 Ibid., Laws of Repentance 2:10.

4 Rabbi Moshe Cordrovero, *Tomer Devorah*.

5 In the *Tefilah Zakkah* that precedes the *Kol Nidrei* service.

6 *Mishneh Torah*, ibid. 2:9.

7 Talmud, Tractate *Yoma* 87.

8 The way the *Shulchan Aruch* (*Orach Chaim* 606:1) codifies the law is carefully worded: "And the one being asked for forgiveness should not be cruel in denying the forgiveness." This is a moral imperative rather than a legal one and is a lower demand than that which is originally codified by Maimonides that he should forgive with a whole heart (*Mishneh Torah*, Laws of Repentance 2:10). The *Shulchan Aruch* also writes that one does not have to forgive one who has sullied your reputation by spreading false information about you. This is because he cannot make restitution by restoring your reputation. Once the information is out there, it is impossible to know who has bought into the false narrative.

JOSEPH TOWARD HIS BROTHERS—A PARADIGM OF FORGIVENESS

After many years of tension, Joseph's brothers sold him as a slave.[9] Joseph is repeatedly sold until he ends up in the house of Potiphar.[10] Having rebuffed the advances of Potiphar's wife, he was thrown into prison, unknown to anyone, a foreigner rotting in a horrible Egyptian jail.[11]

Because of his brothers' actions, years of Joseph's life were spent under the most horrific conditions. Then, in a most dramatic turn, Joseph became viceroy of Egypt.[12] He was now all-powerful and could easily take revenge on the terrible deed of his brothers. And then, lo and behold, he was given just this opportunity when famine forced the brothers to appear in front of him.[13]

However, Joseph never does take revenge. Initially, the brothers are terrified that he was just biding his time. They thought that their father, Jacob, acted as a restraint on him. And then Jacob died.[14] The brothers were fearful that their time had come: "What if Joseph hates us and decides to repay us for all the evil we did to him?"[15] So, they made up a lie, saying that Jacob had left Joseph a message, saying: "O please, kindly forgive the spiteful deed of your brothers and their sin, for they have done you evil."[16] They took the threat so seriously that they flung themselves before him and said, "We are ready to be your slaves," just as they had turned Joseph into a slave.[17]

Short of murder, is there anything worse than turning your own brother into a slave? Can you imagine the years of struggle that Joseph had after he was sold? But Joseph never allowed himself to become

---

9 Genesis 37: 27.
10 Ibid., v. 28.
11 Ibid., v. 20.
12 Ibid. 41:39–43.
13 Ibid. 42:3–6.
14 Ibid. 49:33.
15 Ibid. 50:15.
16 Ibid., v. 16–17.
17 Ibid., v. 18.

a bitter person. He was able to truly forgive.[18] We think of Nelson Mandela in our time, who emerged from Robin Island off Cape Town, projecting forgiveness and the dignity of man. Mandela saved a country, South Africa, by refusing revenge. Joseph forgave his brothers and saved the history of the Jews.[19]

THE SECRET OF FORGIVENESS

Much earlier, Joseph revealed the great secret of forgiveness. When he first revealed his identity to his brothers, he told them that it was a part of God's plan that this should have happened. He said: "Don't be distressed or angry with yourselves for selling me here, because it was to save lives that God sent me ahead of you."[20]

If we believe that everything comes from God, then we will understand that the person hurting us is just one of an infinite number of delivery mechanisms to give us what we need.[21] If God wanted it, what was supposed to happen would have happened anyhow. That this person was chosen as God's messenger to do the action has nothing to do with us.

FORGIVENESS SAVES THE FORGIVER

Joseph did not just save his brothers; he saved himself. There is no more pathetic person than one eaten up by his bitterness. Bitterness and resentment consume our energies; they exhaust our emotional and spiritual capacity to engage in the wonderful world around us, experience wonder and joy, get in touch with our own potential, and to dedicate ourselves to our mission on earth. And hence, it is the victim who gains the most from forgiveness. "When we forgive, we free ourselves from the bitter ties that bind us to the one who hurt us."[22] And this allows us to begin our own process of healing.

---

18 Ibid., v. 15–19 as understood by the Zohar. See however, Rabbeinu Bachaya, ad locum.

19 Ibid. 45:1–15.

20 Ibid., v. 5.

21 *Rashi*, Exodus 4:13, 23:7, based on the *Midrash Rabbah*, Numbers 18.

22 Dave Pelzer, *A Man Named Dave*.

Rabbi Nechunia ben Hakaneh's students asked him on account of which meritorious practice he achieved longevity. He answered that he would never wait for his offender's request for forgiveness. "In all my days, I never derived honor from the shame of my fellow, nor has my fellow's curse risen [with me] onto my bed"; i.e., he would forgive anyone who had cursed him before he went to sleep at night.[23]

Since then, the custom developed that, before going to sleep, we include a prayer forgiving anyone who might have done something against us on that day:[24]

> *Master of the Universe, I hereby forgive anyone who antagonized me or who sinned against me—whether against my body, my property, my honor, or against anything of mine; whether he did so accidentally, willfully, carelessly, or purposely; whether through speech, deed, thought, or notion; whether in this transmigration (gilgul) or another transmigration—I forgive every Jew. May no man be punished because of me. May it be Your will, my God and the God of my forefathers, that I sin no more.*[25]

It is not in our hands to forgive things that were done to others, or to the Jewish nation as a whole, but we can forgive what was done to us. And when we do, we hand the case back to God. Let Him be the judge. Our job is to forgive.

By forgiving, Joseph did not just save his brothers. He saved himself.

No one is saying that this is easy—even for great people. Someone approached the great Rabbi Eliyahu Lopian and asked him forgiveness for speaking negatively about him. Rabbi Lopian told the person that he would have to get back to him. Indeed, he did,

23 Talmud, Tractate *Megillah* 28a.

24 This is a part of the bedtime *Shema*.

25 Many also have the custom to repeat forgiveness just before the beginning of the Yom Kippur service in the *Tefillah Zakkah*—The Prayer of Purity.

two weeks later. He said, "I spent the last two weeks working out my forgiveness for you. I can now say I forgive you."[26]

THE BOTTOM LINE

Hard cases aside, Maimonides states:

> *[I]it is forbidden for a person to be cruel and refuse to be appeased. Rather, he should be easily pacified but hard to anger. When the person who wronged him asks for forgiveness, he should forgive him with a complete heart and a willing spirit. Even if he distressed and wronged him very much, he should not seek revenge nor bear a grudge.*[27]

But what if the offending person is not even sorry for what he did? Jewish law says that, for strategic reasons, one can hold back forgiveness to ensure that the repentance is sincere.[28] Strictly speaking, there must be no malice and no desire for revenge mixed in the request for forgiveness.[29] But who can be so pure? We are better off forgiving. "Those who forgive others who sinned against them will themselves be forgiven by God for their sins against Him."[30]

In the early 20th century, a holy couple by the name of Rabbi Aryeh and Chana Levin lived in Jerusalem. Once, a thief who had just been set free and had no money whatsoever in his pocket went off to find Rabbi Levine. The Levines welcomed the man like a distinguished guest. They gave him some money and sat him down to a good meal. Then they asked him to stay the night. In the morning, the guest was gone—along with the Levine's wine cup and silver Shabbat candlesticks. Rav Aryeh woke his wife and told her what had happened. "Let us forgive that poor thief completely," he ended. "Let Heaven not punish him on our

---

26 As reported by Rabbi Aaron Leib Shteinman in *Ayelet HaShachar* on the Torah, *Parashat Vayechi*. (See there for some additional elements to the story.)

27 *Mishneh Torah*, Laws of Repentance 2:10.

28 *Shulchan Aruch*, *Orach Chaim* 72:1.

29 *Mishnah Berurah*, ibid. §9.

30 Talmud, Tractate *Rosh Hashanah* 17a, as brought down by the *Mishnah Berurah*, ibid. §8. This is the principle of God repaying people *middah k'neged middah*—measure for measure.

account. Let us promise each other and really resolve in our heart that this little incident will not mean anything for us in the future, and it will not prevent us from inviting other thieves into our home!"[31]

Forgiving might be one of the most difficult things that God asks of us, but He wouldn't ask if it was not within our grasp.

31 Simcha Raz, *A Tzaddik in Our Time.*

51
MODESTY

Rebbi said: Don't look at the container but rather at what it contains.

Ethics of Our Fathers (4:20)

THE BROADENING CHARACTER OF MODESTY

The English word "modesty" does not begin to capture the deep and sensitive concept communicated by the Hebrew word *tzniut*. *Tzniut* really comes from the word "to be hidden." Spirituality is not obvious in this world; it is hidden below the surface. *Tzniut* is our capacity to recognize and connect with that spirituality.[1]

The Hebrew name for "world" is *olam* (עולם), which is related to the word *he'elem* (העלם)—hidden. The world hides God. God operates just below the surface of the reality that we normally see. Without *tzniut*, we would simply accept that what we initially see is all there is.

Spirituality is not obvious in this world; it is hidden below the surface. Tzniut is our capacity to connect with that spirituality.

Tzniut is therefore an enabling trait and not a limiting one—one that broadens and deepens, rather than limits and constricts.

1 *Maharal, Netiv Hatzniut*, chap. 1.

Tzniut is an attitude, a character trait, and an approach to life for men and women alike. It is not a dress code, though our clothing is one of the tools we use to project our own inner self. Our clothing tells others to look deeper if they want to see the real us. However, they are first and foremost a message to ourselves.

Were we able to perceive our bodies as simply the outer garment to the soul, we could walk around naked as Adam and Eve did in the Garden of Eden. Adam and Eve did not perceive each other's bodies as an object of sensuality.[2] However, after the sin, our ability to perceive ourselves as well as others properly meant that *tzniut* and spirituality became inseparable.[3]

The Book of Esther tells us that Esther was beautiful.[4] She actually had a greenish complexion, but a thread of kindness was drawn over her face.[5] She radiated spirituality. Her complexion could have been off-putting, but her inner-self shone on her face, and that is what made her beautiful in the eyes of those who saw her. So too, we need to believe that projecting our inner-self is showing the world the most beautiful part of ourselves.

TZNIUT—ONE OF THE THREE BIG KEYS

Micah the prophet made an astonishing statement: "For what does God demand of you except that you engage in justice and loving-kindness and walking modestly with the Lord your God."[6]

This doesn't make sense. Micah starts off by rhetorically asking what God wants of us. Well, for a start, it would seem that God wants us to do all of the mitzvot. Micah doesn't say that. He mentions only three things: justice, kindness, and walking modestly with God.

Micah wasn't being reductionist, throwing out the whole Torah for just three principles. Rather, this sagely prophet was telling us where

---

2 Genesis 2:25.

3 Ibid. 3:10–11, 21, as interpreted by the *Maharal*, *Netiv Hatzniut*, chap. 1; Rabbi Eliyahu Dessler, *Michtav Me'Eliyahu*, vol. 3, p. 116.

4 Book of Esther 2:7.

5 Talmud, Tractate *Megillah* 13a.

6 Micah 6:8; see Tractate *Makkot* 24a.

to start. What are the keys that will allow us to set on our spiritual journey? If we develop kindness on the one hand and boundaries and self-restraint on the other, we will be able to reach all of Judaism. But, says Micah, there is a third ingredient—a third must. And this is *tzniut*. It is one of the big three.[7]

TZNIUT—THE ABILITY TO BE INNER-DIRECTED

A Torah scroll is covered with a mantle and then kept hidden in the Ark (the *Aron Kodesh*) at the front of the synagogue, which in turn is covered with a curtain. For protection, the Ark alone would be sufficient. The extra layers—the mantle and the curtain—help us relate to the Torah as something whose essence is spiritual.[8] They help us not to get caught on the physical appearance of the Torah. We cover the superficial to allow us to focus on the hidden.

And so, *tzniut* can be defined as the ability to defocus from the superficiality of a person (or a situation) by focusing on the deeper, inner reality of that person—his or her true worth.[9] It is a quality, a trait that takes training and that emerges from deep inside of ourselves.

A person who is *tzanua* (modes) will want to project his or her internal self. But that is only secondary. *Tzniut* begins as a way of guiding our perceptions about ourselves toward the deeper parts of our identity, our holy and spiritual selves that, after all, ought to be our primary identity.

As we gain in our ability to define ourselves non-externally, we become more internally developed people. As our sources of self-worth become deeper and more spiritual, we grow in our positive self-image as someone with dignity and value. Our relationships with others change as they realize that our external selves are not the part that we want them to relate to.

---

7 Micah appears to be putting *tzniut* ahead of mercy, strength of character, humility, passion, truth, and dozens of other traits.

8 It is interesting that the Talmud refers to someone who touches a Torah scroll with their bare hands and not through an intermediary (like a pointer or a piece of clothing) as touching the "naked" Torah; Tractate *Megillah* 32a.

9 *Maharal, Netiv Hatzniut*, chap. 1.

We talk in a more refined way.[10] We dress in a way that guides others away from our sensuous, bodily aspects in order to draw attention to our inner beauty.[11] We radiate honor, grace, and sensitivity.

Contemporary societies have a hard time with this idea. Our media stars—models, actors, dancers, and singers—always project the utmost confidence. But they pay a high price for showing themselves off in an artificial and perfect light. Their real inner selves rarely if ever get a chance to express themselves, and as a result they often feel lonely, empty, and sad. Their character development is sometimes undeveloped just because they are stuck on doing things that solicit approval from others. Many have very poor self-images, requiring constant feeding of their ego.

Tzniut is a way of guiding our perceptions about ourselves toward the deeper parts of our identity.

By contrast, we see that great Torah people have their own internal sources of self-worth and have little need for positive reinforcement from other people. They never look for publicity. They try to hide their acts wherever possible. They see this as the only way to maintain the integrity and internal, spiritual worth of what they are doing. In fact, the Sages tell us that, at any one time, there are thirty-six hidden *tzaddikim*—righteous people in the world in whose merits the world is maintained.[12]

This is why Jacob fights with an angel alone.[13] So too, there was no one to witness Joseph's temptation by the wife of Potiphar.[14] Moses' encounter with the bush was also a solitary, un-witnessed encounter.[15] None of this is coincidence.

---

10 See below in this chapter, "Tzniut is Speech."

11 *Shiurei Daat*, vol. 2, no. 2; *Sefer Hachinuch* 99; *Ramchal, Daat Tevunot*, vol. 2, p. 42; Exodus 28:2.

12 Talmud, Tractate *Sanhedrin* 97b.

13 The *Targum Onkelos* explains that the name *Yisrael* means that Jacob's struggles were only for the sake of God and not for any human audience.

14 Genesis 39:11.

15 Exodus 3:1.

TZNIUT LEADS TO GREAT WISDOM

This leads to a counter-intuitive result. *Tzanua* (modest) people don't dress and act in hidden ways because they lack self-confidence. The opposite is true. Because they are not superficial, they are filled up with the inner content of their lives. They feel more confident about themselves because they are not acting to solicit the approval of others.

DEEP WISDOM IS HIDDEN

This is also why certain types of wisdom, such as Kabbalah, is hidden. Since this wisdom reveals a deeper spirituality, only one who has the quality of seeing below the surface can truly see this wisdom.[16] King Solomon, who knew something about wisdom, said it clearly: "And those who are *tznuim* (modest) will possess wisdom."[17] If one is not modest, one is more subject to surface messages and sensual impressions.[18] One lacks a vital tool to thinking deeply. As the *Maharal* puts it: "A person ought only to relate to the words of Torah according to…its hiddenness."[19]

TZNIUT IN SPEECH

Tzniut is a way of relating to the world. It affects what and how we hear;[20] what and how we see.[21] It also affects what and how we speak. The Talmud relates:

Sensitive language refines our thinking and the way we relate to others.

Reish Lakish said: A person should never allow a despicable word to leave his lips, for the Torah took a detour (circumlocution) of eight letters in order to avoid using a despicable word, as it says: "From the pure animal and from the animal that is not

16 *Maharal, Netiv Hatzniut*, chap. 1, based on Proverbs 11:2: "When pride comes, then comes shame; but with the humble is wisdom." Actually, the *Maharal* says this about all wisdom.

17 Proverbs 11:2.

18 *Netiv Hatzniut*, ibid.

19 Ibid.

20 Talmud, Tractate *Ketuvot* 5b.

21 *Maharal, Netiv Hatzniut*, chap. 2.

> *pure."*[22] *Instead of using the shortest way of saying this, using the single word "teme'ah—impure," the Torah used the longer expression "asher lo tehorah—that is not pure."*[23]

This is unprecedented. Every letter in the Torah counts. Every letter is explained by the Sages as adding to our storehouse of wisdom. Here too, there is a purpose to the increased letters. It is to teach us purity of speech. Clean language affects the whole way we relate to the world.[24] It is, in fact, the language of *tzniut*.

This can best be understood from the opposite extreme—foul language. Foul language in every tongue is explicitly physical. When someone uses foul language against someone else, it has a cathartic effect in the same way that hitting the person does. By associating a person with very physical words, he is reducing the person to a more physical stature. He has indeed done violence—to the person's stature.

So too, with positive, more sensitive linguistic usage, we refine our thinking and our way of relating to the world, and we refine the way we relate to others.

TZNIUT IN DRESS

The reader may find it strange that the entire chapter until this point failed to make mention of dress as an expression of *tzniut*. Indeed, like all our relationships with ourselves and others, the character trait of *tzniut* impacts on how we dress. After all, we wish to project ourselves in such a way that others will perceive our inner essence—our real selves—and not our outer, superficial, physical selves. And this is how we wish to perceive others. But, if our entry point to understanding *tzniut* would be all about the clothes we wear, we are in danger of confusing this profound concept with a mere dress code. Someone who has a highly developed quality of *tzniut* will understand how to apply it to

---

22 Genesis 7:2.

23 Talmud, Tractate *Pesachim* 3a. The Talmud then goes on to bring other examples and asserts that this should apply to all areas of our language, even when we are dealing with the most mundane things.

24 *Maharal*, *Netiv Hatzniut*, chap. 3.

dress as well. They will know how to be dressed well—to be attractive without being attracting. They won't chafe at feeling that something has been imposed upon them. Rather, their dress will be a reflection of their entire world view.

There will come a day, known as the Messianic Era, when we will see how everything forms a grand unity connected back to God. This period will reveal the *kavod*—the glory and honor—of God. In that era, spirituality will be revealed. We will no longer have to peek beneath the surface to see what we must see.

52
HUMILITY

The students of the Kotzker Rebbe asked him where God was. The Kotzker replied: "Wherever you let him in!"

Humility follows *tzniut* (modesty) because even though they are two entirely different qualities (as will become apparent), they are generally mutually reinforcing. Someone who lacks *tzniut* will be focused on the external and the superficial, and will therefore also not understand how humility, which requires the stark realization of the enormous chasm between who we are and who God is, is developed.[1] Humility is also the recognition of the huge gap between who I am today compared with my infinite potential—an inward looking trait.[2]

HUMILITY REQUIRES A POSITIVE SELF-IMAGE

Humility is an enabling quality. It gives me the feeling that I have so much to do that I had better get started right away.

False humility is the belief that we can never be great. A person with a poor self-image is forbidden to work on his humility. Such a person will only increase his poor self-image, which he will use to tell himself that

1 *Netiv Hatzniut*, chap. 1; *Ramchal, Mesilat Yesharim*, chap. 22.

2 *Mesilat Yesharim*, ibid.

he is not capable of doing anything: "Who, me? Who am I to do this?"[3] By contrast, Hillel, famous for his humility, said, "If I am not for myself, who is for me?"[4] By this, he meant that we cannot expect other people to take responsibility for our personal growth. We may have parents, teachers, mentors, and friends, but at the end of the day, it is our commitment to ourselves that will define our spiritual trajectory.

JUST DOING WHAT NEEDS TO BE DONE

Humble people are fine with themselves. They believe in their ability to do things. They just don't think that what they have done is anything special.[5]

Take Moses as an example. Moses was certainly capable of forceful, if not fiery, action. He killed an Egyptian taskmaster.[6] He fearlessly stands up to his rebellious nation, time and again.[7]

Even more dramatically, Moses broke the first Tablets.[8] Then Moses stands up to God Himself: "If you destroy the Jewish People," he tells God, "wipe me out of your Book."[9]

When Moses went with Aaron to Pharaoh, he did not say, "Please, maybe it would be a good idea to discuss the Jewish situation." Even though he had a speech deficit,[10] he acted with the utmost confidence and decisiveness, demanding that the Jewish People be released.[11]

And yet Moses is described as the most humble man on earth.[12] Moses did not attribute anything special to himself when he did all of this. It had to be done, and he had to be the one, and so he did it. He thought that the strength, the inspiration, the moral bearings to do all of this came from God. He also knew that he had done just a part of what he

---

3 Rabbi Chaim of Volozhin, *Ruach Chaim on Ethics of Our Fathers* 4:1.

4 *Ethics of Our Fathers* 1:14.

5 *Mesilat Yesharim*, chap. 22.

6 Exodus 2:15.

7 See, for example, Numbers 16:5–11.

8 Exodus 32:19.

9 Ibid., v. 31; see also Numbers 14:11–19.

10 Ibid. 4:10.

11 Ibid. 5:1.

12 Numbers 12:3.

could be doing. He felt enabled and motivated by that knowledge and hence highly committed to the life that unfolded for him.

Moses affected change because of his authenticity and humility. He served God and His people without personal gain. "I have not taken a single donkey of theirs nor have I wronged even one of them," he declares.[13] Moses' leadership was the power of influence, of changing lives through modeling behavior, through spiritual leadership, and through personal example.

False humility is the belief that we can never be great. True humility is an enabling quality.

The humility of Moses was such that he wanted nothing for himself. He would just as soon have handed the leadership mantel to Aaron.[14] He saw himself as a servant of his nation, not as their boss. He recognized, valued, and honored every single soul. The Torah reveals these things to us not because God wants to act as Moses' biographer, but because these are practical lessons for us, in our families, in our businesses, and in our volunteer and social interactions.

RECOGNIZING GOD'S HANDOUTS

The humble genius thinks, "If my next-door neighbor had my IQ, he would be just as brilliant. This is God's gift. It was given to me as a handout. I am just using what I was given."[15] So too, the humble businessman thinks, "If he had my social networking skills, he would be just as entrepreneurial." The wealthy man is acutely aware that he was given a gift by God, that he is not any better a person because of it, and that his responsibility is to share that wealth. He is aware that everyone else was given some other special attribute that he lacks.[16]

This is what the Sages meant when they said, "If you have learned a lot of Torah, don't attribute goodness to yourself, for this is what you

13 Ibid. 16:15.

14 Exodus 3:10–13; see Chapter 4.

15 *Mesilat Yesharim*, chap. 22.

16 Ibid.

were created for."[17] Rather, you should feel, "What else should I have done? I was just doing what I had to do."[18]

The humble person is not aware that he is humble. Were a humble person to think "Oh, I am so humble," he would actually be arrogant. Neither can you fake humility. You cannot act as if you have it. This will only reinforce your inflated opinion of yourself—that in addition to all your great qualities, you are humble as well. You can only be humble if it begins in thought and ends in action.[19]

Let's take a brief look at another great figure, Abraham. After the near-sacrifice of his son Isaac, the verse says: "And Abraham returned to his young men, and they got up and they went together to Beer Sheva."[20] Why does the Torah tell us that Abraham walked together with the young, unnamed men? Abraham was a sagely man of one hundred and thirty-seven years. He was super-wealthy, a prince amongst men, famous around the world, and now he had just passed the test of the sacrifice of Isaac—a heroic, spiritual act.

Abraham was perfectly aware of his great achievements. Yet, he didn't see his walking with the youth as any contradiction to this. There was no condescension. There was no sense of entitlement. We can sense Abraham thinking, "These are people, and I am a person. They did what they needed to do, and I did what I needed to do. We are all equal."

Abraham related to everyone with such genuine honor and authentic respect that everyone felt that they could be comfortable with him.

No one felt awkward in Abraham's presence. He related to everyone with such genuine honor and authentic respect that everyone felt that they could be comfortable with him. He even addresses an idolater as "my master,"[21] and is perfectly happy to wash this man's feet as well as his two co-travelers.[22] "Whomever possesses three traits," say the Sages, "is of the students of

---

17 *Ethics of Our Fathers* 2:8.
18 *Mesilat Yesharim*, ibid.
19 Ibid.
20 Genesis 22:19.
21 Ibid. 18:3.
22 Ibid., v. 4.

Abraham...a good eye (i.e., sees the good in others), a humble spirit,[23] and a meek soul.[24]

ARROGANCE—CONTRACTION AND EXPANSION

The opposite of humility is arrogance and pride.[25] The arrogant person can never just compete with himself. It is not good enough for him to be great; he must be "greater than." He must lord it over others. He genuinely thinks that his opinion is always the best one in the room. Ultimately, he will find it hard to accept any higher Authority. "And your heart will be raised up [in arrogance], and you will forget the Lord your God."[26]

The Kabbalists refer to the word *tzimtzum*—contraction, to denote God's withdrawal to allow space for the creation to exist.[27] In God's case, what is hidden is the light that comes from Him.[28] Even though it looks like this *tzimtzum* has created a void, it can never be entirely so, for nothing can exist if God is not present to sustain this.

Man's soul also requires a *tzimtzum* of sorts. This is necessary for each individual to develop his own identity, an independent ego. Hence, the seeds of arrogance lie within us all. A growing sense of self is vital to become a functioning adult. Arrogance is the unhealthy extension of that—the idea of the rugged individualist who is fully self- contained and therefore does not need anything from anyone.[29] It is an extreme version of *tzimtzum*, when the individuation leads to total self-centeredness.

In a spiritually healthy person, *tzimtzum* is followed by *hitpashtut*—expansion of the soul beyond self to connect with God. The arrogant person, however, knows nothing of *hitpashtut*. His self fills all of reality.

---

23 Abraham stated: "I am dust and ashes" (Genesis 18:27). Hence, God says to the Jewish People that He has desired them because they don't become arrogant when He provides them with goodness; *Rashi*, Deuteronomy 7:7.

24 *Ethics of Our Fathers* 5:22.

25 *Maharal*, *Netiv Ha'anavah*, chap. 3.

26 Deuteronomy 8:14, see also v. 11.

27 *Zohar* 1:15a.

28 This is called the *Ohr Ein Sof*—the light from He who is without end.

29 Rabbi Shlomo Wolbe, *Alei Shur*, vol. 2, chap. 17.

It is all his doing. "Take care lest you forget God...Lest you eat and be satisfied, and you build good houses and settle. And your heart will become haughty...and you say in your heart, 'My strength and the might of my hand made me all this wealth.'"[30]

THE FIRST SIN—THE SEEDS OF ARROGANCE

The roots of this arrogance go back to the sin of Adam and Eve. The snake appealed to Eve's enormous spiritual and intellectual prowess by saying that upon eating from the Tree of Knowledge, she and Adam will have Godly powers.[31] "For God knows that on the day that you will eat [from the tree], your eyes will be opened and you will be like God, knowing good and evil."[32] The snake fed into Eve's natural and positive trait to imitate God and took it to an evil conclusion.

The truly arrogant person turns himself into a type of God. He ultimately has a problem accepting God because it means humbling oneself to a higher being. It means accepting that God knows best. He cannot do so because he can admit to no weakness; he is the ultimate self-contained man, pretending that he needs no other, let alone God. And just because of this, his vision is truncated. His arrogance stops him from sensing all of his unused potential. Arrogant people have often achieved great things. Their arrogance has worked for them. And hence, they see no reason to change.

CONTEMPORARY ARROGANCE—REALLY POOR SELF IMAGE

There are few truly arrogant people in the world today. Most of those who appear as arrogant are really trying to compensate for a self-image problem. They are hiding their insecurities. Being humble doesn't mean belittling yourself. It means being you—that is small enough.

For a person with a poor self-image, the message must remain: "The world was created for me."[33] My spirituality is enough to justify the

---

30 Deuteronomy 8:11–17.

31 *Rashi*, Genesis 3:5.

32 Genesis 3:5.

33 Tractate *Sanhedrin* 37a.

existence of the world.[34] I need to know the importance of my mission. And yet, I began as a putrid drop and I am destined to rot in my grave.[35] God will determine my birth, He will determine my death, and He will determine all my natural endowments.

Rabbi Simchah Bunim of Peshischa stated, "A person should have two pieces of paper, one in each pocket, to be used as necessary. On one of them [should be written] 'The world was created for me,' and on the other, 'I am dust and ashes.'"

---

34 Rabbi Chaim Friedlander, *Siftei Chaim, middot*, vol. 1, p. 112, in the name of Rabbi Eliyahu Dessler.

35 *Ethics of Our Fathers* 3:1; see also 4:4.

53
SENSUALITY

Envy, sensuality, and running after honor remove a person from this world.

Ethics of Our Fathers[1]

Tzniut (modesty) and humility are traits that develop our inner spirituality and allow us to then anchor our relationship with the world by moving from the inside out. By contrast, sensuality (i.e., the enjoyment, expression, or pursuit of physical pleasure) starts with the outside world that we then try to take into ourselves. It is hard to channel sensuality properly before one has worked on *tzniut* and humility at least to some degree. On the other hand, a *tzanua* and humble person will automatically be less centered on taking things in from the outside world.

FOOD, SEX, MONEY—BOTH GOOD AND BAD

When sensual things become the goal, they make us more physical. And it is the nature of the physical to provide but a momentary pleasure, a wisp of something that is gone in a flash.[2] Sex, eating, or spending based on the desire to take something—as opposed to giving something—can never be built on. Inevitably, they are addictive; over

1 *Ethics of Our Fathers* 4:21.

2 *Ramchal, Mesilat Yesharim*, chap. 15.

time, they require more and more in quantity or in exoticness to provide the same spark. They are part of a futile attempt to fill ourselves up from the outside.

If these things were bad, our answer would be asceticism. However, this is not a Jewish idea, and for good reason. For we are charged with sanctifying our world, not ignoring it.[3] All three primary expressions of the sensual drive—sex, food, and money—have their place in holiness. All can be harnessed.

God's first commands to mankind through Adam and Eve had to do with sensuality, eating, and sex. "From all the trees of the garden you should eat"—a positive command—"but from the Tree of Knowledge of good and evil you may not eat"—a negative command. So concentrated was the holiness of these two commands that they generated the equivalent of our 248 positive and 365 negative commands.[4] In addition, they were commanded to be "fruitful and multiply," also involving sensuality. However, that leaves us with a dilemma, because these things can be both good and bad; it is sometimes hard to make clear moral judgments about them.

The snake speaks to Eve with guile: "Eat. It will be good. You will be empowered."[5] Unlike pride, sensuality doesn't detach us from God. Rather, it distances us from Him by driving us more into the material world. Pride is a separation. Sensuality is a distancing.[6] We may believe in God and be very sensuous at the same time, but we will find it hard to connect.[7] The average person does not spend his every waking hour steeped in sensuality. However, it is insidious; it creeps up on us as the snake did to Eve.[8]

Sensuality distances us from God by driving us more into the material world.

3 See Chapter 29.

4 *Ramchal, Maamar Hageulah*, sect. 2; Genesis 2:15.

5 Vilna Gaon, on the *Taz, Orach Chaim* 59:3. Hence, he writes, the snake is called "*mirma*," which means "guile." See *Mimaamakim*, Exodus 39.

6 Rabbi Tzadok HaKohen, *Machashavot Charutz*, no. 4.

7 Ibid.

8 Vilna Gaon, Proverbs 17:11.

THE ROOTS OF NEGATIVE SENSUALITY

The snake tempted Eve with arrogance: "And you will be like God"—combine your potential with the knowledge of the tree, and you can compete with God Himself! Eve, however, never actually fell for this. She ate the fruit not as an act of arrogance but as an act of sensuality:

> *And the woman saw that the tree was good as food, because it is a sensual experience for the eyes, and that the tree was pleasant for enlightenment, and she took of the fruit and she ate, and she gave also to her husband who was with her and he ate.*[9]

God asked Adam, "Where are you?"[10] Where are you spiritually now? Where are your former exalted heights?[11] "Where are you in creation?" He asks him further: "Did you eat from the tree?"[12] "Did you introduce an anti-spirituality force into the world, making it harder for all mankind?"[13]

The legacy of Adam and Eve's sin is that, from then on, some sensuality would creep into and mix with virtually everything.

From then on, sensuality would be mixed into the noblest of our endeavors, and this became our legacy. As long as the remnants of the sin had not been resolved, some sensuality would creep into and mix with virtually everything.[14] For Jews, this became our primary *yetzer hara* (evil inclination).[15]

9 Genesis 3:6.

10 Ibid. 3:9.

11 Vilna Gaon, *Aderet Eliyahu*, ibid.

12 Genesis 3:11.

13 See Talmud, Tractate *Chullin* 139b.

14 Rabbi Tzadok HaKohen, *Pri Tzaddik* 8.

15 Rav Tzadok HaKohen. This was because Jews attached themselves to the core of Adam and Eve's soul.

ISHMAEL—SENSUALITY AS A DEFINING TRAIT

The story of sensuality is the story of Ishmael, Abraham's eldest son from Hagar, who was sent away to found a new civilization.[16]

Kindness is an expanding trait; the person starts from within his own reality and directs himself outwards to sustain and nurture others.[17] Someone who lacks kindness is simply selfish. But it is also possible for someone to be a giver, but in the wrong way or in the wrong direction. Ishmael inherited Abraham's giving, but instead of directing it outwards to others, he turned this giving inwards, toward himself. This is kindness gone wrong, and it is the root of sensuality.[18] Hence, the Torah calls incestuous sexual relations between a brother and a sister *chessed*—giving or kindness.[19] In fact, this is what happened to Ishmael.

Ishmael inherited Abraham his father's kindness (*chessed*). The descendants of Ishmael throughout the generations were known for their hospitality.[20] But Ishmael also distorted his giving trait by becoming sexually licentious—the idea of taking unlimited pleasure given by others.

The good news about distorted giving is that it is easier to correct than someone who has no kindness to begin with. For if an egocentrically sensual person were to do *teshuvah* (repent), he would already have the quality of giving; he simply needs to change the direction from out-in to in-out. Instead of allowing his heart and passions to speak to him, he must now speak to his heart and direct his passions.

SENSUALITY AND BOUNDARIES

There is another road to sensuality, and that is via arrogance.[21] If I am so great (arrogance), then I deserve to have my every want fulfilled

---

16 Genesis 21:11–12, 18.

17 Rabbi Yitzchak Hutner, *Pachad Yitzchak*, explaining the *Ramban*, Exodus 20:8.

18 Rabbi Eliyahu Dessler, *Michtav Me'Eliyahu*, vol. 2, "The Traits of the Forefathers." See Talmud, Tractate *Kiddushin* 49b.

19 Leviticus 20:17.

20 *Radal*, Ezekiel 17:13, in the note.

21 Concerning the first, the Talmud says: "The Jews only served idolatry in order to permit

(sensuality). And nobody, not even God Himself, is going to tell me what to do. The sexual abuse that reached full bloom in America in the last decades of the twentieth century owes itself to many factors, but what is prominent is that it was predominantly perpetrated by powerful men on vulnerable women who felt that the woman's consenting to the abuse by their silence would be the make or break of their careers. Its source was the arrogant entitlement of people in positions of authority. It was dominance and power expressed in the form of sensuality—the demand for sexual favors.

The problem of sensuality is not only with people in power. Modern man has been sold a myth—a series of myths, really—that self-actualization requires a break from all inhibitions so that each can find his own path and values. Second, we are told that restrictions prevent self-actualization, rather than what they really do in creating healthy boundaries. "Want to keep your virginity until you find that one special life-long partner? Perhaps you are sexually suppressed." A campus culture of coupling tells us to see sex as a momentary act of pleasure, rather than as a profound act of bonding with someone else.

It was inevitable that, in this environment, interpersonal commitments would be weakened and that marriage would now be just one ideal amongst many possible arrangements. This whole package—the idea that I can self-actualize by choosing my own values, by being free of healthy boundaries, by allowing myself to express my sensual urges however I want—has contributed toward the huge plague of self-doubt and poor self-image. The uncertainty of whether relationships will bring one the pleasure they seek from them, and the fear that they will end if they don't live up to their partner's expectations, leave one constantly doubting oneself. Advice columns offer simplistic psychological answers instead of moral growth, i.e., without the heavy lifting of becoming a giver as opposed to a taker.

---

public licentiousness"; Tractate *Sanhedrin* 91a. They wanted to make free love with the Medians. The Torah said no. So, they created a new justificatory ideology that said that this was permitted. Their sensuality led to idolatry. As for pride leading to sensuality, the Sages say in the Talmud (Tractate *Sotah* 4b): Rabbi Yochanan stated: Every person who has arrogance in the end will fall (by having) an adulterous relationship.

ISAAC'S TRAIT

Isaac's trait was *gevurah*, the power of restraint. It is the ability to set boundaries, exert self-control, and push oneself to do the right thing. Whereas kindness must be expressed outwards, strength must be expressed inwards. "Who is mighty? He who conquers his evil inclination." *Gevurah* is a contracting trait; the person turns inwards to exclude from himself all that may not be good.[22] It is a trait of setting boundaries—of defining what is good and within the boundaries, and what is not good and outside of the boundaries—lest one transgress or lest the slightest wrong thought taint one's action with a drop of impurity.[23]

Someone who lacks *gevurah* is morally and spiritually out of control. One who has *gevurah* but turns it in the wrong direction, i.e. outwards, is a tyrant, delighting in the control and manipulation of others.[24] This, in fact, is what happened to Esau, whose blessing became "by the sword you shall live."[25] Instead of wanting to control himself, he wanted to control others. Instead of humbly serving himself, he worships himself. Hence, he wants to lord it over others. This is *gevurah* gone wrong.

THE STORY OF MAN BEGINS

The more we center on ourselves, the less fulfilled we will be. The more we crave quick sensual fixes, the less able we will be to fill the void. Sensuality is a dead end. The only thing that will work is to fill ourselves up with meaning, spirituality, and values, and as we fill up, turn ourselves into givers to others. Here begins the story of every man, the whole world of psychology, and of any other science of man: all must extend from this starting point.

---

22 *Zohar*, vol. 2, p. 157b.

23 *Michtav Me'Eliyahu*, vol. 2, *Lech Lecha*, essay on the traits of the forefathers.

24 Rabbi Chaim Friedlaner, *Siftei Chaim*, Festivals, vol. 3, p. 269.

25 Genesis 27:40.

EPILOGUE

The Impossible Mission of Being Jewish

What we [scientists] strive for is just to draw His lines after Him.

Albert Einstein[1]

To be Jewish is to have a radical view of history. We are charged with drawing God's lines—of completing them, at every level of the cosmos. At an individual level, the various stages of history can be described as stages of the soul becoming increasingly more dominant with respect to the body. With this, the body gets purified more and more.[2] At a global level, Jews believe that their holy mission is to repair the world, thereby ushering in the Messianic Era.

In a world of so much evil, this is an exceptionally ambitious agenda. But, as Jews, we don't just believe; we do.

At first glance, Judaism appears small on fundamental beliefs—the Thirteen Principles of Faith can be printed on one page—and big on actions. Yet, those beliefs are so concentrated that, in their expanded form, they have provided a monumental guide to Jews throughout the ages.

1 Quoted in Martin Buber, *The Knowledge of Man*. This, said Einstein, is the purpose of science.

2 However, there will always be a slight difference between the body and the soul; *Ramchal, Daat Tevunot* 80 (p. 67), last paragraph.

The world has not been kind to the Jews, but this has never dented our commitment to achieving our destiny and the destiny of the whole world with it. It is remarkable that we have survived at all. This is the secret of doing the impossible. God challenged us, and we took up the mantle.

When we left Egypt, we were commanded to build the *Mishkan*—the Tabernacle. This required goldsmithery, silversmithery, intricate weaving, and other skills. The Jews were a bunch of ignorant ex-slaves[3] whose legacy left them with rough hands unsuited for fine work.[4] Moreover, there was no one around who could teach them. The Jews had only their great passion[5] and intuitive wisdom. Yet somehow, they found within themselves the means to engage and complete this highly professional work.[6] Their success was against all the odds. It was mysterious. Moses bestowed his great wisdom on those tasked with the work,[7] and God did the rest.

The key here was, "whoever raises up his heart," let him volunteer. It was the passionate committing of their hearts to do the seemingly impossible that opened them to the Divine inspiration that led to them knowing what to do.[8]

The Torah calls the men and women who built the *Mishkan* "wise of the heart,"[9] people who are filled with "the spirit of wisdom."[10] They raised up their heart to their impossible mission,[11] just as Jews have been doing impossible things ever since. We have been building Jewish communities and institutions under conditions that seemed like sheer insanity. We built from the ashes across the former Soviet Union. We rebuilt core Torah institutions in Israel and America after World War

---

3 *Ramban*, Exodus 31:2.

4 Rabbeinu Bachya, Exodus, ibid.

5 *Ramban*, ibid.

6 *Ramban*, ibid.

7 *Kli Yakar*, Exodus 28:3.

8 The *Netziv*, *Haamek Davar*, Exodus 36:2.

9 The various words use for those who helped to build the Tabernacle can be found in Exodus 35:10, 25; 28:3; 31:6; 36:1.

10 Exodus 28:3.

11 *Ramban*, Exodus 35:21.

II. We reestablished communities across a Europe devastated by the Holocaust. And we built a new country—Israel—from scratch on barren earth and surrounded by powerful enemies. What was our secret?

Israel's first Prime Minister, David Ben-Gurion, seemingly alienated from Judaism, nevertheless sensed the secret. In a lecture he delivered in 1950 to the high command of the IDF, he stated:

> *Our spiritual advantage has supported the Jewish People in every generation for four thousand years now, and only if the Israeli nation...continues to preserve our spiritual, moral, and intellectual advantage, which was the secret of our survival over thousands of years, we...will win from among the enlightened world friends and partners in the vision of the eternal redemption of humanity, a vision that beat in our hearts through all time, and which was revealed in the Book of Books that served as a light unto nations.*

To be Jewish in our day and age, and to be committed to its implications, is to dare to dream of that which others have long predicted could not be done. In pursuit of our mission, we have defied the laws of history to show that below the surface of an often-insane world lies a whole expanse of spirituality. If engaged, this spirituality will bubble to the surface, affecting not only ourselves but everyone and everything around us. We will truly make the world a better place.

The fact that we not only survive but thrive defies the normal rules of history. It defies the demographers. This is what we are: tenaciously jumping into whatever and wherever our calling goes.[12] It is a wonderful and mysterious thing, this Jewish idea. It is available to whomever wishes to begin the journey.

---

12 See the *Meshech Chochmah*, Exodus 36:30.

APPENDIX

Brief Biographies of Some
Primary Authors and Their Books

In this appendix, authors are listed by their first names, followed by their family names (without the title "rabbi" preceding the name), unless they are famously known by another name, e.g., Maimonides. Included in the list as well are names of well-known books, followed by the name of the author and his biography. The choice of authors was determined primarily by the frequency with which they were quoted in this book, and not all authors mentioned in the book are listed here.

Akiva—see *Rabbi Akiva.*

Alter Rebbe of Chabad—*see Tanya.*

Ari—Rabbi Isaac (ben Solomon) Luria Ashkenazi (1534–1572), commonly called "The Ari" (the lion), also referred to as *Ha'Ari Hakadosh* (the holy Ari) and the *Arizal* (the Ari, may his memory be blessed). He lived in Safed at the same time as the author of the *Shulchan Aruch*, Rabbi Joseph Karo. He was a master of the Kabbalistic work, the *Zohar*, and it would be impossible to understand the *Zohar* without him. The *Arizal* himself never wrote any books. However, his words were faithfully recorded by his student Rabbi Chaim Vital in the *Kitvei Ari*, the "writings of the *Arizal*."

Chafetz Chaim—Rabbi Yisrael Meir Kagan (1838–1933). Author of *Mishnah Berurah*, a codification of certain laws that summarizes the halachic process of the previous four centuries, and many other works. He is called the "Chafetz Chaim" (lover of life), based on his work on the laws of proper speech. He lived in Radin, which is today in Belarus, where he established a famous yeshiva. He traveled Europe extensively to strengthen Jewish observance.

Chaim of Volozhin (1749–1821)—A student of the Vilna Gaon, Rabbi Chaim of Volozhin was the founder of the Lithuanian-style yeshiva system that we have to this day. He authored *Nefesh Hachaim*, a book that shows the profound impact of every action that any human makes. He was born and died in Volozhin, in Belarus.

Chatam Sofer—Rabbi Moses Schreiber (1762–1839). Primarily remembered for his extensive responsa, as well as his strong stand against watering down Judaism in Hungary, the *Chatam Sofer* was the leading halachic authority of his time. He had a difficult life. As rabbi of Pressburg, he oversaw the rebuilding of the Jewish community on four occasions—three after fires, and one after the invasion of Napoleon. He lost his first wife at the age of fifty without any children. However, he then married Seril, the daughter of Rabbi Akiva Eiger. Together, they had eleven children.

Chinuch—*see Sefer Hachinuch.*

Dessler, Rabbi Eliyahu (1892–1953)—Born in Gomel, Belarus, Rabbi Dessler grew up in Eastern Europe. At thirteen, he was one of the youngest yeshiva students in Kelm. He entered business with his father, and declined a position as a rabbinical judge in Vilna. His father lost all of his wealth in the Russian Revolution. Rabbi Dessler consequently moved to London in 1928, where he served as a community leader before moving to head the Gateshead Kollel in 1940. In the late 1940s, he became the spiritual leader of Ponevezh Yeshiva in Bnei Brak, Israel. His mulit-volumed work, *Michtav Me'Eliyahu* (portions of which were translated as *Strive for Truth*), is a compilation of his speeches and writings, and has become possibly the most influential Mussar work of the 20th century. This work draws on Mussar and philosophical sources, as well as Kabbalistic and Chassidic sources.

Hirsch, Rabbi Shimshon Raphael (1808–1888)—He was the founder of the *Torah im Derech Eretz* school of German Jewry in

Frankfurt-on-Mein. This approach encourages total commitment to Torah while still maintaining professional and other engagements by showing how everything can be seen through Torah eyes and sanctified. His commentary on Chumash (in particular), *Horeb* on the mitzvot, and *Nineteen Letters* on the philosophy of Judaism, continue to have an enormous impact on our understanding of Judaism today.

Hutner, Rabbi Yitzchak (1906–1980)—Author of the *Pachad Yitzchak*, a deep work of Jewish thought centered around Shabbat and the festivals. Rabbi Hutner was a leading rabbi in the latter half of the 20th century. Born in Warsaw, he studied Torah in Slabodka in Europe and then with a group from that yeshiva in Hebron, Israel. In 1929, he was away for the weekend during the Hebron riots. After a brief stint in Europe, he settled in New York in 1935, where he headed the Chaim Berlin Yeshiva. Later in life, he relocated to Jerusalem and founded the Pachad Yitzchak Yeshiva. His work is known as a blend of Chassidic, Mussar, and deep Jewish thought.

Isserlis, Moshe—see *Rama*.

Karo, Rabbi Joseph—see *Shulchan Aruch*.

Kook, Rabbi Avraham Isaac (HaKohen) (1865–1935)—A Torah genius who felt that the State of Israel, though established by those alienated from Judaism, was nevertheless a good thing. Through his deep and esoteric writings, he articulated a vision of the Jewish nation going through its final pre-Messianic stages, and the changes in historical principles that applied to this generation. He addressed the full range of the issues of the age. Rav Kook was the first Chief Ashkenazi Rabbi of Jerusalem in 1919, and became the Chief Rabbi of Palestine in 1921.

Kuzari—Written by Rabbi Yehudah HaLevi (1089–1140), one of the greatest Jewish poets and thinkers of all time. It is in the form of a dialogue between a king in search of the right religion and a rabbi. The king asks probing questions, the answers to which have led to one of the most important books on Jewish thought. He wrote the work in Arabic, and it was translated by Yehudah ibn Tibon into Hebrew. Rabbi Yehudah HaLevi was also a prolific poet and a doctor. He left

Spain to fulfill his spiritual aspiration to live in the Land of Israel; in Jerusalem, he was run over by an Arab on a horse. Among his famous songs was "My Heart Is in the East, Though in the West I Live," describing his longing to Israel.

Luria, Rabbi Isaac (ben Solomon) Luria Ashkenazi—see *Ari*.

Maharal—Rabbi Judah Loew ben Bezalel (1520–1609): Chief Rabbi of Prague, best remembered for his many books on Jewish thought (*machshavah/machshevet Yisrael*), in which he gives deep and profound insights into seemingly every issue. He is one of the most influential thinkers on Jewish ideas overall. The *Maharal* produced many books. Some of the more frequently quoted ones in this work are *Gur Aryeh*, his commentary on *Rashi* on the Chumash; *Tiferet Yisrael*, on the Written Law; *Gevurot Hashem* on the Exodus; *Beer Hagolah* on the Oral Law; *Derech Hachaim* on *Ethics of Our Fathers*; and *Netivot* on a wide range of subjects. Perel, the *Maharal*'s wife, was brilliant in Talmudic law in her own right.

Maimonides—Rabbi Moshe ben Maimon (1135–1204), also known by the acronym *Rambam*: "From Moshe (Moses) to Moshe (the *Rambam*), there was none like Moshe." After fleeing Spain, he became the head of the Jewish community in Egypt and worked as the Sultan's physician by day, while a long line of Jews was waiting for him when he got home every night to ask him questions on Jewish law and ask for guidance on life issues. The *Rambam* wrote *Mishneh Torah*, which was the first comprehensive codification of halachah (Jewish law), and became the basis of all future legal works. It is a work of staggering greatness. He also wrote *Moreh Nevuchim* (*Guide to the Perpexed*), a book on Jewish thought that even great non-Jewish philosophers throughout the ages study. His other famous work was a commentary on the Mishnah. The *Rambam* was considered a leading medical expert of his time, and produced the standard text books on the subject, significantly updating Galen's works. He is buried in Tiberias.

Midrash—These are a series of Aggadic literature—stories, homilies, historical incidences, and parables—written according to the order of the Chumash. They generally quote the Sages from the time of the Talmud. The most extensive of these midrashic collections is the *Midrash Rabbah. Midrash Rabbah* is divided into the five divisions of the Torah, hence the *Midrash Rabbah* on Genesis might be called *Bereishit* (Genesis) *Rabbah*, the work on *Kohelet* (Ecclesiastes) *Kohelet Rabbah*, and so on. Other important midrashic words are the *Tanchuma* and the *Yalkut Shimoni*. In addition, there are halachic midrashim (which deal with Jewish Law), prominently the *Mechilta* (on Exodus), the *Sifra* (on Leviticus), and the *Sifri* (on Numbers and Deuteronomy).

Mishnah—The short statements of the Tanna'im, put together in its final, written form by Rabbi Yehudah HaNasi (Rabbi Judah, the Prince) (135–217 CE), also known simply as Rebbi and as *Rabbeinu HaKadosh* ("our holy rabbi"). He did this because there was great concern that, in a state of open-ended oppression and exile, the Jewish nation might compromise an accurate recall of the oral tradition. Many of the great sages had been executed by the Romans, and in fact Rebbi was born on the very day that Rabbi Akiva was killed by them.

Moshe Chaim Luzatto—see *Ramchal*.

Moshe Isserlis—see *Shulchan Aruch*.

Nachmanides—see *Ramban*.

Pachad Yitzchak—see *Hutner*.

Rabbeinu Yonah—Rabbi Yonah ben Abraham Gerondi (1180–1264): He lived in Spain and Montpellier in the south of France. Author of *Shaarei Teshuvah* (*Gates of Repentance*), the classic work on *teshuvah*. But he was prolific in other areas of Torah as well, writing on all of the Talmud (most of which has been lost), *Ethics of Our Fathers*, Proverbs, and other ethical works.

Rabbi Akiva—Akiva ben Joseph (50–135 CE): Rabbi Akiva only started studying Torah at the age of forty, but nevertheless became one of the greatest sages of all time, mastering all areas of Torah wisdom. He was responsible for the famous saying, "Love your neighbor like yourself. This is a great principle of the Torah." Rabbi Akiva died tragically at the hand of the Romans, who raked his skin for teaching Torah, while he gave strength and faith to his students and said the *Shema*. He is buried in Tiberias.

Rama—Rabbi Moshe Isserlis (1530–1572) wrote the Ashkenazi customs that differed from the *Shulchan Aruch*, which were later incorporated into the printed *Shulchan Aruch*. His work became known as "the *Mappah*" ("Table Cloth") for the *Shulchan Aruch*. On his tombstone is written, "From Moshe (Maimonides) to Moses (Isserles), there was none like Moses (Isserles)." He lived and is buried in Kraków, Poland.

Rambam—see *Maimonides*.

Ramban—Rabbi Moshe ben Naḥman (1194–1270): Also known as Nachmanides, *Ramban* wrote major works on the Talmud, works of Tanach, and Jewish thought. His commentary on the Chumash often uses *Rashi* as a springboard, and is considered the second-most important Chumash commentary. He was a Kabbalist and a physician. He lived in Spain, though at the end of his life he moved to Jerusalem, re-establishing a community there in what would eventually be called the Ramban Synagogue, which he made from an old ruin. It is still extant today in the Jewish Quarter of the Old City. While in Spain, the *Ramban* was forced into a debate to defend Judaism against the apostate, Pablo Christiani, in front of the king. Losing this debate may have led to the forced conversion of all of the Jews and would certainly have led many Jews to give up hope, but this did not happen. This debate was recorded by the *Ramban* and is known as *Ha'Vikuach*—"the Argument."

Ramchal—Rabbi Moshe Chaim Luzatto (1707–1746): Lived mostly in Italy. The *Ramchal* (an acronym for Rabbi Moshe Chaim Luzatto) translated Kabbalistic ideas into a language and idiom that made very important ideas accessible to even those without a background in Kabbalah. He had a unique ability to write both beautifully and precisely at the same time. His work, *Mesilat Yesharim* (*The Path of the Righteous*), is the most studied work on character development. His work, *Derech Hashem* (*The Way of God*), is a concise but deep overview of the structure of man and the universe and of how man fulfills his purpose. In *Daat Tevunot* (*The Knowing Heart*), the *Ramchal* gives a deeper insight into humankind's communal responsibility and goals, in our partnership with God, and much more. Several others of his works are quoted in this book.

Rashi—Rabbi Shlomo Yitzchaki (1040–1105): Considered to be the greatest Biblical commentator of all times. His commentaries on the Tanach (the Bible) and the Talmud are characterized by their conciseness, and are so great that it is difficult to imagine the study of Chumash and Talmud without his commentaries. He was born and died in Troyes, France.

Sages—This is a broad term that refers to the rabbis who lived throughout the time of the Talmud.

Salanter, Rabbi Yisrael—(1809–1883) Author of *Ohr Yisrael.* He was the founder of the Mussar Movement, which led to a renewed emphasis on character development and authenticity in all areas of Jewish observance. He encouraged people to learn ethical teachings with great emotion (*limud ha'mussar be'hitpa'alut*), in which one takes an ethical statement of the sages and repeats it over and over with great feeling and concentration on its meaning until the idea enters the realm of one's subconscious. He established *batei mussar*—locations dedicated to this. Rabbi Salanter was legendary in his Torah brilliance, in his interpersonal conduct, and in his tireless love for the Jewish People. He was a decisive leader, famously ordering that Yom Kippur be desecrated during the cholera epidemic of 1848. That Yom Kippur, Rabbi Salanter ordered that all Jews must eat in order to maintain their health. Some claim that, to allay any doubts, he himself went up to the synagogue pulpit on that holy day, recited the Kiddush prayer, drank, and ate as a public example for others to do the same. Rav Salanter also engaged in outreach, spending time in Paris to reach alienated Jews there.

Sefer Hachinuch—Attributed to Rabbi Aharon HaLevi of Barcelona (1235–c. 1290), though we are not sure. Also known just as "the *Chinuch*," it was written by a father to his son upon reaching the age of bar mitzvah. It discusses the 613 commandments according to the portion of the Torah in which they appear. It brings the main laws of each commandment, as well as the underlying philosophy of each one.

Sefer Hayetzirah—The oldest Kabbalistic work, written by Abraham. It deals with how the letters and the words were used by God to create the world.

Seforno—Rabbi Ovadiah ben Jacob Seforno (1475–1550) was an Italian rabbi, Biblical commentator, philosopher, mathematician, astronomer, and physician who came from a long line of rabbis. He ran a yeshiva in Bologna. His unique commentary on the Chumash combines clarity, brevity (*pshat*) with depth, and focuses on the thematic continuity of the Biblical narrative. He also wrote on other parts of *Nach* and *Ethics of Our Fathers*. Possibly the greatest non-Jewish scholar of the time, Johannes Reuchlin, was taught Hebrew by the Seforno. This led to Reuchlin's preventing the burning of the Talmud in Germany when he declared that it was not harmful. The Seforno also befriended the future king of France, Henry II.

Shimon bar Yochai—see *Zohar*.

Shneur Zalman of Liadi—see *Tanya*.

Shulchan Aruch—(lit., the ready table), written by Rabbi Joseph Karo (1488—1575). This was the great codification of Jewish law, which is authoritative for all Jews. He lived in Spain, Portugal, various North African countries, and then his last forty years in Safed, which at that time had many great rabbis and was a center of Kabbalah. There, he headed the most important *beit din* in the world at the time. His other great works were the *Beit Yoseph* on the *Tur*, of which the *Shulchan Aruch* is a summary, and *Kesef Mishnah* on the *Rambam*. Rabbi Karo is often referred to as *Hamechaber* (the author) and as *Maran* (our master) by Sephardim. The *Shulchan Aruch* originally gave the laws for the Sephardi Jews; contemporary printings include the glosses of Rabbi Moshe Isserlis, known as the *Rama*, which explained the Ashkenazi custom (see *Rama*).

Soleveitchik—Rabbi J.B. (Yoseph Ber) Soleveitchik (1903–1993), also known as "the Rav," was the leader of Modern Orthodoxy in America and the Rosh Yeshiva of RIETS. He was a descendant of the famous Brisker dynasty and a brilliant Talmudic scholar. He gave deep and profound insights on Judaism, which resonated with the many Orthodox living in the modern world. Two of his famous works were *The Lonely Man of Faith* and *Halakhic Man*. He significantly upgraded the level of Jewish study for women, in particular at YU's sister school, Stern College. Around 2,000 rabbis were ordained by him, and these became the backbone of many communities around the USA.

Talmud—The Talmud is divided into short statements called the Mishnah, which were made by the Tanna'im, and the commentary on them several generations later, called the Gemara, which was discussions by the Amora'im.

Tanchuma—see *Midrash*.

Tanya—Authored by Rabbi Shneur Zalman of Liadi (1745–1813), the founder of the Chabad or Lubavitch movement. Later he moved from Liadi to the town of Lubavitch, both in the Russian Empire. He wrote the *Shulchan Aruch HaRav*, a work which has a major impact on halachah. His most famous work, *Tanya* (also known as *Likutei Tanya*), is a profound description of how man is built and how he should act in the world. His siddur, *Torah Ohr*, was compiled according to the *Nusach Ha'Ari*, and is the standard Chabad siddur today.

Vilna Gaon—Also known as the *Gr"a* (HaGaon Rabbeinu Eliyahu) (1720–1797). Considered by many as the greatest of the rabbis of the Acharonim (since after the time of the *Shulchan Aruch*). He wrote sharp and deep notes on the entire Babylonian Talmud, Shulchan Aruch, Mishnah, all of Tanach, and much of Kabbalah. It is difficult to comprehend one person encompassing so much knowledge and depth of understanding. The Vilna Gaon led a very holy and ascetic life. He encouraged his students to settle in the land of Israel, which involved enormous hardship in those days, and many did. He felt that man must actively participate in the process of the final redemption. He himself set out for Israel, though he felt compelled to turn back.

Wolbe, Rabbi Shlomo—Was considered the greatest of the Mussar leaders in the second part of the 20th century. He came from a non-observant family and became a *baal teshuvah* as a student at the university of Berlin. He later became a close student of Rabbi Yerucham Levovitz of the Mir Yeshiva. Due to WWII, he settled for a period in Sweden before moving to Israel, where he was first the spiritual leader (*mashgiach*) of Beer Yaakov Yeshiva, and later the Mir Yeshiva in Jerusalem. Amongst his works, the *Alei Shur* became one of the classic Mussar texts in Lithuanian style yeshivas.

Yalkut Shimoni—see *Midrash*.

Yehudah HaLevi—see *Kuzari*.

Yehudah HaNasi—see *Talmud*.

Zohar—The primary Kabbalistic work, written by Rabbi Shimon bar Yochai (d. 160 CE). The *Zohar* means "the bright shining". It is so called because of the light it radiates. It explains the world of spirituality in all its many levels. Rabbi Shimon bar Yochai wrote it with the light of Moses' soul. Until then, the *Zohar* had been oral, but the oppression of the Romans caused a situation where its accuracy was in danger of being compromised. This, despite the dangers involved of people misunderstanding the secrets of God and the Torah. At one stage, the *Zohar* was hidden in a mysterious manner and then rediscovered, for it was intended to provide us support when the light of spirituality was most hidden. Rabbi Shimon bar Yochai died on Lag Ba'Omer (the 33rd day of the Omer). Today, on the anniversary of his death, hundreds of thousands of Jews go to Meron in the upper Galilee, where he is buried. Rabbi Shimon's principal teacher was Rabbi Akiva. Rabbi Shimon's student in turn was Rebbi, Rabbi Yehudah HaNasi, the compiler of the Mishnah.

INDEX

Key: *The numerals that follow the index entries represent the number of the chapter in which the concept is discussed.*

D

E

F

S

W

Y

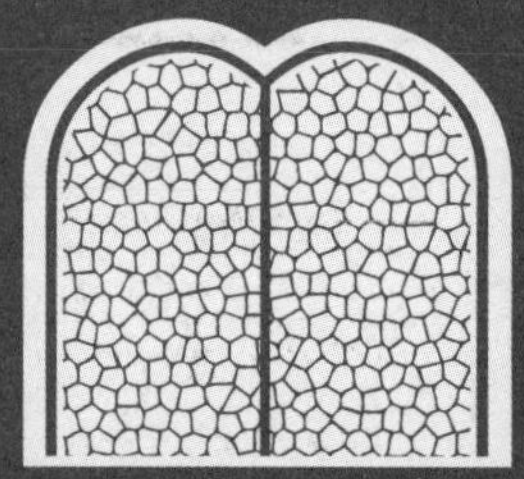

BOOK PUBLISHERS

Elegant, Meaningful & Bold

info@MosaicaPress.com

www.MosaicaPress.com